The
MANAGER'S GOOD
STUDY GUIDE

The
MANAGER'S GOOD
STUDY GUIDE

edited by Ken Giles and Nicki Hedge

published by The Open University

oubs.open.ac.uk

The Open University

Book Trade Department

Walton Hall, Milton Keynes MK7 6AA

First published 1994. Reprinted with amendments 1995. Reprinted 1996, 1997, 1998, 1999, 2000, 2002

ISBN 0 7492 4950 1

Edited, designed and typeset by The Open University.

Printed and bound in the United Kingdom by Bath Press, Glasgow

For further information about Open University Business School courses and packs, please write to the OUBS Information Team, Course Information and Advice Centre, PO Box 724, The Open University, Milton Keynes MK7 6ZS, UK. tel: (+44) (0) 1908 653231.

oubs.open.ac.uk

1.9

Contents

About this book

'...there are few differences between managing a business and managing a hospital, a university, a government agency or a trade union ...' Drucker quoted in *Professional Manager*, September 1993, page 7.

This book sets out to help you improve your study skills, whether you are just starting to study, or have been studying for some time. Although it is not a book about management as such, the practice of management informs our approach to study skills. It is aimed at people working in the public, private or voluntary sectors. Particularly, the book is aimed at managers studying 'in service' or who want to move into a management career. The emphasis is on the needs of managers who are working towards management qualifications. Our approach is informed by the needs of students studying by means of supported, home-based distance-learning methods, such as those long used by The Open University's Open Business School. The guidance is equally applicable to young people and others studying full time in more traditional settings. The book also helps Master in Business Administration (MBA) students who are returning to study after a long break.

We recognise that those of you who are managers already may find it difficult to think of yourselves as 'students' but we have been unable to find an appropriate alternative.

We have organised the book to make it easy for you to look up specific topics. You can use it as a reference book to which you can return regularly as you continue your study of management courses. Even if you are an experienced student and are getting on reasonably well, you should still find that this book has something to offer you – for example, it may help you to improve your writing skills, or to plan your strategy for a forthcoming exam.

It is not a book of quick, 'off-the-shelf' remedies for study problems. It is written in the belief that acquiring good study skills is a long-term process involving changes to habits of working and ways of thinking about what you are trying to achieve.

Use this book to suit your own purposes. Reading through the contents pages will give you a reasonable idea of what each chapter is about. However, it is often worth turning to the chapters themselves to glance at the detailed contents pages, sections and Activities. For example, Chapter 2 contains material about areas which you might not at first sight see as essential to your study skills concerns. None the less it contributes substantially to the process of becoming an effective student. Similarly, although English may be your first language, you may find Chapter 6 useful for further exercises in reading and for the information it contains on time management and active learning. Use the index at the back of the book to further guide your progress – for example, you will find several references to note-taking in different chapters.

Young students and those not in employment may need to draw on case study material and other examples from their course, or from other relevant contexts such as voluntary activities to apply their learning.

The book is based on practical exercises and examples, and you are encouraged to apply your learning to your work situation. You are asked to explore and start to identify the methods of studying that work most effectively for you. You are encouraged to work out approaches to study that will suit your way of learning and your circumstances. You will find that you are expected to work actively on the text by undertaking Activities. Usually this will require you to have access to a notebook, but sometimes you will be encouraged to write in the book itself – assuming, of course, that it is your own copy. If it is, you will probably want to write on and highlight parts of the book anyway. If, in a few weeks' time, it still looks as good as new, you're probably not using it properly!

Finally, in an age when management is becoming more international, the book also aims to cater for people studying in English but for whom English may be a foreign language. For those studying for UK qualifications, it should also help to clarify the demands and expectations of what may be a radically different educational experience from that in their own cultures. We realise that British examples and case studies will be unfamiliar, but in the end we are forced to recognise that a Greek example, for instance, is likely to be equally as 'foreign' as a British one to a German or a Belgian person.

The idea for this book is based on Andrew Northedge's highly successful *The Good Study Guide*, published by The Open University in 1990, on which we have drawn extensively. We are greatly indebted to him for his content, inspiration and approach, particularly with respect to Chapters 1, 2, 7 (sections 1–6) and 8. *The Manager's Good Study Guide* was edited by Ken Giles and Nicki Hedge for the Course Team working to produce the Open Business School course B600 *The Capable Manager*.

Note to readers

To get the most out of the practical exercises in this book you will find it very useful to have photocopies of certain pages of the book. The items you should photocopy are as follows:

■ Reading appendix 1 'Successful versus effective real managers' (page 269)

■ Reading appendix 2 'Germanity – reflections on a people' (page 279).

Acknowledgements

The following people have contributed to this book in various ways and particular thanks go to them.

Richard Mole, the Open Business School (OBS), Consultant Editor

Professor Brian Moores, External Assessor

Andrew Northedge, author of *The Good Study Guide* (*GSG*)

Ian Williams, Open University, East Midlands Regional Centre, overall Developmental Tester

Authors

The introductory section 'About this book', Chapter 1 'Getting started' and the final chapter 'What next?' were co-authored by Ken Giles and Nicki Hedge. The authors have therefore referred to themselves as 'we' in those chapters. The authors of the remaining chapters have referred to themselves as 'I'.

Chapter 1	Getting started	Ken Giles and Nicki Hedge, OBS, drawing on *GSG* Chapter 1
Chapter 2	Learning opportunities	Rosemary Thomson, OBS, drawing on *GSG* Chapter 3
	Section 3 'Learning from a mentor' and Appendix 2.1 'A mentoring action plan'	Karen Dolan, OBS
	Section 'Learning from electronic media'	Gilly Salmon, Open University East Anglian Regional Centre
	Section 'Learning from case studies'	Draws on material in OBS courses B789 *Managing Voluntary and Non-profit Enterprises* Course Guide and B500 *Study Skills* pack.

The Chris Hampson case study, developed by Don Cooper and Rosemary Thomson, OBS, appeared originally in the OBS course B784 *The Effective Manager* and is reused in the OBS course B600 *The Capable Manager*

Chapter 3	Reading	Nicki Hedge
	Text labelling activities adapted from work led by Florence Davies, University of Bristol	
Chapter 4	Effective writing	Nicki Hedge
Chapter 5	Writing assignments	Nicki Hedge
	Section 'Report writing'	Ian Williams
Chapter 6	Studying with English as a foreign language	Nicki Hedge
Chapter 7	Working with numbers	Jon Billsberry, OBS, drawing on *GSG* Chapter 4
	Diagramming	Ian Williams
Chapter 8	Preparing for examinations	Ken Giles, drawing on *GSG* Chapter 7
Chapter 9	What next?	Ken Giles and Nicki Hedge

Developmental testers

Yochanan Altman, Alan Clarke, Mike Green, Malcolm Hughes, Sheila May, Pam McNay, Jo Miller, Harry Mole, Sylvia Sklar, Mike Thompson, Don Ward, Ian Williams

Open University production team

Giles Clark *Book Trade*
Jenny Cowan *Course Manager*
Harry Dodd *Print Production Controller*
Kathy Eason *Editor*
Rich Hoyle *Designer*
Roy Lawrance *Graphic Artist*
Cherry Martin *Secretary*

Grateful acknowledgement is made to the following sources for permission to reproduce material in this book:

Text

Chapter 7 (pages 210 to 212) adapted from Henry, J. and Martin, J. (1987) *Practical Creative Thinking*, Meta © J. Henry and J. Martin; Reading appendix 1: Luthans, F. (1988) 'Successful versus effective real managers' Academy of Management Executive, vol. 2, no. 2, Academy of Management; Reading appendix 2: Stern, S. (1992) 'Germanity – reflections on a people', European Foundation for Management Development Journal *Forum*, 92/4, EFMD.

Figure

Figure 7.1 adapted by courtesy of Euromonitor Publications and Salomon Brothers Inc.

Chapter 1 Getting started

1 How to use this book

This is not a book you sit down with and read from cover to cover. It is a book to dip into and select what you need; to begin now and return to many times. Study skills are not something you can read about once and instantly understand and make your own for all time. You learn them gradually through trial and error, through repeated practice, and through stopping to reflect on your experience. You will need to return several times to the sections of this book that are relevant to *your* particular study concerns. The way that you choose to approach challenging study activities, such as note taking, or writing, will change as your abilities develop and as your study needs change. It is therefore quite likely that the sections that discuss these skills will take on new meanings as you return to read them again over a period of perhaps several years.

Indeed, the topic of study skills is not one for beginners only. Whatever the level of your study skills, there is always something to gain from going back over your techniques and attempting to refine them. Moreover, you do not necessarily need very different advice when you are more expert at something. There are often basic truths about performance which you need to return to periodically and understand again at a new level.

For this reason, it is not easy to grade the various sections of the book as 'beginners' material', or more suitable for 'intermediate' or 'advanced' students. As you read, you will find some ideas relevant immediately because of the particular study tasks in which you are engaged. You may also find them just as relevant again in a year or two's time.

This book is therefore intended for beginners as well as more experienced students. This chapter starts with the assumption that you have not studied for a long time, but the following chapters include both introductory level discussion and more advanced ideas. It is up to you to pick out what is useful to you at the stage you have reached.

The contents list is fairly detailed in order to help you find your way to what you need, and there are also chapter contents lists and an index at the end of the book. Spend five minutes scanning through to find those topics that, at first sight, are particularly relevant to your needs.

ACTIVITY As a manager or potential manager, you will be familiar with the need to manage yourself effectively, to plan and to control the use of your time. This applies as much as anything to your use of this book. To help you to do this, we suggest you think carefully about your aims and objectives, having scanned the contents lists and index, by completing the following sentences:

My aim in using this book is:

Having worked through the book, I would expect to:

My aim in reading this chapter is:

Having worked through this chapter, I would expect to:

We can now assume that you have decided that your aims and objectives justify your reading on. If you are motivated enough to put in the effort to succeed, if you have the time and if you are clear about your objectives, then we aim to give you the right sort of help to improve your skills in the areas where you feel there is the greatest need. We will also help you to check on your progress, so that you achieve your aims.

If you have done the first in-text Activity, you have already taken a first step towards using the book properly. You have made it your own by writing *your* thoughts in it and you have begun to demystify the contents. After all, the book *is* yours. We hope that you will now continue to use it in this way, sticking bits of paper in, using a highlighting pen, drawing diagrams, writing notes and comments in the margins, such as 'yes' or '✓', 'surely not' or '?', and even 'rubbish' where you strongly disagree! In this way it will become a live and personal learning aid.

When we were writing this book, someone objected strongly to the idea of writing in books. Of course, only do this if the book really *is* yours.

The text has been organised with the main points picked out in boxes, the idea being that you can skim through, reading just the brief summary boxes if that is all you need. 'Key points' boxes look like this:

Key points

Use key points to find out what was considered important in the previous section.

However, if you are looking for a fuller explanation, you can settle down to work through the main body of the text. In many places, the text includes closely worked examples to show exactly what is meant. To get the most out of these examples, you will sometimes need to stop reading and carry out an Activity. You have already done this once. Frequently we provide suggested answers to Activities. Use these as a guide – your answers will often be as good as the suggested ones. Occasionally, when an Activity asks for a purely personal opinion, we do not provide any feedback.

These boxes and Activities allow you to read the book at different levels of detail, depending on what you currently need. In fact, each chapter goes into a fair amount of detail and this is another reason why you shouldn't try to take everything in at one attempt. In any case, you need to mix *reading* about studying with *practising* it.

The Manager's Good Study Guide was written specifically for use in conjunction with courses offered by the Open Business School at the Open University, based in Milton Keynes, England. The ideal way to use the book is as part of a course, whether distance learning or conventional, where you benefit from contact with a tutor and other students, rather than working at it all on your own. Discuss your problems and successes with your tutor, another student and in self-help study groups. The book will also work perfectly well on its own if that is what you need. You will, however, need to work out a plan of attack.

Key points

- If you are starting to study for the first time in many years, you will probably find that this book goes into a lot more detail than you need at first.

- Don't be put off. Take a little at a time. Skim through and find the sections that relate to what you are currently working on, or what is of immediate interest to you.

- Expect to take two or three months to work your way through the book.

2 Why read about study skills?

Why should you need a book on studying anyway? It seems to be a fairly straightforward activity. But perhaps it isn't always so simple …

Michael looked up again and saw it was now 7.20 pm – nearly an hour since he'd started and still he was only on page two. Only another hour and he'd have to go and collect Fran from her class – and would he ever get started again after that?

'Early start tomorrow morning – can't afford to be too late tonight. And there's the thriller on TV from 9 till 10 o'clock – only two more episodes to go – can't miss this one. I wonder what was significant about that car waiting opposite the flat?… No! I must get back to the course text – or perhaps a cup of coffee would help the concentration a bit – the last one didn't though – and that was only 20 minutes ago anyway.'

He looked at his note pad. The title 'leadership' was neatly written across the top. The rest was blank.

'They said you should make notes as you read – but notes of what? No point copying out the book. "Sum up what you have read." How?… What is there to sum up? Is it totally obvious, or have I missed the point?… apart from those needlessly long words, which don't make sense even when you read the definition in the dictionary. Typical of academics. Why am I bored? I was expecting to be stimulated. The book looked quite attractive. Now I can't seem to get through it. … Perhaps I should sort out my desk before going any further …'

The phone rang. It was Robert …

He brought back another cup of coffee and sat down again.

'Only half an hour left now. Must concentrate. Let's go back to the top of page two – on second thoughts, I may as well go right back to the start and try to get some notes down, since I can't remember a word of it … Oh forget it!… It's too late to get anywhere now. I'll slip out for a quick jog before getting Fran. I can always try again later on, after the TV serial … But at this rate I can't see either improved job performance or a management qualification looming very large …'

Michael is not alone in his difficulties …

Eva dropped another crumpled ball in the wastepaper basket and stared blankly at the pad. What now? She had made half a dozen starts and hadn't once reached the middle of the page before rolling it up in disgust.

'How can I be stuck when I've hardly started? It won't ever be done at this rate! "Write a report for your line manager on what makes meetings effective. Use examples from a recent meeting you have attended to illustrate your answer." How do you start on a subject like that? I don't go to any meetings … apart, that is, from the Friday morning so-called Staff Meeting where Charlie dominates the whole proceedings and we can't get a word in edgeways. Surely they can't want me to use that in any way? Perhaps I could just alter some bits from the course text and string them together …

but on second thoughts the tutor would probably spot that and tell me it wasn't really my own work … I could try unrolling some of those balls and see what I wrote. How about looking up "Meetings" in the dictionary and starting from there? …Why am I doing this to myself? …'

Of course, it's not always like that and we've exaggerated for the sake of effect. On the other hand, there are occasions when things do look pretty bleak. Although Michael and Eva are fictitious, their problems are real enough. Such problems are faced not only by new students, or 'weak' students. They are general problems we all face when we study: problems of getting started and of keeping going, of struggling to understand, of managing time, of completing a task, and of keeping up one's morale.

One of Michael's problems is finding enough time for study between his social commitments, his work commitments, and his leisure interests. Both Michael and Eva have problems using what little time they have as effectively as possible. Both are concerned about what they should be doing and how long it should be taking them. Both are stuck and cannot see a way forward. Michael is repeatedly distracted – by a phone call, by his own thoughts, by making coffee, by tidying his desk, and most of all by the boredom he experiences when he reads the text. Eva is distracted by her dejection when she reads her own words and by her general feelings of inadequacy as a student. So she is approaching the report in a very tentative way, casting around in desperation for almost any way forward. Both are feeling fed up and have lost the enthusiasm they had when they started their course. They are in danger of giving up and wasting all those good intentions. They need some help with their study skills!

There appear to be four broad forces acting against Michael's drive for success in his studies: social commitments, work commitments, poor understanding of the task, and a poor use of time. We can represent the relative strength of these four forces and those acting in favour of Michael's success by a diagram such as Figure 1.1. The strength of the forces is represented by the length of the arrows.

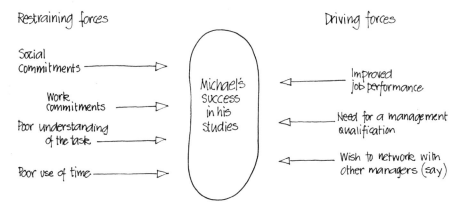

Figure 1.1 Forces acting for and against Michael's success in his studies

Michael's success in his studies might have been subject to other driving and restraining forces we don't know about, such as failure to make progress on a previous course. But, whatever the forces might be, the driving forces seem to be weaker than the restraining forces at present! All in all, Michael's motivation for success is low. He needs help to strengthen the driving forces and reduce the restraining forces and if possible convert them into driving forces if he is to succeed.

Now what about you? Do you know what is driving you towards success in your management studies and what is likely to restrain you? If you want to succeed in your studies, you will also need to think about ways of strengthening the driving forces and relaxing the restraining forces.

ACTIVITY Try to analyse your own situation in terms of driving and restraining forces. One driving force might be a supportive family. Another might be encouragement from your boss. You may feel that a restraining force might be the length of time since you last studied seriously. Another driving force might be a new responsibility at work where you are encouraged and well placed to try out some of the course ideas. At the same time, the new job might be a restraining force in that it may make unforeseen extra demands on your time and energy. Try to capture your situation on a sheet of paper and represent it as a diagram such as the one we drew for Michael. Don't forget that the length of the arrows you draw should indicate the relative strengths of the forces. This is technically a 'force field' diagram.

An alternative way to represent the relative strengths of the forces would be to vary the thickness of the arrows.

When you have finished, have a look at how you represented your situation. If you are unhappy with it, how can you strengthen the driving forces and moderate or convert the restraining forces?

In Eva's case, her initial motivation to succeed, and the effort she is putting in, is being adversely affected by her lack of real understanding of the task and her lack of training in study skills. She's not at all clear about what would constitute a good outcome. As a result, she is unable to finish her report, and the evidence of a mounting pile of failed attempts is reducing her motivation to grapple with the task … it's becoming self-defeating. We can represent this in diagrammatic form as shown below in Figure 1.2.

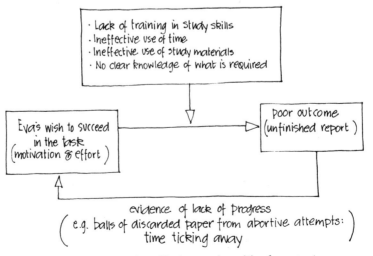

Figure 1.2 Eva's decreasing effectiveness in writing her report

On the other hand, both Michael and Eva may be doing better than they think. Studying often feels like a struggle, and it is in the process of struggling that important learning starts to happen. It might help you to understand the process in which you're now involved if we think of your career as a management student as a river – although your river might be nothing like the one shown here in Figure 1.3.

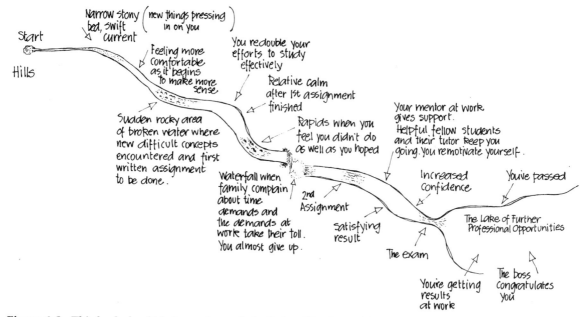

Figure 1.3 *This book should help you to reach the Lake of Further Professional Opportunities*

You too, if you are a typical student, are likely to experience moments of despondency as well as elation, and times when the pressures on you seem overwhelming. But in time you too will probably look back on the experience and wonder why you ever entertained a moment's doubt about your eventual success.

Many managers say that studying gives them not only greater knowledge and understanding of the management process, but also more confidence and purpose at work. This is another reason why it is very worth your while to study this book.

Key points

- Although studying is frustrating and tough, it is also very rewarding and satisfying.

- Developing a wide range of study techniques and strategies will not only help you to succeed as a student, but will also strengthen your capacities as a manager.

What follows now will provide valuable guidance, not only for the likes of Michael and Eva, but also for you.

3 Managing yourself

Practical arrangements

Many people find it important to establish a place where they regularly sit down to study. Ideally, you need to be able to work undisturbed in a place with good lighting and heating where you have enough space to have easy access to your study materials. You may not be able to arrange all these, but it is important to try to get as close as you can, if you are to give yourself a reasonable chance. If you do not have regular access to a place where you can study undisturbed, you will find studying rather frustrating and ineffective.

You will also need the following equipment: a good supply of pens, A4-sized notepads, a box of index cards, computer disks if you use a PC, cardboard pocket files or ring binders, labels, shelf space and a good dictionary.

Figure 1.4 An ideal 'study kit'

If you study for any length of time, then you will soon begin to accumulate large amounts of printed material, including hard copy back-up if you use a PC, handouts, your own notes, old written assignments, and so on. It is important to start being systematic about how you store all this material at an early stage in your studying. As one student put it facetiously, 'It is essential to develop a good piling [sic] system.' Better still, use labelled folders, or ring binders, or boxes so that you can lay your hands on what you need when you need it.

Other people often don't realise just how hard you need to concentrate when you are studying; or else they simply cannot resist the delights of your conversation. Unless you can arrange to be left alone while you study, you (and, in due course, those around you) are in for a very hard time. Thinking with the intensity required for making sense of ideas which are new to you requires a great deal of effort. It will repay you to make absolutely sure that the people around you understand your study plans and know when to leave you alone. An answerphone can be a useful gatekeeper if you don't want to be distracted by telephone calls while you are studying.

4 Developing a systematic approach

When you first start to study, it will be very difficult for you to make any real progress until you have developed some kind of system for studying. Until you have a general feel for what needs to be done, and when, you may spend a lot of unfocused time, starting one thing and then another and wondering whether you are getting anywhere at all. Effective studying is just one instance of learning to manage yourself. You need to plan and schedule your work as you would any other management task. Michael was clearly suffering from the lack of a well thought-out purpose and plan. One of his main problems was how to manage his study time.

Managing time

Michael had two related problems with time: finding enough time, and more importantly, using his time effectively. His problem is captured in a poem which did the rounds of our offices some years ago.

> 'It isn't that I'm indolent
> Or dodging duty by intent;
> I work as hard as anyone,
> And yet I get so little done,
> The morning goes, the noon is here,
> Before I know the night is near,
> And all around me, I regret
> Are things I haven't finished yet.
> If I could just get organised!
> I often times have realised
> Not all that matters is the man;
> The man must also have a plan.'

Finding time

Michael had social commitments (picking up Fran, talking to Robert on the phone), work commitments (an early start the next day), and leisure interests (watching the thriller). All of these things are important, but

Michael now needs to find time to study. Effective study often requires quite a lot of time and time in fairly good-sized chunks, not just for reading and writing, but for thinking and mulling over ideas. You have to *make* space for it in your life.

We all plan our time at work, for example you probably keep a diary to arrange and keep track of your appointments. Many diaries have monthly planners and you will find it useful to have one of these, not only at work, but for home use as well – to ensure there are no clashes between, say, completing written assignments on time and some other commitment. Forward planning can help you get the most from your social life as well as from your studying, whilst taking your work commitments into account as well.

Management students may have to make very difficult choices between competing calls on their time. It is likely that the time required for study will displace some other activity. And yet we all know the result of 'all work and no play'. So you have to become an expert at *creating* time. One way to set about this is to draw up a chart of your typical week and see where there is room for manoeuvre.

	Sunday	Monday	Tuesday	Wednesday	Thursday	Friday	Saturday
Morning							
Afternoon							
Evening							

Figure 1.5 *Sample chart for indicating a typical week's activities*

ACTIVITY Draw an expanded version of the chart as shown in Figure 1.5, perhaps including more divisions under morning, afternoon and evening. Work out the total study time you can reasonably expect to set aside and mark where in the week this falls, using the symbols L (leisure), W (work) and S (study). Try to identify where clashes are likely to occur and where you may have to rearrange or cut back on some other things. Some managers choose to get up very early and work either at home or at the office, or to study at work after hours. Others choose late night working at home. Don't neglect to include commuting time when you may, for example, be able to work on the train at appropriate tasks.

Don't be alarmed if you found this Activity almost impossible. It is. Life is usually extremely messy. What is more, having made a plan, it is even harder to stick to it. But sticking to it is not necessarily the point. Even if you find that you are constantly having to change your plans, it is still worth making the effort, because the decisions you make in changing your plans force you to think about what you are doing and why. Planning helps you think *strategically* instead of just drifting.

Try to draw up longer-term strategic plans as well as shorter operational ones. At the end of each week, review how you have performed against your plans. It would be worth keeping and comparing your weekly plans over a period to see if there are any significant trends indicated.

Using time

Michael was experiencing difficulty not only with finding enough time but also with making effective use of time. He could not decide what tasks to take on in the two-hour period available to him. By flitting about rather inconclusively he ended up finishing the session early, without really having achieved very much. To avoid this, you need to develop ideas about how much time you need for particular types of task and how long to stick at them when you are running into overtime. You will find you can do some tasks (such as reading a difficult passage or writing a section of a report) only when you are reasonably fresh and have a reasonable period of free time ahead of you, while other tasks, such as organising your notes, or reading through a draft of a report, can be squeezed into odd moments, or managed when you are more tired. *People vary a lot in their patterns of working, so these suggestions may not be the right ones for you.* The point is that, to get the best out of yourself in the time you have available, you need to stop occasionally to reflect on whether you could parcel out your study time in different ways to get better results. Don't just plod on vaguely hoping for the best. You need to manage yourself more actively than that.

Figure 1.6 below gives an indication of how you are likely to perform over a period of study time. You need to try to arrange a 'best fit' with the study tasks you have to undertake.

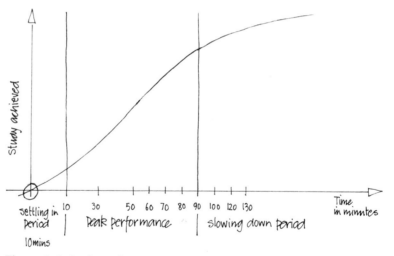

Figure 1.6 *Study performance over time*

In thinking about and planning your work so that you are most effective, you need to be aware of the things that are essential for your success. There are things you *must* do to succeed; things you *should* do; and things you *could* do when you've completed the first two tasks effectively. We might think of your studies as a target with a bullseye which you must hit to gain the highest number of points, as shown in Figure 1.7. This applies not only to your work on your course as a whole, but also to your individual study sessions. You need to start each session in the context of your overall study plan in which you have specified your aims and objectives, but be prepared to modify your session study plan in the light of feedback on how well you are achieving your goals for the session. You should specify what you *must*

11

do, what you *should* do and finally what you *could* do. So, for example, in terms of this book, 'must do', number 3, would be to read a key section of a chapter on a study skill where you are weak; 'should do', number 2, would be to do an in-text Activity in the section; and 'could do', number 1, would be to skim read the rest of the chapter in preparation for the next stage. Don't prevaricate by time-filling on the 'could-do's at the expense of more important work. You need to work efficiently to be effective.

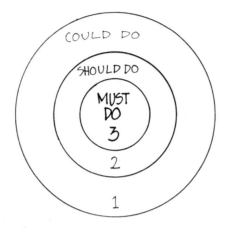

Figure 1.7 Study target

Finally, remember that 'the best can be the enemy of the good': there comes a time when to say 'that's good enough' and to go on to other things is a better use of time than to continue to work on a task that is already well enough achieved. There's a lot of truth in the marketing adage that you achieve 80% of your results with 20% of your efforts, and conversely expend 80% of your efforts on achieving the remaining 20%. You need to ask yourself whether the last 20% of results is really worth the time that could be devoted to other tasks.

Completing a task

So far we have talked as though studying came neatly bundled into clear-cut tasks. Unfortunately, as Michael found, a lot of what you have to do as a student is weakly defined. Indeed, it is a crucial part of your job to create the shape and size of the tasks you have to do. You have to define tasks for yourself.

Defining tasks

The first thing is to have an overall aim for what you are hoping to accomplish in a given week. But you also need to break this down into a list of smaller task objectives, such as 'reading the rest of the chapter', so that you can decide how much time to give to each and so that you can manage yourself, that is:

■ get yourself started,

■ keep yourself going, and

■ decide in the light of feedback on your progress when to stop and move on to another task.

It is important to be able to relate the tasks to the time you think you need to spend on them. In the first place, you will want to have some idea of how much time to set aside. Secondly, by relating the tasks to time spans you can measure progress: this nearly always increases your control over your study and, very importantly, your confidence in yourself as a student.

As for breaking down the overall task into smaller chunks, a satisfying result of doing this is that it puts you in a more powerful position, for it changes the balance between the size of the task and yourself, and puts you firmly in control.

When you have set yourself a defined task, it is easier to focus your attention on it and to keep yourself working your way through it, resisting some of the distractions Michael found himself prey to. Moreover, it is particularly important with a big task, such as writing a report, to be able to break it down into a series of smaller tasks – otherwise you may find yourself reproducing Eva's behaviour.

Why it is so easy to be distracted when you are studying

When you don't really understand the text you are trying to read, and don't really know what you are trying to do, you feel restless and uneasy. Distractions offer you the chance to focus your attention on familiar matters and so escape from the uncertainties which studying often brings. The urge to avoid uncertainty is very strong. That is why it is so important to define clear-cut tasks for yourself to create a shape and a meaning for your work.

If you find that you keep stopping when you are working, it's an indication that you need to reset your targets: try setting yourself a smaller and more tightly defined task, particularly one with an active component in it. For example, if you keep drifting off as you read, get a highlighting pen and search for a key word or phrase in each paragraph. This will help you to focus on a concrete task and to emphasise the flow of argument.

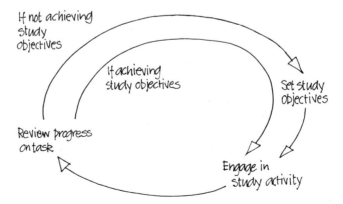

Figure 1.8 Study plan feedback loop

Typical study tasks that you can define for yourself, and for which you will need to set time limits, include:

- Read the next two sections of the text you are studying.
- Make notes on an article you have read recently.
- Plan your next written assignment.
- Gather together notes and ideas for your next written assignment.
- Write a first draft of the main section of the assignment.
- Go over your study plans for the coming week.
- Make contact with other students.

By written assignment we mean an extended piece of writing such as a report or 'essay' which is part of course assessment.

You will get a fuller picture of the range of tasks you can define for yourself as you work through the rest of the book.

Having given some shape to your studies by identifying a number of tasks that need to be accomplished, you then need to divide the time you have available between these tasks. It is doubtful whether you could ever do this in a precise way and then stick exactly to your plans. Study is too unpredictable for that. But you can set broad targets which will help you to decide when it is time to stop doing one thing and start on the next.

Time versus task

Time management and *task management* are closely related, and you need to balance one against the other. If you become too obsessed with time, as Michael was, then you tend to think in terms of the 'hours put in' rather than what you have achieved. You may then find that you start 'filling up' the time with relatively unimportant tasks on your list in order to while time away until you can finish your session feeling virtuous. To avoid this, you need to try to finish a certain task or tasks (even if you don't always succeed). On the other hand, if you focus too much on the task, you may let it drag on for much too long. That is why you need to switch your attention between both *task* management and *time* management to get a reasonable balance.

Procrastination is the thief of time.

The Complaint: Night Thoughts Edward Young (b.1683–d.1765)

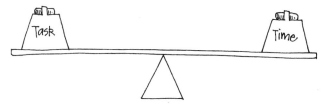

Figure 1.9 *The balance of task and time*

Key points

As you start on your studies, you need to think carefully about the following things:

■ Managing your time, which involves:
  – finding time by planning out your week
  – using time effectively by doing work of different kinds in the most suitable time slots.

■ Defining tasks for yourself, then:
  – allocating time to them, and
  – monitoring your progress as you attempt to complete them.

■ Setting up a place to study.

■ Equipping yourself.

■ Organising things so that you can find them.

■ Sorting out arrangements with family, friends and colleagues.

5 Managing to study

Being a student

As a management student, you have to take responsibility for your own studies. In our years as schoolchildren, our teachers were prepared to take a lot of the responsibility for what we learned and how we learned it. At school level, there is a general understanding that if pupils do badly in an exam their teacher is also open to criticism. By contrast, as an adult, it is up to you to decide that you will study management and to decide how much effort to put into studying it. No one else assumes responsibility for telling you what to learn from the available resources, nor how to learn it, and no one remonstrates if you fall behind in your study plans. You have to 'manage' your own study by yourself. You have to decide your own priorities, set your own targets, and work out your own strategies for achieving them.

This is likely to be particularly so if you are studying by distance learning. You will be working mainly on your own with your course materials at home, without the more obvious and frequent progress markers that characterise some other forms of study.

You also have to accept responsibility for deciding what views to hold. As school pupils, much of what we were given to study was presented as facts. We gained marks for the accuracy with which we could repeat what we had been taught. Adult students find that the truth about things is far less certain. Tutors expect you to form your own judgements about the strengths and weaknesses of various management ideas. Your studies are an enquiry into the nature of the management world in which you are participating. You have to be able to weigh up ideas and test them against your experience, something which youngsters lack. You have to be able to argue for one idea against another.

You and your fellow students will bring with you a considerable fund of relevant knowledge and experience already accumulated over your adult life, which helps to make you the people you are. Your tutor and the course material will respect and draw on this knowledge and experience. You are not an empty vessel to be filled with knowledge. You already have views and ideas about and experience of the management world, against which to test new knowledge. Part of the learning challenge for you is fitting this new knowledge into the framework of your existing knowledge. You will find yourself changing and reordering your perspectives as a consequence.

This does not happen all at once. If you are returning to study after a long break, it is likely to take quite a long time to adjust. Nevertheless, your target is eventually to become an independent learner: to be able to find your way round a subject for yourself. Instead of jumping through hoops held up by other people and then waiting to find out whether you have 'passed', you set your own agenda. You study to find out whatever it is that *you* want to know.

> Younger students and those not in employment may need to draw on case study material and other examples from their course, or from other relevant contexts such as voluntary activities.

ACTIVITY Ask yourself what, if anything, you have learned since you opened this book.

Almost certainly you will have an idea about the contents of the book. More fundamentally, though, have you read anything that has encouraged you to say 'Yes, that's me' or 'I'd never thought about that', or 'I wonder what I'd do in that situation'?

Make a note of anything you feel you've learned so far.

> There's more about active learning in Chapter 6, Section 3.

This reflecting on learning and asking yourself what you want from your learning (remember the first Activity you did in this chapter) all helps to make you an active seeker for understanding.

Learning

The purpose of studying is to learn, and learning consists of:

- Taking in new ideas (and by taking in we mean making sense of new ideas, not simply hearing and memorising them).
- Thinking through new ideas, testing them and fitting them alongside your existing ideas so that you build up a better general understanding of management.
- Expressing newly formed ideas by talking and writing about them.
- As a management student, endeavouring to apply ideas to the real world by, for instance, analysing case studies and writing course assignments.

ACTIVITY Think back to the Activity you've just completed. To what extent did the learning you considered involve these four features of learning? If any were not involved, can you think of a reason why?

Taking in new ideas

Learning is not simply a matter of cramming lots of facts into your head. Learning in this memorising sense is a very restricted form of learning. It may come in useful for learning the vocabulary of another language, but its place in most courses of adult study is very small indeed. It may be the case that clever people often do know lots of facts – but the reason some people can recall facts quickly has to do with how well they have the facts organised in their minds. What really distinguishes people who know a lot about a subject is the understanding they bring to bear on it and the ideas they have available for discussing it.

Chapters 2, 3 and 4 are largely about absorbing new ideas.

Thinking

Thinking is not a thing you would often sit down to do in its own right. It happens while you are busy doing other things. In fact, you think a lot when you are getting on with writing notes on what you are reading, discussing contentious or difficult ideas with others, jotting down ideas for an assignment or summarising your course notes into a concentrated form for exam revision. These kinds of activities may seem like extras which are tagged on to central study activities, such as reading and writing. But they are not at all marginal aspects of study. The odd moments when you are jotting down notes for yourself are often times when you are doing a lot of thinking and testing out ideas, and you should not undervalue them.

You can give free rein to your ideas in all sorts of unlikely and unexpected circumstances and situations where you are free to mull over or play around with thoughts and ideas creatively. Merely relaxing in a chair at home, in a train, doing the ironing, using an exercise bicycle, swimming or jogging can provide excellent opportunities for making unexpected but creative connections. It's amazing how often a useful thought about, say, a troublesome written assignment will pop into your mind at an unexpected moment. But don't neglect to write it down as soon as possible! There's nothing more frustrating than remembering later that you had a brilliant thought ... but can't quite remember what it was.

Finally, the advice to sleep on a difficult problem is often valuable. The solution may even occur to you, seemingly spontaneously, in the middle of the night or be there next morning. Again, you need to write it down.

Expressing ideas

The third aspect of learning ideas is to be able to use them. Speaking and writing are not just things you have to do to show what you have learned. Expressing ideas is part of the learning. Until you can use ideas to say things for yourself, you have not really mastered them. The time you spend speaking and writing is just as crucial to your progress in learning as the time you spend listening and reading. Separate chapters are devoted to these topics. Finally, as a management student, you will be expected to apply the ideas to managerial work in case studies and course assignments.

One thing these aspects of learning have in common is that they are all active processes, requiring purposeful action on your part. Even seemingly spontaneous insights will be the result of previous purposeful activity.

Key points

- When you study you have to:
  - take in ideas
  - sort out the ideas in your mind
  - express ideas
  - apply ideas to the world of management.

- As a management student you have to:
  - decide your own priorities
  - set your own targets
  - work out your own strategies, and
  - make up your own mind about ideas.

This book is all about these processes.

---

6 Summary

Study skills cannot be neglected. The study skills of adult learners are rather different from those skills that were expected at school. The term 'study skills' covers a range of capabilities, some of which you can develop quickly, while others take a long time. Many study skills involve thinking about how you learn and reflecting on the usefulness of your study habits.

To summarise, you should now understand that:

- It is worth refreshing your study skills from time to time, both before, during and after a formal taught course.

- Study skills cover a wide range of capabilities; these are likely to develop progressively as you become more accustomed to thinking about how *you* learn.

- This book should be used as a resource; you are expected to skim the sections of little immediate interest and to find and work on sections that are relevant to your current needs.

- Struggling to understand, coping with inevitable set-backs and keeping going, managing one's study time in the context of social, domestic and professional obligations and pressures, and completing study tasks to an appropriate standard are all universal problems and experiences.

- It is worth paying attention to practical study arrangements: set up a place to study, think about what supplies you will need to organise yourself to greatest effect, and negotiate arrangements for undisturbed periods of concentration.

- You are responsible for setting your own study priorities, monitoring your progress and instituting any actions that are required to stay on top of your study programme.

Study skills are not a painless short cut or formula which, when learned and applied, will automatically ensure success. They are part of a process to which you yourself must add the vital ingredient.

Now, before reading on, look back at the first Activity. Have you achieved your purpose in reading this chapter? If not, consider any further steps you could take.

Chapter 2 Learning opportunities

1 Introduction

Reading a book, such as this one, is one form of learning opportunity and, in distance learning courses, text may well be the primary study material. Research on learning approaches has shown that people learn in different ways, at different speeds and from different sources. You may be aware, for example, that you learn more effectively from visual media such as video, pictures and diagrams than from text or listening to lectures. It is important for your self development to identify which ways of learning suit you best and to build on these experiences as part of your learning strategy.

In this chapter we will be considering learning opportunities which do not involve reading as a major element; study through reading is covered in Chapter 3. I hope to convince you that studying is essentially to do with getting hold of new ideas. You absorb new ideas by making sense of them, by thinking through the ideas, questioning them and fitting them alongside ones you already have in your mind. You learn to use the ideas by putting them into practice in the context of your work as a manager and by expressing them verbally and in writing.

There is ample evidence that adults learn more effectively if they can relate what they are studying to their experience. It is easier for most managers, therefore, to learn about management than to study, for example, a new foreign language or an unfamiliar skill. Management theories make practical sense when managers are encouraged to associate them with their own work. It is essential to give ourselves time to *reflect* on what we have learned as we go along. Adult learners have a far greater store of past experience than children; children form what they learn into experience while adults embed their new learning into what they have already learned, making connections with past experience and building on it. Taking time to reflect on what you have learned will help these connections to be made and to stay with you.

If you are not yet a manager, you can still draw on case study material, your experience of voluntary and other organisations you know, and so on.

However, as we know from long experience, while many managers can relate what they study about management to what they are doing, they often find it harder to write in formal written work or examinations about what they have learned. You will get some help with these aspects of study in Chapters 5 and 8.

Key points

In most courses of study you are concerned with learning:

■ ideas

■ ways of questioning and expressing ideas

■ ways of putting ideas into practice.

Before you read any further, I suggest you think about what you want from this chapter by attempting the following Activity.

ACTIVITY My aim in reading this chapter is:

Having worked through this chapter, I would expect to:

Don't forget to check back to this Activity when you have completed your work on this chapter.

2 Learning from your own experience

What factors affect how much you enjoy a learning experience? What determines whether you experience a sense of achievement? I made the point earlier that people learn in different ways. This is related not only to the different sources of learning – text, audio-visual media, other people – but to *how* they learn. For example, do you learn better if the room is quiet and there are no distractions or do you need to listen to music as you study? Do you prefer to be alone or learning with a group of people?

ACTIVITY At this point, think about and note down two learning experiences which you felt were particularly productive at school, at work or anywhere else. The first of these should be a learning experience when you were on your own; the second should be one where you were learning with others in a group.

Now try to identify what it was about each of these experiences that encouraged you to learn and what it was that made them memorable for you.

Obviously, your examples will be specific to your own experience but you may have noted some of the following characteristics:

Solo learning experience:

- *peace and quiet which encouraged concentration*
- *subject matter which interested me and was relevant to my particular learning needs*
- *learning material which was well managed, structured and easy to assimilate*
- *a sense of challenge and achievement*
- *time in which to think about what it was I was studying.*

Group learning experience:

- *a group with shared interests and commitment*
- *a non-threatening environment*
- *wide experience and knowledge in the group*
- *a commitment to learning rather than to individual agendas*
- *opportunities to reflect on what we learned as we went along.*

These are the kinds of characteristics which actively foster learning and if the ones you listed differed from those listed above, this reflects your individual preferred learning approach. You may also have realised that, for you, learning on your own is more productive than learning in a group, or vice versa.

One of the most important factors in any learning experience is reflecting on what you have learned – taking time to make connections between new ideas and those you already possess and relating these to your work as a manager. To help you do this as you study, you should be adopting a critical stance, considering for example where this information (or this idea) has come from, whose interests it serves, whether it is based on dubious assumptions and so on.

Key points

In order to learn effectively you need to:

- identify and replicate productive learning experiences
- take time to reflect critically on what you are learning
- think about how what you have learned relates to your job as a manager.

Making sense of new ideas

Making sense of new ideas is not at all straightforward. For example, you cannot make much sense of a discussion about a topic until you understand the questions the discussion is trying to address. But you cannot really get hold of what the questions mean until you have engaged with some of the discussion. Learning new ideas is a matter of circling around, picking up the gist of what is going on.

However, having picked up the general gist and some notion of the new ideas which are being put forward, you need to challenge their validity and their relevance to your own learning needs. Just because something is new does not automatically mean it is good or right for your situation. The following case study illustrates this point.

Clare was sent on a training course by her manager to improve her skills in selecting staff. The trainer was very enthusiastic about 'assessment centres', which were considered to be much more reliable than interviews in selecting the best person for a specific job. Clare was excited by the idea and took copious notes about the kinds of ability and performance tests which were involved, the accuracy of scoring them and ways in which they could be designed to replicate actual performance of particular tasks. She wrote up a very comprehensive report for her manager when she returned to work.

Three days later her manager asked her to come and talk about these new ideas, which she did at great length, proud of her new knowledge. He listened carefully, taking notes as she spoke.

Eventually, he said, 'Clare, these ideas are all very well and very interesting. But we are a small company and only take on about five new staff at most in any one year. We would need to have individually designed tests for each job vacancy since these occur at different levels and involve different skills – for example, at this point we need a new Marketing Director and we also have a vacancy for a Purchasing Clerk. We'd also need someone who was qualified to run and grade the tests. I don't want to discourage you, but assessment centres are just not practical or cost effective in our case.'

Clare realised she had been acting like a sponge. She had absorbed every new idea the trainer had offered without questioning whether it was appropriate for every situation, without asking about costs or assessing it against other selection methods.

So, picking up the general gist, while essential to helping you understand new ideas, is not effective learning. Taking a critical approach to these ideas, questioning and challenging them, and putting them into context is what really matters.

ACTIVITY Can you think of one or two examples of situations when you or your colleagues failed to take time to reflect on a new idea or an apparently good decision which later proved difficult or impossible to put into practice?

The spoken word

Tutorials, group discussions, TV and radio programmes, and audio and video cassettes are all examples of the spoken word and are very valuable in giving you a chance to sit in, as it were, and overhear ideas in action. They present you with samples of the kinds of debates going on in the field of management. They let you hear how the arguments work. Even when you get lost or confused, you can still make valuable progress in:

- hearing how the language of the subject is used
- hearing the kinds of questions that are asked, and
- getting a sense of the kinds of arguments that are used.

Asking your own questions and putting the ideas into your own context will help you to make sense of them.

When you read, it is *you* who has to shoulder the whole burden of pushing the meaning along. If you get tired or confused, the process of understanding comes to a halt. With the spoken word, it can be the other way round. Speech has its own forward momentum so that when other people are speaking, meaning sweeps along independently of you. Of course, you may not always be able to keep pace with the meaning, so that you are left floundering at times. But if you question what has been said, meaning can be made to 'happen' as a shared social event, rather than just as a private process inside your head. In this way the burden of making meaning and of driving it forward is shared with other people. You have the opportunity to be involved in a line of thinking by participating in and learning from discussion.

It is not unusual to read, quite passively, ideas that are laid out neatly in a text and then to believe that you have grasped what they are about. But when you hear another manager speaking around those ideas, you may begin to realise there is much more to be understood than you realised at first. You may begin to see new possibilities for using the ideas.

You may find, as you reach for ideas during discussion, that they slip from your grasp and dissolve, or that they emerge in a garbled form. You may want to re-read or engage in further discussion until you gradually get on to reasonable working terms with elusive ideas. Later, you may struggle to achieve a further degree of mastery over the ideas, as you use them to write an answer to an assignment question for your course. By the time you have done all that, ideas which seemed quite slight and straightforward as you read them on the page will have acquired layers of extra meaning and become integrated into a wide range of other related ideas which you already held in your mind. By constantly challenging and questioning the ideas for yourself, you begin to make sense of them. They are not just something 'out there' on a page, which you chose to memorise. They have become part of the way you think and understand.

Key points

Modes of study that use the spoken word:

- help you to get the general gist of new ideas
- drive you on through difficult arguments
- help you to challenge your previous thinking, and
- help you to build newly acquired ideas into the way you think about a subject.

Internalising ideas is a complex process which does not happen in a single moment or through a single activity. It develops unevenly over time and over a range of activities, surging forward at some times and hanging back at others.

Other people may be pleased to be asked to help. For example, you may be unsure of working with figures, but a friend or colleague may be able to explain a numerical problem to you better than any textbook. Or someone in your family may have a particular skill which they can teach you. However, in some circumstances, the nature of your relationship with another person can actually block learning. For example, the emotional nature of a partnership between two people can create problems; one partner teaching the other to drive a car is a famous example.

ACTIVITY Make a list of people – friends and acquaintances – who might be in a position to help you learn. Make a point of asking for their help when you need it.

3 Learning from a mentor

Most work-related learning opportunities can be enhanced through having a mentor. The Concise Oxford English Dictionary defines a mentor as 'an experienced and trusted advisor'. A mentor is a person, usually in the same organisation, who is willing to devote some time to the development of other managers and who can provide advice and expertise related to managerial work. The mentor may be formally responsible for overseeing the career and development of another person outside the normal manager/subordinate relationship, or rather less formally, may be a friend, advocate and guide through important life and career events, offering advice, encouragement and support.

Mentoring is now recognised as an important area for attention in any field where the nature and direction of a person's development is a matter of concern. Indeed, many large organisations in both the private and public sectors are now either experimenting with, or are fully committed to, mentoring programmes. A mentor may help a person to achieve his or her potential in terms of both career and academic qualifications. A mentor can help that person to identify with the organisation or profession, make sound judgements and gain the right experience whilst at the same time being noticed and appreciated within that organisation.

The role of the mentor

If you have a mentor, in addition to the provision of advice, encouragement and acting as a role model, you may expect other forms of support. It is important, however, not to harbour unrealistic expectations. Figure 2.1 below should help you to discriminate in this area.

Your mentor can:	Your mentor cannot:
■ assist you in making connections between your learning on the course and your organisation	■ take responsibility for your career development or progression
■ provide you with objective and trustworthy support	■ arrange peer-group support sessions
■ help you to attain a self-managed approach to learning and development	■ assess your coursework or learning style
■ encourage, stimulate and reinforce your self confidence, particularly if you are experiencing difficulty with some aspect of the course	■ arrange supplementary tuition or reading materials
■ help you to resolve any issues arising from applying learning at your workplace	■ arrange assignments and practice opportunities
■ help you obtain access to information and people within your organisation	■ prepare you for the examination

For advice on choosing a mentor see Appendix 2.1.

Figure 2.1 *The role of a mentor*

4 Learning from lectures and talks

Lectures have traditionally been the main mode of teaching in higher education, although this is less true in the field of management education, where small group tutorials tend to be preferred. By a lecture or a talk I mean a situation in which the lecturer or speaker makes a formal presentation, largely uninterrupted by the audience, although there may be opportunities for questions at the end. There are many opportunities to hear guest speakers at, for example, Institute of Management branch meetings or at a conference, and these occasions can be very valuable in supporting and broadening your learning. On the other hand, lectures are not normally an integral feature of distance learning courses but you may find them useful in enhancing your learning experience.

Perhaps I need to make a distinction here between teaching and learning. I said lectures were a mode of teaching because any initiative on content is taken by the speaker (the teacher). In learning, however, the initiative is taken by you, the learner. You can sit through a lecture and learn nothing! To learn, you need to be receptive and active, listening with attention and taking notes.

The lecture is not a very good method of delivering a lot of detailed information. It is too unreliable. Essential information is better presented in print, where it can be set down correctly, where you can study it when you are ready to take it in, and where you can return to it when necessary. There is a tendency for lecturers to expect their audience to listen to their words of wisdom with passive acceptance. But, like all learning opportunities, you should be prepared to be critical in your judgement and to question assumptions – your own and those made by the speaker.

Lectures and learning

The lecture comes into its own by helping you to understand how the ideas in the subject are used. The lecturer can project meaning into the words through tone of voice, gestures and facial expression. Devices such as diagrams, slides and notes on a flipchart can also be brought into play. By orchestrating all these different modes of communication, the ideas you are grappling with in the course can be presented to you much more explicitly and forcefully.

Lectures are an excellent counterpart to reading – where you can stop and think over points which puzzle you, and go back to re-read them if necessary, and where you have time to make notes thoughtfully. When you are learning unfamiliar material, both approaches are useful. One drives you on into new territory; the other lets you get your bearings and take time to map out the ground around you.

Alternatively, a lecture might shake up all your thinking on a subject, so that you are not sure what to think. You might simply end up with a new set of questions. But this could be exactly what you need to help you make more sense of a written text. Good lectures offer live discourse: words spoken in a social setting which engage directly with the thoughts in your mind and help you to get inside a subject. Lectures can be a springboard for further learning because they have opened up your mind to new possibilities.

Problems of learning from lectures

If you are to learn from a lecture you will have to complete three challenging tasks.

- You will have to attend to and make sense of a line of argument.
- You will have to think critically about what is said to gain any real value.
- Unless the lecturer provides handouts, you may have to take notes of some kind to encapsulate the new knowledge and use it as a basis for further learning.

Since you can't effectively do more than one task at a time, the best you can aim for is to switch quickly from one task to another. In an odd way the urgency of the struggle to cope with this mental juggling act is helpful. By putting you under pressure, lectures force you into taking leaps and short cuts. These force you to seize the initiative in making sense of the subject. When you are reading you may tend to hold yourself at a respectful distance from the ideas in the text, painstakingly summarising them in note form. In a lecture you haven't time for that. You just have to pitch in and make what sense you can quickly, because the scraps you get down are all you will take away with you at the end. You have to learn to think on your feet.

But how do you develop this juggling act? Clearly, you cannot afford to leave the primary task of paying attention to the lecture for very long or you will lose the drift of the whole argument. On the other hand, you are bound to miss some of what is said because listening intelligently will make you stop and think critically from time to time, as you make connections with other ideas already in your mind. You have to find out how to make a trade-off between listening and thinking that enables you to keep in touch.

Appendix 2.2 sets out some helpful advice on how to take notes during lectures.

Perhaps the most significant thing you can do to keep your mind on the lecture is to develop a good note-taking strategy.

Since the notes are made in time 'stolen' from listening and thinking, it matters a lot how time-consuming and how effective your note-taking strategy is. You have to weigh up quality against speed. To strike a suitable balance you have to think about your broad objectives:

- What is your purpose in being at the lecture at all?
- What do you hope to gain by making notes?

You will then need to try out a number of different approaches and afterwards look back over the notes you have written in order to see whether they serve your objectives.

Key points

The strength of the lecture lies, not in presenting information to you, but in:

- engaging your mind with the debates going on in the subject

- showing you how the explanations work

- letting you hear how the language of the subject is used.

The weakness of the lecture for the learner lies in:

- encouraging passive acceptance of its content

- expecting you to follow the argument, while simultaneously thinking about the subject matter, and making notes

- lacking any real opportunity for discussion around the issues unless explicitly provided at the end.

ACTIVITY   In this section I have emphasised the importance of reflection in effective learning. Take some time now to reflect on what you have learned from reading so far, and note down your own key points.

5 Learning in groups

We learn throughout our lives by engaging in discussions with other people. This is particularly important in management. As well as giving us access to the ideas of others, discussion helps us to clarify our own thoughts. In the effort to explain a point, you may quite frequently hear yourself expressing ideas in a form you had not quite been aware of before. In short, discussion helps you to think.

Learning with others, sharing experiences with other students, is a major factor in the motivation to study. Without access to other people, the 'long-distance learner' can feel isolated, defeated by problems of time and family management, worried about difficulties with the learning material. Even a telephone conversation with someone else who is taking the same course can restore confidence and regenerate the enthusiasm to go on.

Sharing the thinking load

When you are thinking by yourself you have to do two things at the same time. You have to hold in mind what you are thinking about – the frame of reference – and you have to work through the thought itself – the content. This puts limits on how far you can go, since it is easy to lose track of one while you attend to the other. However, when you are discussing with other people, you share the responsibility for holding on to what the discussion is about – the frame of reference. This means you can pursue thoughts of your own and then tune back into the discussion to remind yourself of the point of it all.

One advantage, then, of group discussions is that the frame of reference is looked after by the group as a whole. Another is that the frame keeps moving onwards, with the result that the thoughts in your mind are constantly being presented against a slightly different background. This allows you to consider them from a wider viewpoint. A disadvantage, however, is that the discussion can be taken over and diverted by other group members.

Learning in a tutorial group

The tutorial approach outlined here is typical of The Open University's Open Business School. The approach may differ in detail in other institutions. For some students raised in other educational traditions, the approach may take time to adjust to.

As I have pointed out, lectures and talks are likely to be only a small part of distance learning management courses, whereas 'tutorials' are likely to be important. The tutor in a group tutorial acts as a facilitator of your learning experience and you should expect to be actively involved. You are, after all, an adult with useful experiences to bring to the group. This doesn't mean that your tutor won't lecture for part of the tutorial time in order to explain the main ideas of a particular topic, so all the advice about how to get the most out of a lecture or a talk is still valid in tutorial situations.

However, at a tutorial, you would expect typically to be in a group of up to 20 managers, depending on the purpose and circumstances. You would expect there to be plenty of opportunities to ask questions or request clarification of what has been said. You would also expect to participate actively by engaging in individual tasks and to work in pairs or in small sub-groups which might discuss a topic or a case study. What is more, when you meet the same people regularly, the group's handling of the subject matter evolves. The frames of reference become more subtle.

But learning from tutorials involves some input from you. You will be expected to prepare for the tutorial by completing a particular part of the course work, or by reading specific parts of the text. This is so that everyone in the group is at the same stage and common problems can be addressed at the tutorial. If you, or others, have not reached that stage, your contribution to the group's learning will not be particularly valuable, nor will you get full benefit from this learning opportunity. However, don't miss out on the tutorial as a learning opportunity, even if you are behind. The tutor and the group will help you to catch up and restore flagging enthusiasm.

Your tutor is an extremely valuable resource. He or she is likely to have had management experience and to be able to relate theory to practice as well as pass on examples from personal experience. In a distance learning system, tutors can usually be contacted by telephone, increasingly by fax, or sometimes through an electronic mail system, if you get stuck when studying on your own. Your tutor can help by exploring the issues with you when you encounter a study problem. Anxiety about contacting your tutor over something which you may feel is relatively trivial will only build up and cause frustration. Tutors are accustomed to being asked for help and advice – that is what they are there for – *but they cannot provide it unless you*

29

ask for it. It may help you to remember that you are probably not the first student to have a question about a particular issue: often the fault is in the learning materials, not in yourself. If yours *is* the first time a question has been raised, the tutor will find it particularly interesting to explore it with you. Tutors will also mark assignments and provide essential feedback on your performance on written work. Your tutor will also have a general idea of what the examiners will be looking for and be able to offer you valuable advice if you have not taken a formal examination for some years.

Key points

Tutors:

- facilitate learning rather than lecture
- are a source of knowledge and experience
- need input from you
- can offer advice and help
- expect to be contacted if you have a problem.

The combination of private study and regular discussions is a powerful one. Discussion benefits from the ideas individual members contribute to the group as a result of prior study. Conversely, the development of understanding through discussion helps the individual member to make more sense of their studies.

An equally important benefit of group-based learning is that it helps to keep up your morale. Many people say that the best thing about attending a tutorial is discovering that others are experiencing exactly the same difficulties as themselves. It is easy to feel stupid, inefficient and inarticulate when you study on your own. Just talking with others about the disarray of your study programme and your confusions over the reading, and so on, helps to put these worries into perspective. Studying is a tough challenge, and everyone finds it difficult. You need to keep reminding yourself of this; talking to other members of your group who are facing exactly the same tasks is by far the most convincing evidence.

Of course, you can do more than just commiserate. You can actually help each other. You can share tips about how you cope. You can exchange plans and strategies for approaching the work ahead. You can even share out some of the work. Learning is not a competitive activity. You can often collaborate very effectively with other people, checking different sources of information for a project, comparing plans for an assignment, or cross-checking notes from a book or lecture.

Networks of mutual support can make the everyday challenges of study much more manageable. When you run into a crisis, as most people do from time to time (from pressure of work, moving house, domestic complications, etc.), such networks can make the difference between struggling through and dropping out altogether.

Collective progress

A tutorial group which meets over a period of time gradually develops a shared understanding of the subject matter. The discussion doesn't go back to first principles each time. It builds on the achievements of previous meetings. This means that as your own thoughts on the subject matter are gradually becoming more developed through working on the course, so the shared understanding within the group also becomes more sophisticated and the collective frames of reference that the group constructs during discussions become more powerful. This means that you are able to take part in discussions which increasingly approach the level of the ideas you are reading in the texts.

I have stressed the practical help you can get from studying in a group. But meeting other people can be an end in itself. Tutorial groups often bring together people from a wide range of backgrounds, whose only common characteristic is an interest in the subject matter of the course. The pleasure of social contact and of taking part in challenging discussions may turn out to be the most rewarding part of studying. It can be a very significant social experience as well as an intellectual one.

ACTIVITY Have you studied in a group? Note down some of your thoughts about how you can ensure that a group learning experience is productive.

Key points

The value of participating in tutorial groups includes:

■ learning from other group members

■ sharing the work of advancing your thinking

■ building a deeper understanding based on a shared frame of reference

■ providing social support for your studies.

Tutorials: how to enjoy taking part

Discussion is a highly flexible process which can accommodate a wide range of needs and interests. It can veer from the stimulating and illuminating to the dreary and stultifying, and back again. It is sometimes hard going and confusing, but then it is suddenly exhilarating when you glimpse a new perspective. You need to understand its inherent unpredictability if you are to make effective use of group learning. Don't expect too much or too little.

When a group begins to discuss a topic, the boundaries are limitless. But every minute you spend on one issue is time denied to others. So there is always uncertainty as to how long the group should spend pursuing any given point and uncertainty over the best direction to follow next. Indeed, members of the group will have different views on these matters. There will also be uncertainty as to what right each group member has to influence the direction of the discussion and how such influence should be exerted. Thus, the flexibility which is a core strength of discussion is also a problem. It is never absolutely clear what is and what is not a useful contribution to the discussion, or where the debate as a whole is supposed to be heading. The 'intellectual agenda' is always uncertain.

Even more tricky is the 'social agenda'. Only one person can speak at a time. How is the group to determine who should speak and when? Taking turns would be very mechanical and would work against the whole idea of pursuing a train of thought or arguing out the differences between two views. But anything else requires group members to make judgements about the value and the timeliness of their own potential contributions. Some people are much more optimistic about this than others. Some are inclined to doubt the value of anything they might contribute and prefer to take the safe option of staying silent. Others happily throw in thoughts without very much concern about their relevance. So there can be a very uneven pattern of contributions. It is unsatisfactory for the group as a whole when the full range of insights is not made available. It is particularly unsatisfactory for those members who are not getting a chance to try out their own ideas.

To establish and maintain a social and an intellectual agenda for group discussion requires some form of management of the process. Overall responsibility for managing tutorial discussions often falls to the tutor. But it is not a task the tutor can accomplish unaided. It is in no one's interest, for example, to allow one or two people to dominate a whole discussion, yet it is very difficult for the tutor to prevent this without taking over and dominating the discussion him or herself. On the other hand, the tutor can't make the other group members talk. A direct question to a quieter individual, for instance, tends to shine the spotlight too suddenly and too brightly and can create embarrassment rather than encouragement. In the end, tutors have to rely on people coming forward more or less spontaneously to make contributions (whatever the reservations they may feel). They also value assistance in drawing out the less confident members of the group and in keeping a check on the more enthusiastic ones. In other words, a good group discussion relies on active participation and a sense of shared responsibility. It is an exercise in co-operative learning and all present should try to avoid attitudes, actions and roles that do not positively encourage this process. Examples of these are:

- aggressive behaviour
- blocking, that is cutting off or preventing a member's contribution for no good reason
- dominating
- being competitive
- withdrawing
- seeking sympathy
- pleading for a pet idea
- indulging in distracting behaviour, for example talking aside to an individual member of the group
- adopting distracting physical poses and facial expressions.

A study group discussion is a challenging social process. As managers, most of us are eager to speak effectively and to show the force of our ideas, but at the same time we are concerned not to appear foolish. So we often feel quite ambivalent, particularly at the first few meetings of the group – keen in principle to contribute, but also quite reticent. In the early meetings it is easy to form the impression that most of the other people are more articulate, more hardworking and more confident than you are.

All groups go through a number of stages – although not all groups go through all stages. These are as follows:

Forming At this stage the group is coming together for the first few meetings and is still a collection of individuals. People are polite to one another, guarded in what they say and worry about what impression they are making on other group members.

A group member may wish to manipulate the group for purposes which he or she is reluctant to disclose. Such a member has a hidden agenda.

Storming This stage is characterised by conflict when individual members test their strengths, and disagreements arise. It is – or should be – constructive conflict so that hidden agendas are aired and recognised and the group can proceed to the next stage.

Norming By now, the group has become more cohesive and members are open with each other. The group can now establish roles and procedures to make it perform effectively.

Performing This is the final stage, but is not always achieved. Group members work productively together, recognising and accepting individual strengths and weaknesses.

There's more about group processes in the section 'Learning from self-help groups' on page 35.

Your feelings about working in a group are probably the same as everyone else's and they are probably related as much to the particular stage the group has reached as to the subject under discussion.

A discussion in a tutorial group is not set up as an ordeal to test you. It is part of the study package for which you have paid your course fee. Don't let yourself be intimidated. It is *your* discussion, arranged in order to help *you* learn. Don't just sit on the fringe of the group. Push your chair right in so that you can see everyone's face and hear what they are saying. Give yourself a chance.

Saying the simple thing

You may feel that you ought to wait until you have something really important to say – a penetrating new insight, a telling illustration of the theme, or a lucid summary of the debate – before taking up the group's time by speaking out. If you raise the stakes to this high level, you will only create problems for yourself. For a start, it will be a very long time before you attempt to speak. As you wait, poised for the right moment, the discussion will drift on to other topics, so that when you finally speak it is no longer clear what, exactly, you are referring to. By then you will also be too wound up by the significance of the occasion so that you tend to say too much too quickly, and other people will find it hard to follow your train of thought. They will then have difficulty responding to what you have said and incorporating it into the flow of the discussion. Think for a minute or two about one or more occasions when you have acted in a way similar to this. Remember that, at some time, we have all had this kind of experience.

Rather than entering into this cycle of inhibition, it is much better to set your sights low. Just ask the simple question, make the obvious point, and offer the mundane illustration. What seems ordinary to you will often be more interesting to other people. In any case, the group does not *need* brilliant contributions to have a good discussion. It just needs everyone's mind focused on the main theme and a steady flow of contributions. You all work together to move the discussion on to new levels of understanding and analysis. Individual brilliance isn't necessary.

In any discussion, you are likely to be confused occasionally – to be unsure of what, in general, the discussion is about or of what, in particular, has just been said. This may make you feel rather inadequate, but don't let it. You may be quite right. The whole group may have lost its bearings and the person who has just spoken may have made little sense. These things happen frequently. Simply saying that you don't understand is a useful contribution because other people are probably worrying about the same thing. Just ask a simple question, such as 'What are we talking about?', or 'What would be an example of what you just said?' In going back over a few points, the whole group, including the tutor, may reach a new level of clarity about the issues being discussed and be extremely grateful to you for helping them achieve this. Of course, you *will* tend to be confused if you have not done any reading in preparation for the discussion. It is very important that you try to do this in advance, or at least skim over some of it, so that you can tune your thoughts into the subject matter and make a useful contribution to the discussion.

I keep six honest serving-men
(They taught me all I knew);
Their names are What and Why and When
And How and Where and Who.

I keep six honest serving-men, Rudyard Kipling

Being a 'quiet' group member

You may sometimes find it difficult to contribute simply because so many other people are eager to speak. There isn't time for everyone to say a lot and some people are just more talkative and more thrusting in groups than others. So don't feel self critical if you say very little in some discussions. You can get a lot from a discussion by listening very closely and participating silently – agreeing or disagreeing with what other people say. It certainly isn't the case that the people who speak most in a discussion necessarily know the most. You ought to try to join in some of the time. But don't worry if you find yourself cast in what you feel is a relatively minor role. Groups need their support players just as much as the big shots. The important thing is for you, or any quiet group members, to feel you can contribute when you want and that you feel involved in what is going on. You can contribute as much by nodding agreement as by saying 'Yes'.

Finally, if for any reason you find that you are unable to arrive in time for the beginning of a tutorial, or have to leave before the end, don't feel you have to miss the whole meeting. Just let the tutor know your difficulty and arrive or leave discreetly when you have to.

Key points

In tutorial discussions:

- Don't be anxious about the quality of your contributions. Other people are usually more concerned about what *they* say than what you say.

- Don't wait for 'the big moment' before you speak; ask the simple question, give the obvious example.

- Share in the responsibility for keeping the group going.

Try as best you can to do the relevant reading before the tutorial but don't skip the tutorial if you haven't been able to manage it.

Learning from self-help groups

This section draws on material from The Open University's Open Business School's Study Skills pack (B500).

Even when group tutorials feature as part of the formal course structure, you should also expect to form and participate in other discussion groups outside the tutorials when the tutor is not present. Self-help groups can arrange to set their own agendas and meet at places and times which suit the circumstances of individual members.

If self-help groups are to be successful, however, they need commitment from everyone who attends and agreement on a firm agenda to avoid unproductive discussion. While no one likes to appear too thrusting and self important, particularly when the group members don't know each other well, someone has to be prepared to accept at least a share in the role of leading a self-help group, perhaps on a rotating basis. Once the group has met for the first time, subsequent meetings and their agendas can be arranged in advance.

Successful self-help groups benefit from a leader who takes responsibility for setting up meetings, sending out reminders and checking up on group members who don't attend. As with group discussions, there is a social aspect to self-help groups and a need to address the 'domestic factors' in meetings. These include arrangements for tea and coffee, a place to meet which is free from distractions and disturbance, room for everyone to spread out papers and books and so on. The leader should also ensure that the group doesn't wander off the point or descend into anecdotal recollections. However, the leader should not be so dominant that he or she dictates the form and content of the discussion and overrides the needs of other people in the group.

As with tutorials, attending to group processes is important for success. All group members will need to consider the following points.

Initiating

When a lull occurs someone has to break the silence. The reluctance most people feel about doing this usually stems from their unwillingness to risk saying something others might reject.

Giving and asking for information

Group members should be prepared to ask questions to help clarify their own understanding of the subject, and the other members must be prepared to share *their* understanding. Remember that self-help groups are an exercise in co-operative learning and understanding. There are no points to be scored and there is no one to be 'put down'.

Giving and asking for reaction

When a member does share his or her understanding of a point, groups often treat it as a conversation stopper and remain silent or move on without comment. For learning to take place some reaction should be volunteered or requested. A dynamic group thrives on interaction.

Re-stating and giving examples

This is really a specific type of giving and asking for reactions. If a member re-states what another has said, or offers an example, this is feedback to the original speaker.

Mis-statements

Misinformation and mis-statements must not be allowed to pass. Suggesting that someone else's statement is not entirely accurate requires some skill and determination. Too often it is allowed to pass to save embarrassment of either the speaker or the critic. Given that group members are being encouraged to test their understanding in the presence of the group, it is inevitable that the whole group will not always have gained the same impression from the course material.

Clarifying, synthesising and summarising

Even with apparently simple material, groups can get themselves tied in knots and from time to time someone should be prepared to summarise and draw together the ideas which have been discussed. This often has the effect of drawing a discussion to a close. In a self-help group it is not necessarily the job of the chairperson, although he or she should be prepared to recognise that the discussion has come to a natural end.

Self-help groups tend to be practical and focus on the next written assignment or revision for the examination. They should also, however, include a review of what has been learned over the weeks since the last meeting and discussion of any problem areas. This helps everyone to reflect on the learning experience. As the members of the group get to know each other better, individual strengths and weaknesses become apparent and these need to be recognised. Expertise can be shared and everyone can benefit.

Although, by definition, self-help groups meet without a tutor, it is often worth talking to your tutor about your plans. He or she may be able to give you advice or tips about agenda items or make some time available in the tutorial for feedback from your group.

Finally, as with any management activity, don't forget to review the progress you make in achieving the objectives of the group. Appropriate remedial action will ensure that the group continues successfully and doesn't lose direction or enthusiasm.

6 Learning from electronic media

Learning from video

Some people find it difficult and boring to learn from text alone, and appreciate the opportunity of a change to visual media such as television programmes and video cassettes. Now that a high percentage of homes, at least in the UK, possess a video recorder, most people can watch specially prepared training videos whenever they wish, and they can also record television programmes for detailed attention later. However, it is important, from the outset, that you are aware that learning from these media is not just a case of viewing and listening in the way normally associated with them as a form of entertainment. They have a different purpose which will involve you more actively, and you should assume the same questioning stance as you would towards any other learning materials.

There are two major categories of video which are of particular value to managers. The first is the stand-alone training video, which is often used as a catalyst for group discussion. Often, this type of video contrasts 'good' and 'bad' management practice and succeeds in putting across a simple set of messages in a humorous way.

The second type of video is the kind produced by the Open University in conjunction with the BBC which is integrated into the course and provides an illustration or expansion of the ideas presented in text. For example, it may show a graphic demonstration of a difficult concept such as a financial break-even analysis, a role play in which actors portray fictional characters in a management situation, or a real-life case study of an organisation in which managers take part. In the latter case, you have the privilege of 'eavesdropping' on events as they are actually happening and on situations to which you might not otherwise have access, such as senior management discussions. An effective video draws the viewer into the action and discussion so that he or she feels part of it.

The advantage of video is that you control when and how you watch it. Some video programmes are designed so that there are pauses in the action to allow you to reflect on what you have just seen, or to respond to a question. Even when this facility is not built in to the programme, you can stop the tape, rewind and replay it to suit your personal learning needs. If you didn't grasp the idea the first time, you can replay the cassette, or selected parts of it, as often as you wish. Videos can also provide a shared frame of reference for discussion of issues at tutorials.

Video is particularly valuable in understanding the dynamics of processes. With writing or speech alone, it often takes many words to represent the unfolding of a dynamic process. Verbal explanations tend to have a somewhat static quality. Moving pictures offer great potential for representing the world in terms of 'processes' rather than 'objects'. Thus, video can develop and convey a different kind of knowledge from 'book knowledge' – a more rounded and dynamic understanding.

In order to gain the maximum benefit from learning from video, particularly that which is part of a text-based course, you may be required to undertake some preparation before you watch it. As with most forms of study, you also need time to watch and, possibly, you may need to negotiate when you can have uninterrupted use of the family television set. There may be accompanying notes you should read beforehand and exercises to carry out or questions to answer, after you have watched the video. Therefore, you may need to:

- Read about the topic in the text beforehand.
- Read any associated programme notes.
- Be prepared to make notes as you watch.
- If necessary, replay the video, either in part or in full, to ensure that you have understood it.
- Carry out any associated activities.
- Reflect on what you have seen and how it connects with the rest of your learning.

Key points

Video has the advantages of:

- being a visual medium
- being able to depict a range of real-life situations
- being under your control.

Problems of learning from video

Some of the problems associated with learning from video are logistic and concerned with making time and finding space in which to watch in peace. It is difficult, too, just as with live lectures or talks, to make notes, listen and watch at the same time. This can be even more problematic if you have to watch television in the sitting-room with other people around you, the telephone ringing, a friend dropping in for a chat and so on. There is also a danger of relying on video as a main learning medium just because it suits your learning approach. In most courses which contain a video element, the text contains the core information and the video is used to illustrate some key point. Where video recordings of actual lectures are provided in place of text, as is the case in some institutions, this can add considerably to the amount of notes you need to make and, unlike a live lecture, there is no opportunity to question the lecturer or ask for clarification. However, you can at least replay material you have not understood and discuss the content with others, as well as undertake preliminary and follow-up work.

Finally, people with visual impairment are at a disadvantage when major learning is restricted to video, although it is sometimes possible to obtain Braille transcripts of television programmes and video recordings.

Learning from audio

As with video, there are two categories of audio cassette which you are likely to find useful. The first is designed to be interactive – that is, you are expected to stop the tape at intervals and carry out an activity. Using audio cassettes interactively with texts helps to vary the texture of your studies, offering a change of activity and a change of pace. Open University research has shown that many students like audio tapes that are cross-referenced to text. This can be a powerful way of talking you through a complicated diagram or table of figures which features in the text. This is not the kind of audio cassette to play in your car when driving on the motorway!

Although the audio cassette player in the home may have been replaced by a CD player, most car and personal stereos still play cassettes. Travelling time can be particularly valuable for study purposes when using this medium. For example, you might like to record your notes on cassette and play these back on your way to work.

Many managers appreciate the non-interactive kind of audio recording to listen to while travelling, often bringing together experts or senior managers to discuss issues of common interest. It tends to be easier to concentrate on abstract arguments because you are not attending to visual images at the same time. A 'philosophical' debate, for instance, can be very arresting, when you have nothing but the words to focus on. This kind of cassette can also be designed as a revision aid, picking out the main points raised in the text and reminding you of what you have been studying. Indeed, the flexibility of audio cassettes means you can make such tapes yourself, particularly of key points you wish to remember for, say, an exam.

ACTIVITY Can you think of any ways in which you could improve your time management by using audio cassettes as a learning medium?

Key points

Audio cassettes can support your learning by:

- talking you through complex ideas or diagrams
- bringing together a number of experts
- transforming travel time into learning time
- acting as an aid to revision.

Problems with learning from audio

The interactive audio cassette requires associated materials to be at hand and a commitment of time to tackling the activities which go with it. The more discursive type of cassette may also require you to make notes. People whose hearing has deteriorated find audio cassettes difficult if there are no accompanying visual stimuli to supplement their impaired hearing (again, it may be possible to obtain written transcripts of audio material). When more than two or three people are talking on an audio cassette, it becomes increasingly difficult to differentiate between them and to remember who they are. Is that the Managing Director or the Sales Assistant making that contentious remark ...?

Using the telephone in learning

In distance learning, because of the geographical dispersion of course tutors and students, face-to-face contact for some students is difficult, or even impossible. Letter or fax have their place but the telephone can often provide an effective tutorial substitute.

In its simplest form, the telephone tutorial is merely a link between the tutor and one student. In this case a constructive dialogue is easily established since you have experience of this form of individual contact in everyday life. However, you may not be experienced in its use as a medium for learning. Good preparation is of vital importance in this form of contact, particularly when it involves problem solving, diagrams or other such material. This applies whether the contact is pre-arranged or you are telephoning because you need help from your tutor.

Problems in using the telephone for learning

- You may not have met your tutor face to face – in which case there's a sense of impersonality.
- The lack of visual contact, such as a smile or a puzzled look – the voice alone has to carry the message.
- The pressure of time – a feeling that the interaction moves more quickly than in a face-to-face situation – and on the telephone time is money!
- The element of surprise or, indeed, possible intrusion for the tutor and the awareness of this on your part unless the call is pre-arranged.
- The unfamiliarity with or nervousness about the use of the telephone for such a purpose.
- The awkward siting of some domestic telephones.

Key points

It is possible to overcome most of these drawbacks.

- Don't forget to put yourself in the other party's shoes when you need to make telephone contact with them.

- Prepare carefully – have any necessary materials to hand and jot down the points you wish to raise in advance.

- Use more voice cues to compensate for lack of visual contact – words and phrases such as 'Can you expand on that point?', 'OK so far?', 'May I have a think about that for a moment?', 'Yes' and so on all help to move the conversation along smoothly and reassuringly.

- Listen sensitively – give the tutor a chance to articulate her or his points.

- Remember that your tone of voice carries a clear message in the absence of visual cues – a smile can't be seen to modify the message of the voice.

- Remember that you can write or take notes as well as listen.

- Give your tutor a chance to give a thought-out response to a query if you have telephoned unannounced – to take a note and arrange to telephone back. This gives your tutor time to think about an answer, to jot down what he or she may wish to say and to bring any necessary course material or papers to the telephone. If your tutor is not personally available, leave a short clear message so that he or she can prepare before contacting you.

- Don't be afraid of silence – you can always check what's going on by a question such as 'Did you understand my last point?' or 'Do you need to think about that?' People need time on the telephone to think, just as they do face to face.

- Finally, don't forget to check back over what you've learned as you would do for a normal tutorial.

Learning from electronic media

This section is a very basic introduction to some of the ways in which personal computers can help people to learn. If you do not know anything at all about computers, you have no need to worry. Modern personal computers are so much easier to use than hitherto and there are a range of starter courses available to help you become familiar with their operation. Even if you don't see yourself using a personal computer in the near future, this section should at least introduce you to the possibilities if you eventually decide to use one.

Of course, many managers today are quite familiar with the uses and applications of computers and this ability to use word processing, spreadsheet and database tools can extend their learning capacity. These tools cut down the time spent on note-taking, information searches and writing tasks and can greatly improve the quality of written communications. Using a computer as a communication tool can also provide access to data, messaging and conferencing facilities across networks.

Word processing has had a profound impact on writing style. The sheer speed with which you can get words down and move them around in a document has transformed the writing process. In addition, the ability to edit as you write, check the spelling, or look up a word in the computer's thesaurus encourages the production of documents that are legible and easy to read. As you become more proficient, you can change the typeface, underline, embolden or italicise particular words or phrases, box headings and tables and add charts and graphs. The resulting documents can look extremely professional.

More advice on the use of a word processor in writing tasks is given in Chapter 5.

However, not everyone finds they can accomplish mentally demanding writing on a word processor. Others find they write too much because it is so easy to produce words, or they keep moving bits around until their writing loses coherence – the fact that only a certain number of lines of text can be displayed on the screen at one time is no help at all. Like any other medium, then, using a word processor is a matter of personal preference.

If you have to sit a written examination as part of your course you will be disadvantaged if you rely too heavily on word processing. I advise that, if you use a word processor as part of your everyday office equipment, you practise the lost art of handwriting before the examination. Writing and word processing are two different skills and you don't want to add to the stress which examinations tend to create.

A *spreadsheet* is a tabular arrangement of data, organised in rows and columns. The entries in the table are known as cells and each cell can hold some text or figures or, more importantly, a formula that calculates a value for that cell from values held elsewhere in the sheet. You can alter the value of one cell and all the dependent values in the other cells will change automatically. For example, if you want to know what effect an increase in sales figures would have on your profit, you can play around with changes to sales and see immediately what effect any increase or decrease will have.

Spreadsheets are an invaluable learning aid when it comes to trying out the effects of changes in, for example, budget figures or numerical data. In your written work you may want to support an argument by showing what effects these changes can have on related figures, particularly in areas such as costing, budgeting, marketing, sales or production figures.

Computer *databases* consist of files containing records, rather like a filing cabinet but much more convenient. Each record holds data in a structured manner about, for example, a product, department or person. You can organise this data so that it can be recalled for different purposes; for example, you might want an alphabetical list of clients, or a list of clients living in a particular area, or a list of clients seen in February. The same basic data can provide all these lists within a few minutes. There is obviously scope for utilising a database for study purposes, perhaps through key words as you go through the course or for indexing relevant journal articles you have read; it can be particularly helpful in making connections.

ACTIVITY   Can you think of ways in which word processing and the use of spreadsheets or databases could help to increase your learning and/or be of value to you when you are studying?

The opportunities offered by CD-ROM (*Compact Disc-Read Only Memory*) for gaining access to information are immense; it is like having a library of electronic books at your fingertips, expertly stored and indexed for you to browse through. Some encyclopaedias, dictionaries and other reference sources are available on compact disc, and for managers, there is the opportunity to look at industry or sector data comparisons.

In addition, *library catalogues* are nearly always held on computer. This has transformed the activity of hunting for relevant books, journals and articles that can be used for help with your learning on advanced courses. It is now possible to carry out searches for source texts much faster and more flexibly than before. Open University students, for example, have library access through the computerised AIMS system. There are enormous benefits in being able to access information in this way.

AIMS gives students access to external databases, including those of other university libraries.

Personal computers are increasingly used as communication tools for purposes such as *electronic mail*, a system in which managers on the same computer network can exchange information electronically. Circulation lists can be created and stored to enable a message to be sent simultaneously to everyone in a specific group. Instead of laboriously ensuring that messages are sent by hand to everyone on your circulation list, you can despatch them electronically with a single computer command and arrange for replies to be automatically returned to a file in your computer. A group of managers on the same course can communicate with each other electronically, saving valuable meeting time and paper.

So-called wide-area-networks, connected through the public telephone system, also allow you to participate in a *computer conference*, which you could perhaps use to set up an electronic self-help group. The computer in this situation acts in effect like a notice board on which people pin messages. One person puts up a message and then other managers, or the tutor, put up other messages in response. You might check the 'notice board' every few days to read the new messages that have been put up in the various currently active 'conversations', and add comments of your own. In this way, a group of managers on the same course can arrange to hold a computer conference about various management issues, or, more narrowly, about the next piece of written work to be done or revision strategies for the examination.

Networking extends your learning opportunities by enabling you to appreciate the contribution of others and by facilitating the discussion of your own views and ideas. Using computer conferencing enables you to tap into a vast resource of other students and tutors who will have differing backgrounds, experiences, jobs and geographical locations from yours.

Electronic conferences are organised so that there are areas which focus on particular topics or interest groups, equivalent, perhaps, to traditional teaching rooms or seminars, as well as 'chat' areas, equivalent, perhaps, to the common room in a bricks-and-mortar university. You can browse electronically around these, glimpse all kinds of issues being discussed, and choose to join in on any aspects that interest you or where you have a contribution to make.

If this is a new medium for you, you may be tempted to give up before getting to the learning benefits. As with any new piece of software, you'll need to put aside some time to learn what it can offer you and how to use it effectively.

Once into the conferences, some basic idea of protocol may help you:

- Let other people know you are there – put in a brief statement saying who you are and what your interest is. Don't forget to 'sign' your name – others are more likely to reply to you.

- Electronic networking is a cross between verbal and written communication. Don't think that you must produce essay standard writing, but you do need to practise conciseness and clarity.

- Keep each message or comment to one topic area, and try not to use more than one screenful of text. This will help to keep interest lively and lead to further discussion.

Key points

Electronic media can help your learning through using:

- the flexibility of word-processing facilities for writing assignments

- the spreadsheet facility to show the effects of changing cell values

- databases for information searches

- electronic networks to facilitate contact with other students.

---

7 Learning from case studies

Case studies as examination questions are referred to again briefly in Chapter 8.

Case studies are widely used in management teaching to bring ideas and course concepts to life in a relevant and interesting way. They may also occur in assignment or examination questions to give the student the opportunity to demonstrate a broad knowledge of the subject matter.

A case study is a concise description of a situation which exists, or a series of events which have taken place, in an organisation. The events, whether from real life or fictional, together with any diagrams and tables, provide a *scenario* on which you may be asked to base your analysis and comments. You are not required, in most case studies, to display expert or in-depth knowledge of the particular organisation. Typically, your task will be to identify a number of things that have gone wrong or important things that may not have been done and to make recommendations for addressing these.

You will be expected to identify the principles and concepts related to what you have been learning, and base your analysis and recommendations on these. They will provide a framework within which the case will have a deeper meaning for you than would appear to the casual reader. Indeed, you may wish to make brief notes to remind yourself of key course concepts and ideas, perhaps in a brief sketch or diagram, before even reading the case study. This will alert you to the sorts of things you might expect to feature and will help to inform your approach.

It is worth keeping the following general points in mind when you tackle a case study.

These points have been adapted from the Open Business School course B789 *Managing Voluntary and Nonprofit Enterprises* Course Guide.

■ Management problems are rarely neat and self-contained; they are usually related to other problems and issues. For example, a problem of an overloaded job (job redesign) may have implications for the organisation's reward and career systems, for staff motivation, for inter-departmental relations and how the organisation is structured. Typically, a case study will contain several *interrelated* problems and issues giving you scope to use a variety of course ideas in analysing it.

■ Remember you must show that you understand course concepts, ideas, techniques, etc. and that you can use them to *analyse* the case study and come up with *realistic* recommendations. Be aware of the danger of advocating grand solutions that are very difficult or impossible to implement, or simplistic analyses in which most of the people involved are acting foolishly or in bad faith. Typically, the case study will allow several different interpretations and you should be prepared to recognise some of the uncertainties and ambiguities. Don't stop after identifying one theme or problematic aspect of the situation – look for several strands.

■ Based on your analysis, develop a set of *realistic* recommendations for tackling the problems or issues that you have been asked to address. Often it will be helpful to point to potential pitfalls and difficulties associated with your recommendations. Or you may simply indicate how you would set about tackling the problems because it would be important to gather information and support in working out actual solutions.

■ Make sure that you give *evidence* from the case study to support your analysis and recommendations. This is one way in which you can show that you really understand the concepts you are using.

Case studies need to be approached systematically. The following steps will help you to get the best learning experience – and a good assignment answer.

Don't be afraid to use the margins of the case study for quick jottings.

How to read questions effectively is tackled in Chapter 5.

First, read the case study through fairly quickly to get a general feeling for the story line. Certain points may leap from the text; make a brief note or highlight them immediately if this happens. Then re-read the case study more carefully, bearing in mind that every paragraph has probably been designed to contain something of relevance for you to consider and relate to the course. Make brief notes during this second reading about problems which seem to be occurring and any major issues you can identify. Now read the questions that accompany the case study to ensure that you are clear about what you are being asked to provide in your answer. Then, *look for the underlying issues* – what issue or issues seem to be causing the problems described in the scenario? If several problems are apparent, then you should try to find links and common causes. For example, in a scenario about a department, 'problems' might include increasing absenteeism, poor performance and persistent lateness. From your reading of the case, you would probably deduce that staff motivation is low – but what is the underlying cause? Perhaps the jobs are boring and repetitious, maybe a recent change in working practice proved to be unpopular, or the departmental head's management style might be inappropriate. It is these underlying issues, rather than the consequences, that you need to identify from your analysis.

At this point, you may find it useful to construct a simple matrix which you can use to make sense of any case study. You need a focused, systematic analysis. To attempt to answer the question by returning frequently to the text will slow up your thought processes. Indeed, you may well lose track of what you intend to do as you try to disentangle salient points from the mass of text – and, more crucially, have to take them in the order dictated by the text, rather than in the order best suited to your answer.

If you look at the sample matrix in Figure 2.2, you will see that it has four vertical and four horizontal headings. The horizontal layers relate to the levels within an organisation. Working from the top down, you can see the levels descend from the organisation as a whole, or factors outside the organisation, through departments or groups of people to the individual; the fourth level is in the mechanical or technical areas where systems or machinery are involved.

Level	Main issues	Related problems	Relevant course concepts	Specific actions
Environment/ Organisation				
Department/ Group/ Inter-group				
Individual				
Technical/ Technological				

Figure 2.2 *A matrix for analysing case studies*

The first two headings across the top of the matrix are related to what was said earlier about identifying 'issues' rather than 'problems'. The third heading is concerned with concepts or ideas from the course you are studying which can be used to explain the underlying issues and why they are causing the observable problems. Under the final heading can be listed specific actions that can be taken, related to ways in which course concepts can be applied to resolving the main issues in the case study.

Below is a short case study. Read it through carefully before turning to Figure 2.3, where I have used the matrix to help analyse (a) what issues and problems are involved, and (b) which management concepts are relevant to these issues. You may not be familiar with some of the language or concepts at this point, but you should have no difficulty in getting a general idea of how to use the matrix. Remember that you can start anywhere within the matrix and that you don't need to fill in all the cells.

When you have completed the matrix, you are ready to form a coherent view of the case. You have identified one or more underlying issues at one or more levels within the organisation and it is these which need to be tackled if the situation is to be improved. Your plan should identify the main issue or issues and use relevant course concepts to analyse the problems arising as a result. It should also recommend a course of action using course concepts you have identified. Most case study questions will require you to undertake this kind of analysis and recommendations for improvement. You also need to retain a sense of realism; not everything can be put right immediately and you should make practical recommendations for phased improvements. Finally, you should think about how you could write out a plan for your answer as clearly and succinctly as possible.

Your plan may be in note or diagrammatic form according to preference. Planning answers is considered in Chapters 5 and 8.

When you have produced a first draft of an outline plan which identifies the problems and the major underlying issue(s) and how these should be tackled, you should re-read the case to decide if you need to modify your plan. In particular, you should ensure that you have covered *all* the questions you have been asked to answer about the case study. Make any changes necessary. Then go ahead and write a final draft of your analysis of the case study in an appropriate format, such as a management report, checking back to the question from time to time to make sure you are on track.

The following case study has been approached in this way.

Case study

Chris Hampson is the Sales Manager at Barset Motors and was promoted to this job six months ago. The General Manager will be holding a six-month appraisal interview with Chris in a week's time.

Chris has worked for Barset Motors for four years and, until recently, had always enjoyed the work, having been successful in the used car section and, later, selling new models. 'I enjoy selling,' Chris explained. 'I get a real kick out of it.' Colleagues and customers respected this expertise and Chris was a popular member of the sales team with a list of regular customers.

Most people are delighted with promotion and Chris was no exception, but things were not working out as well as was expected. Much of the time, Chris was to be found in the showroom, eager to hear about the staff's current sales and purchases and hoping to keep the respect of the sales staff in this way, as well as to be a good manager.

Distractions seemed to be never-ending and there did not seem to be time for all the office work; in fact, it became necessary to take work home. The General Manager had asked for some ideas for a big Promotion Week, but Chris, having agreed the deadline for this paper, found it much harder to write than he had expected. When the paper was ready – the day before the deadline – the typist was sick. There had been some difficulties in finding someone else to type the paper and other things had started to go wrong.

On another occasion, at a simple ceremony when a young sales trainee was being presented with a certificate, Chris, having spent some time talking to an old customer, had been late, and had not had time to prepare a speech. Once or twice a member of staff had been on leave when, according to the chart in Chris's office, he should have been at work. There had been several reminders from the Personnel Officer about the manufacturer's training programme for showroom staff – Chris's nominations were late. There had been other reminders to make a case for an extra salesperson in the used car department. (To make such a case required an analysis of the sales figures over the past year and the compilation of a careful and convincing forecast for the next year, but Chris had not yet had time to deal with this.) Once or twice some important letters had remained in Chris's tray, unsigned, for some days.

Finally, this morning, there had been an unsettling exchange with one of the sales staff. Chris had told him that the price he had offered for the customer's car was too high and the salesman had become angry at what he saw as the manager 'always interfering'. He had said he was an experienced salesman and that he was going to see the General Manager.

As it happened, the General Manager was away for the day and the salesman cooled down, but he and Chris kept their distance from each other and Chris felt troubled by the episode which seemed to express all the difficulties that had arisen since that welcome promotion six months earlier. Being a manager did not seem as easy as being successful at sales and nothing seemed to have turned out as expected.

(B600 *The Capable Manager*, Open Business School Professional Certificate in Management)

Now look at my matrix in Figure 2.3. Because I am using this case for illustration, I have deliberately not used any jargon. Neither have I assumed that you have read any management course materials at this juncture – so if you are an experienced or well trained manager you may well be able to add significant insights and pointers to my table.

Level	Main issues	Related problems	Relevant course concepts	Specific actions
Environment/ Organisation	Policies on promotion and training		Staff development and training	Management training for Chris
Department/Group/ Inter-group	Inappropriate leadership	Anger from subordinate Not acting like a manager	Conflict Management style	Need for Chris to appreciate that the old selling job was past history
Individual	Work overload	Taking work home Speech not prepared Nomination late Unsigned letters	Time management	Setting achievable goals Delegating Prioritising
Technical/ Technological		Inaccurate chart	Planning and control	Making plans to achieve better time management and monitoring these

Figure 2.3 *Using the matrix to analyse the case study of Chris Hampson*

To do this exercise, I began by noting down the problems at different levels in the second column. Although the problems relating to the subordinates stemmed from the manager's individual style of leadership, I felt these were problems at a *departmental* level since they related to relationships with staff. I then noted down relevant course concepts before finally deciding on the main issues and my recommendations for action. As you can see, I did not use all the cells in the matrix.

I was then ready to write a report in which I would first identify the main issues at the three levels shown in the matrix, showing that these were underlying the problems described in the case study. Using relevant management concepts from the course, I could explain *why* these issues needed to be addressed. Those in the last column I could use as a set of recommendations to improve the situation.

Key points

■ Case studies typically provide a scenario of an organisation where there are problems that course concepts would help to address.

■ You are asked to identify the main issues, analyse the problems which arise and make recommendations for action.

■ You *must* use relevant course concepts to buttress your analysis and recommendations.

■ You need to tackle the case study systematically, using a tool such as the suggested matrix before planning and writing your answer.

Finally, to continue the theme of reflecting on what you have learned, write your own summary for this chapter using the section headings from the Contents list.

Appendix 2.1 A mentoring action plan

The role of the mentor complements the role of your line manager in helping you gain a wider perspective on management in your organisation, and complements the role of your tutor by helping you to connect your academic development to the world of work.

How to use a mentor

When and where to meet your mentor is a matter for negotiation between yourselves. You may wish to use an informal setting, such as a meeting over lunch, or you may prefer a more formal meeting in a more private situation, such as an office. There are no rules dictating how long such mentoring sessions should last. However, a reasonable estimate is one to one and a half hours per month. You may also find that telephone conversations may be used to supplement face-to-face meetings – reliance on telephone contact alone may be necessary for some students whose mentor is geographically distant.

In order to gain the most benefit from a mentoring session, you should:

- plan carefully beforehand what you want to know and what questions you want to ask
- aim to keep your mentor informed of your general progress on the particular course
- share information with your mentor on your progress and what you are learning
- discuss how you would wish to apply this new knowledge and skill to your work.

Remember, your mentor will not necessarily be familiar with the course you are studying nor have all the answers!

Choosing a mentor

Because of the confidential nature of the relationship, you should be encouraged to choose your own mentor, if at all possible. You may wish to raise sensitive issues in the context of relationships with, and attitudes to, superiors,

colleagues and the organisation itself. It is vital, therefore, that you can rely absolutely on the confidentiality of your discussions with your mentor. At the outset, you and your mentor should agree that either side can terminate the arrangement if it is not working.

I recognise that you may not have a wide range of potential mentors in your organisation. However, the following guidelines may be helpful. Try to select someone who meets at least some of the criteria set out below. If you do not have direct contact with someone who might be a potential mentor, it may be worth requesting assistance from your personnel department or training officer, or your course sponsor.

Ideally, your mentor will be someone who is:

- normally *not* your line manager
- from a different discipline or management line
- senior to you or substantially more experienced in management
- located within your organisation
- rather older than you.

It would also be beneficial if your mentor:

- has recent experience of mentoring
- works in the field of developing and training staff
- has recent experience of studying a management course.

Finally, at a more personal level, a good mentor should possess some, if not all, of the following attributes:

- experience to help you identify learning opportunities and to turn theoretical learning into practical ability
- commitment to making themselves available and giving sufficient time to performing the mentoring role
- trustworthiness to provide the personal and supportive relationship necessary
- objectivity to stimulate and nurture effective managerial practice without the constraints of the line relationship
- patience to listen to and assist with difficulties you may have in managing your own learning

- interpersonal skills to build up a good rapport
- commitment to the whole area of continuous personal and professional development.

You would be very fortunate indeed to find someone who possessed all the attributes on this list, if, indeed, such a paragon ever existed. Use common sense here; it is more important that you and your mentor establish a productive interpersonal rapport than that he or she fulfils the 'ideal' image of a mentor.

Appendix 2.2 Taking notes in lectures

There is no single best way of taking notes. Some people scribble busily throughout lectures and write several pages, while others take down no more than a few key points set out diagrammatically. Both of these approaches can be very effective. It depends on the context in which you are attending the lecture, on the kind of lecture it is, and most of all on the way in which you work and learn.

If you are attending a course that uses lectures as the main teaching medium, then you may have to write down a lot to be sure of getting hold of what you need. On the other hand, if the lectures are backed up by handouts and by good textbooks (or better still by 'teaching texts', structured to help you to learn), then you may need very little in the way of a written record.

Equally, if the lecture itself is delivered in a formal and monotonous way and is packed with detailed information, you may find that you have to write down a lot just to keep track of it. If, on the other hand, the lecturer has a lively style and gives striking examples and illustrations of the main points, you may find that you learn a lot by concentrating on listening and just writing the occasional notes of the key points and the topics covered.

The most important factor, though, is you – what sort of lecture listener are you? Do you tend to daydream in lectures? Do you tend to feel anxious about whether you are understanding enough? Are you the sort of person who prefers to rely on the printed text for any ideas you need to work on in detail, so that you can concentrate on listening in lectures? Do you feel confident that a few phrases here and there will be enough to remind you of the points you need to hold on to? Or do you find it too difficult to decide which points are important as the lecture is in full flow? Do you feel that, unless you are writing most of the time, you will miss something crucial? You need to analyse your own reactions to listening to lectures, so that you develop a note-taking strategy which suits *you*.

If writing a lot helps you to allay anxiety and if it keeps you actively 'working' with what is being said, rather than just letting it wash over you, then it may be the right approach for you. On the other hand, if you try to write *everything* down, you will probably learn very little during the lecture itself. Most of your work will still lie ahead of you at the end, in that you will then need to read the notes to find out what is in them. This will be quite difficult and time-consuming if you didn't have time to spare to take in the central theme of the lecture. It is worth stopping to ask yourself whether, in practice, you will find time to read your voluminous notes. Perhaps it doesn't matter, if the writing helps to keep your mind on the job. However, if you do decide that you are *not* likely to make much sense of mountains of notes, this releases you from the burden of writing endlessly and allows you to listen and take notes more selectively.

How do you know which points to write down?

The beginning and the end of a lecture are particularly important times for note-taking. At the start you are likely to be able to get down the main points of the lecture. The lecturer will often give clues in the form of slides, notes on the flipchart or handouts, which reveal the broad structure of the lecture. At the end, you should try to draw out some conclusions. Again, the lecturer may give you direct help with this by summarising. For the first and last 10 minutes, then, you might set yourself the task of taking quite full notes, while allowing yourself to be more relaxed and your note-taking more sporadic in between. All you may need are a few headings and the occasional word or phrase to remind you of the general area covered and the main themes.

Note down any examples and illustrations the lecturer gives. They will help to remind you of the workings of the arguments and explanations. Often you won't need more than a word or two to bring these back to you. On the other hand, when you want to note a key point which is more abstract, you may need to get the whole thing down in detail, if you are going to be able to make sense of it afterwards. Note the names of major writers who are mentioned and the dates of their work. This will help to give you a sense of who the main figures are in your field of study and enable you to make connections with what you read. Make a point of writing down any questions or comments that occur to you as you listen. After the lecture, you may find that your comments are more use to you than the words of the lecturer in reflecting on what was going through your mind at the time.

If you take listening and thinking seriously, you cannot expect to make very full notes in a lecture. In fact the process of deciding what is important enough to write down and what is not may actually be more valuable to you than the notes you end up with. It keeps your mind alert and makes you think about the subject.

Styles of note taking

What you select to write down and how you position it on the page will impose a structure on the material presented in the lecture. This in turn will help you to understand it and to remember it. Don't be stingy with your paper.

Spread your notes across the page generously and use dividing lines, arrows, brackets, boxes and so on, to emphasise divisions and links in the material. You might, for example, put your own remarks and queries over the right-hand side of the paper, or enclose them in square brackets [like this]. Some people find it helpful to use diagrams, putting the topic of the lecture in a circle in the middle of the page and then drawing lines branching out for various sub-topics as they arise.

Of course, you cannot expect lecture notes to have as much structure and clarity as notes you make when you read. You need to try to develop your own style of shorthand, one which makes sense to you. Don't worry if your notes are untidy – this is natural when you are listening and watching at the same time as writing. You can sort them out into a better arrangement after the lecture is over. This has two advantages:

- It helps you to go through what you have noted down and it may also help you to recall other aspects of the lecture.
- You can put your notes into a logical arrangement.

Making notes after the lecture

An hour spent at a lecture is a significant investment of your study time, but the return may seem disappointing if, a day or two later, you cannot recall what the lecture was about, or make much sense of your notes. It is sometimes said that what you get out of a lecture is not determined by what you do during the lecture so much as by the work you put in before and after it. Depending on the circumstances, you may find that lecture time occupies a small percentage of your total study time.

Chapter 3 Reading

1 Introduction

Reading will form a crucial part of your study – you will be required to read a lot of material and you will need to understand what you have read to help you to write assignments and to pass examinations. This chapter focuses on reading for study purposes, and examines the reading process in order that you will understand more about your reading. Reading strategies are described and illustrated in Activities that you can experiment with now, and then use as appropriate during your study programme.

ACTIVITY   Having read the contents list for this chapter, what are your aims in reading this chapter? What, if anything, worries you about reading? What do you hope to gain from this chapter?

Remember to return to this Activity when you have worked through the chapter.

Some of you will be avid readers, whilst others will think that you read very little. As a busy manager, you may find you have little time to read for enjoyment. Perhaps you have difficulty in finding time to read the newspaper every day. Perhaps you feel that most of your reading time is taken up with ploughing through junk mail or circulars at home, and with an ever-increasing pile of papers at work. All of us read things every day, often without even registering that we are reading. Initially, in this chapter, we will consider reading in its widest sense, in order that we can start to think about the process of reading and how we read what we read.

ACTIVITY List everything you read yesterday. As you do so, note *why* you read it – in other words, note *what* you read and your *purpose* for reading it.

Here is a part of my list:

What I read yesterday	Why I read it
Road signs	to go in the right direction and to abide by the law
Newspaper	to see what was on the television and to keep up to date with the main news in a spare 10 minutes
Article in a computer magazine	to see what had been written about an area of specific interest and to learn about the latest developments at work
Recipe book	to choose two dishes that I needed to prepare for the end of the week
Sub-titles on TV	to understand a Japanese documentary film

If you look at your list you will probably see that some of yesterday's reading tasks required a lot of concentration; others required very little. You can also distinguish between reading that resulted in an immediate action or behaviour, such as following road signs and directions, and reading that resulted in an increased understanding of a topic.

Possibly I will remember the road directions I followed, but if not, it doesn't really matter because I can just follow the signs again next time. Hopefully, I will have internalised much of the computing article because I made careful notes as I read it through. I then re-read it and concentrated on improving my detailed understanding.

Road signs require very little effort. But course texts require much more effort and, I would suggest, a different sort of effort. A virtually instant understanding is required with road signs, although you don't really need to make any great effort to remember and to 'learn' a sign. Once you have studied the Highway Code for driving in the UK, you are quite likely to remember what the common signs mean. You will frequently meet these signs and, additionally, the signs themselves should be easy to understand because the symbols were carefully chosen to make the message comprehensible. Course texts and academic texts, by contrast, carry a longer and more complicated message. They may not be instantly comprehensible and you don't usually have to act on them immediately. The associated in-text Activities may be the only occasions when you act on what you have read.

Now think again about your list of yesterday's reading. How long did you spend on any of your reading activities? Did you sit down and read uninterrupted for more than 15 minutes or were you simply taking in information, such as the road signs, as you did something else, for example driving? Were you trying to learn the information, or were you just reacting to it, or were you reading for relaxation? Were you thinking only about what you were reading or were you also thinking about something else? Were you aware that you were concentrating or was your concentration automatic? Try to think about these questions during the next few days. Ask yourself what sort of reading you do and try to decide how your purposes for reading affect your way of reading.

Your feelings about reading are important. How much of yesterday's reading did you enjoy? How much of it really interested you?

2 Your attitude towards the topic

The first thing that affects your attitude to reading is your level of enthusiasm for the topic. In your leisure reading you can be selective and spend your time reading what you like. But once you have chosen to study on a particular course then you are provided with a set of course materials, and some of the materials may not appeal to you at all at first sight. This is potentially a problem.

Key points

You cannot learn effectively unless you can become interested in the subject matter.

Most subjects can be interesting if looked at in the right way. Whether you are interested depends on what is currently on your mind. If you are starting on a subject you are not initially interested in, the first thing to do is pitch in and hope that the writer is able to show you some interesting angles. If you are unlucky and the writer does not succeed, then you need to shift your strategy and work out a way to create an interest in the topic for yourself. One way is to try to figure out why other people have found the topic interesting. What questions were they concerned with? Ask yourself if the topic has any relevance for you as a manager. How does it relate to you in your place of work? Try to pose such questions to yourself as a way of making the subject more interesting to you.

3 Your feelings when reading

How do you feel about reading study texts – text books, journals and articles?

ACTIVITY What are the essential differences between academic texts and, say, newspapers? List five or six differences.

Academic texts require you to be a critical reader. Additionally, they require you to read them in an unbiased way that will allow you to judge the text on the basis of arguments put forward and ideas proposed. This does not mean, however, that your feelings and your ideas are unimportant. You should not ignore your feelings and attitudes but be aware of them as you are reading. If you disagree with a text, or part of a text, try to decide why you disagree and always ask yourself if you are being appropriately critical or if you are just reacting because of bias or prejudice.

4 Reading as an interactive process

Purposes for reading should dictate how you read. Reading for study purposes will require you to read a lot of material. It will require you to learn from material. It will require you to understand material. It will require you to think hard and to relate texts to real life. In other words, reading for study purposes is active reading.

When you read about a management concept you will understand it by setting the new information in the text alongside the ideas and knowledge you already possess. In this sense reading is interactive. Additionally, you will read more actively if you interact with the text. Asking questions of texts, and in a sense entering into a dialogue with texts, will help you to become fully involved with what you are reading. So good study reading is interactive in two important and related ways: a *personal* interaction is required with the text and an *information* interaction is required with your existing knowledge.

ACTIVITY This Activity highlights the personal interaction required of good readers. The paragraph opposite is about the advantages of distance learning for managers. Before you start reading, consider the following:

1 What, for you, are the advantages of distance learning?

2 What, for you, are the disadvantages of distance learning?

3 For you, do the advantages outweigh the disadvantages, or vice versa?

Now read the paragraph below and, bearing in mind your responses to the three questions above, see if the text persuades you that you are right, or makes you think about any new ideas, or simply confirms your views. Do you agree with the writer of the paragraph, or do you think she's 'got it wrong'? Do the advantages suggested apply to your own situation?

The advantages of distance learning for managers

Distance learning has a number of advantages for the busy manager. It can, almost always, give managers control of their learning. Unlike traditionally taught, face-to-face learners, distance learners are free to choose when and where they study. If managers are up to their necks in budget forecasts or resolving crises during one particular week, then, as long as they make up the time the next week, their study time does not have to suffer. Study can be fitted in and around the demands of a busy work schedule and, essentially, distance learners do not have to give up their jobs whilst they are studying. Unlike their counterparts who are taught face to face, distance-taught managers can usually relate what they study to their immediate work situation as they are learning. They can read about a management concept and then see if it makes sense at their place of work the very next day. Similarly, research in the workplace can be easily undertaken in support of course work and assignments, and constant exchanges of theory and practice are facilitated. Also, at the end of their studies, the distance-taught managers simply carry on working, whereas their colleagues who have been taught face to face may have to pick up the threads after a prolonged period of absence.

So, what do you think now? The paragraph might well have made you say 'Yes, but …!' or you might have agreed wholeheartedly with the writer. Inevitably, the paragraph leaves out the disadvantages. You might like to list a few now. To be a critical reader your own personal interaction can help you to see and to 'fill in' the gaps in the writer's argument. The same applies to all academic texts. Perhaps it's years since you read a textbook, and perhaps the concepts of management seem alien to you. Don't panic! You have work experience and practical understanding and skills, and you probably have your own ideas and views on management practices and techniques. Use them as part of your personal interaction with texts.

Key points

Reading is an active process. It is interactive in two senses:

- Personal interaction is required. Try to create a dialogue between yourself and the text.

- An information interaction is required. Try to use the information and ideas in your head to check and to help you understand information in the text.

5 Good readers: facts and myths

Any course of study will require you to read a lot of material. Time is of the
essence. You are no doubt a busy person and you need to learn excellent
time-management skills in order to cope with the demands of adding a
programme of study to what is probably already an overloaded timetable.
I have said that your studies will require a lot of reading. Inevitably, then,
you may be considering ways in which you can speed up the reading you
need to do. Occasionally, managers are sent on speed-reading courses. Even
if you've never been on such a course, you may now be thinking about it,
or perhaps you have read one of the speed-reading books available in most
bookshops. The trouble with speed-reading courses is that they often ignore
critical variables. Familiarity with a topic, the way in which a text is
written, familiarity with the type of text, the varied purposes for reading
the text, and the level of personal interest in a text all act as critical
variables influencing the speed of reading. We need to consider such
aspects of reading before going any further.

ACTIVITY I want to examine some facts and myths about reading. Read
through the statements below and decide if you think they're true or false.
You might think the statements are only true sometimes. This isn't a test.
Make a quick decision as to whether they are more true than false (T) or
more false than true (F).

		T	F
1	Good readers read faster than poor readers.	❏	❏
2	Good readers never sub-vocalise – they never read aloud to themselves in their heads and they never mouth or even speak aloud the words in the text.	❏	❏
3	Good readers ask questions of texts.	❏	❏
4	Good readers never regress – they read smoothly through the text and they avoid going back to an earlier sentence or paragraph.	❏	❏
5	Good readers make notes as they're reading – either on the text itself or on paper.	❏	❏
6	Good readers are not put off by apparently difficult or boring texts.	❏	❏
7	Good readers keep in mind their purposes for reading as they read.	❏	❏
8	Good readers decide on their purposes for reading before they start to read.	❏	❏
9	Good readers do not change their purposes for reading once they have started to read.	❏	❏
10	Good readers try to memorise what they're reading as they read.	❏	❏

My responses are given below. You may disagree and of course you are free to do so. However, do take a little time to think about reading. Just because an 'expert' has told you something is right and something else is wrong, this does not necessarily mean you have to agree with them (or with me).

1   Good readers read faster than poor readers.

TRUE: Generally speaking this is true, although some fast readers fail to understand the text. Thus, it would not be true to say that poor readers always read more slowly than good readers. Some good readers read very slowly.

The speed of reading should depend on your purposes for reading and on how familiar you are with the topic of the text. At the start of your management course, you will probably read more slowly than at the end of your course. The difficulty of the text also makes a difference and so too does your familiarity with the genre or type of text you are reading. The more familiar you become with academic texts and reading for information, the faster you will be able to read. Don't try to run before you can walk. Accept that, initially, reading will take longer than you might like. If you are concerned about your reading speed, note how long reading activities take and try to set yourself goals – say, to reduce reading time by 5 minutes per 30 pages in the next week.

You may have read recommended times for reading, but I'm not going to suggest 'good' speeds. I suggest that you are critical of any such advice from other sources. It depends too much on what and why you are reading. What I do suggest, however, is that you get to know for how long, at any one stretch, you can read effectively. Don't try to spend two hours reading continuously, as you'll probably just lose concentration. However, do make sure that you've set aside enough time to allow yourself to get into the flow of the text or texts you're studying. Think about this. If I'm reading quite complicated academic texts, I read best for periods of about 30 minutes. What about you?

2   Good readers never sub-vocalise.

FALSE: Good readers in trouble with texts, or parts of texts, frequently vocalise, in their heads or out loud, in order to unravel some of the text. One rather complicated book on English grammar advises its readers to do this if they're in trouble with comprehension. Try it.

3   Good readers ask questions of texts.

TRUE: This is one of a range of active reading strategies. Moreover, good readers ask questions of themselves when they are reading. They monitor their own reading by frequently asking themselves questions such as 'Do I understand this?', 'Does this make sense to me?', 'Am I reading too fast or too slowly?', 'Do I need to go back and re-read something/everything?', 'Do I need to make a note of this?' Good readers ask questions about the information in texts and about their progress and comprehension during and after reading.

Key points

Good readers ask questions of themselves when they are reading. They monitor their progress through the text and take appropriate action if necessary.

4   Good readers never regress.

FALSE: Good readers know when they haven't understood something and they know that returning or regressing might help them. Reading for study purposes frequently requires you to regress through text in order to check your understanding, to re-read points of particular interest or importance, and to take notes that you didn't make on a previous reading.

5   Good readers make notes as they're reading – either on the text itself or on paper.

TRUE: But many good readers read through a text once first, in order to get its general meaning, and then they go back and re-read and take notes or highlight particular sections of the text.

6   Good readers are not put off by apparently difficult or boring texts.

FALSE: All readers can be put off by difficult or boring texts. If this happens, try to follow the advice on page 55.

7   Good readers keep in mind their purposes for reading as they read.

TRUE: This is good study reading strategy.

8   Good readers decide on their purposes for reading before they start to read.

TRUE: This is another good study reading strategy.

9   Good readers do not change their purposes for reading once they have started to read.

FALSE: Good readers may have to change their purposes as they read. Let's say your tutor has advised you to read an 'important' text and to use the information it contains in order to prepare for an assignment. You set your purposes, for example telling yourself that you need information on X, Y and Z. As you start reading, however, you realise that you don't know enough about A, B and C. The text makes it very clear that A, B and C are important underpinning concepts to X, Y and Z. If this happens, you should change your purposes, concentrating first on A, B and C – then, and only then, you might return to your original purposes for reading.

10 Good readers try to memorise what they're reading as they read.

FALSE: Good readers try to understand what they're reading as they read. This effort to understand will, in itself, help you to remember, but remembering is a later stage. Of course, if you're revising for an exam, you might then be reading in order to remember, but if you are trying to memorise, then it would be better to do this from your own notes.

I hope that the Activities you've completed so far have helped you to start thinking about reading and about the reading process. Reading is often taken for granted. This is inevitable because, for most of us, once we have learned to read as children then much of our reading becomes automatic. Reading is a hidden skill; it often takes place in private and always involves a cognitive process. Exactly what goes on during reading may never be fully understood. However, most of us have had to read texts that present us with problems of one sort or another. The sheer amount of reading required on a management course can be daunting. If you have not studied for some time the academic language of texts can seem off-putting and difficult, and reading to learn from texts presents its own challenge. A range of *reading strategies* will help you to meet this challenge and, used appropriately, will ensure that you read for different purposes, in different ways, and in order to arrive at different outcomes.

6 Identifying your own reading strategies

A reading strategy is an 'operation' you put into action according to your purposes for reading and according to your progress when you are reading. If you are asked to read and to comment on a company report, then you will probably need to read that report from cover to cover. If you are reading the newspaper for relaxation, however, you will probably read selectively, spending time only on those articles that look particularly interesting. Deciding what to concentrate on and what to omit or skim read is just one reading strategy. Making decisions and taking action if you encounter difficult phrases or words is another reading strategy, and one that might be particularly important when you start reading academic texts on your management course.

You need to become aware of your own particular reading strategies. What, for example, will you do if you meet difficult words or phrases? Will you try to ignore them, will you re-read the difficult part, or will you stop and consult a dictionary? As noted earlier, good readers monitor their progress as they are reading. Do you do this? Do you sometimes pause, for instance, to gather your thoughts, to relate texts to your experience, to question your comprehension? Do you sometimes decide to re-read a particularly important or difficult part of a text? If you tend to read without monitoring your progress, then make a point of doing so next time you read something. Remember, though, that your purposes for reading will determine how much you need to understand. Always keep this in mind.

The next section looks at the following reading strategies:

- Working out difficult words and phrases
- Defining purposes for reading
- Getting your head round the topic – making initial hypotheses
- Using the text – checking hypotheses
- Using headings and sub-headings
- Using introductions
- Reading selectively
- Highlighting main topics
- Using labels
- Personal interaction.

The reading strategies in this section can be added to and perhaps you use others. The list here is not exhaustive. It just gives you a start. You can find the text used in this chapter at the end of the book in Reading appendix 1 'Successful versus effective real managers'. Either work through the strategies here first *or*, if you want to, read the text now. If you do read it now , you may need to re-read it as you work through the strategies below.

Working out difficult words and phrases

As a rule of thumb, you will need to understand a word or phrase if it is used frequently in a text and if, without understanding it, you are unable to understand the entire sentence. However, some writers paraphrase their ideas so that, for example, if you continue reading, you can understand what they meant in the previous sentence. Sometimes, too, your purposes for reading will mean that it is not necessary for you to understand every word. Don't waste time if you don't need to.

On other occasions, however, it will be important that you work out what a word or phrase means. If this is the case, try the following procedures:

1 Decide whether, according to your purposes for reading, total comprehension is essential.

2 Re-read the difficult word or phrase in the sentence. See if you can make an intelligent guess about its meaning from:

   (a) what you already know about the topic

   (b) what you've read before

   (c) what you read after the difficult part.

3 If you still can't get the meaning and if you've decided you need it, then use a dictionary or ask someone to help.

Remember that every time you stop to consult a dictionary you will be interrupting the 'flow' of your reading. Sometimes this is inevitable, but on other occasions you might be able to ignore or to guess the word and still be able to understand the sentence and the overall message. Let's try with a few examples taken from Reading appendix 1.

In the example below, I've underlined some words that, hypothetically, might cause problems. The exercise is somewhat artificial as I've chosen the 'difficult' words – you may have no problem at all with them. However, if you read through the examples and the suggested solutions this will alert you to some possible strategies for use when, and if, you encounter difficulties.

> ### *Example 1*
> They believe that although managers who are successful (that is, rapidly promoted) may be <u>astute</u> politicians, they are not necessarily effective.

If you ignore the word 'astute' you don't really get an understanding of the sentence. Let's assume you decide to check in the dictionary. Do so now, if you don't understand the word; a good test of understanding is whether or not you can paraphrase the word. Having read your dictionary definition, now re-read the sentence. Making sense of the word in context is essential.

Example 2

Starting with the <u>landmark</u> work of Henry Mintzberg, observational studies of managerial work have found that the <u>normative</u> functions do not hold up.

With the word 'landmark' I think you can make an intelligent guess. What is a landmark? If someone's work is described as a landmark, what could it mean? Re-read the sentence and try to paraphrase 'landmark'. (I'd use 'very important', 'highly significant', or 'pioneering'.)

Now look at 'normative'. Earlier in the text we are told that another writer, Henri Fayol, had defined five management functions. Now, suddenly, these functions are described as 'normative'. Do you really need the dictionary? Look at the word. Do you recognise anything? What about 'norm' as in 'normal'. Here the word is used to describe 'function' and so it's an adjective. Can you think of other adjectives ending with 'ive'? (I would suggest formative, subjective, objective, incisive, recursive.) Now re-read the sentence and paraphrase 'normative'. (I tried out: '... found that the so-called normal functions' but I'm not very happy with this as the original is so much better.)

Example 3

Instead of Fayol's five management functions, Mintzberg portrayed managers in terms of a <u>typology</u> of roles.

Again, look at 'typology'. Do you recognise anything in the word – 'typ' from 'type'? Check with the dictionary and then re-read the sentence and paraphrase 'typology'. (I'd say: '... a categorisation of roles'.)

Example 4

These <u>empirically derived behavioural descriptors</u> were then conceptually collapsed into the four managerial activities of real managers.

This one's a real mouthful, isn't it? Most of the texts you read will not be so complicated, but let's work with this sentence for practice. We need to find the 'head-word' – the word that's being described by the other words. Then we can work backwards in order to understand the whole phrase. The head-word is the last word – 'descriptors'. You'll recognise the 'descrip' part and if you think about other nouns ending with 'or' (such as orator, professor, sailor, tailor, supervisor) you'll realise that adding an 'or' to a verb forms a noun referring to the person or thing that does that action.

Now we can go back to the other words that act as adjectives to clarify and describe the head-word 'descriptor'. You may need to look for 'empirically' in the dictionary. Do that now.

Now look at 'derived'. If something is 'empirically derived' it must mean it is 'obtained' (derived) from data drawn from observation.

Now only 'behavioural' remains. Again, look at the word. You'll recognise 'behaviour' with an 'al' ending (like architectural, natural and political). You should be able to see that 'behavioural descriptors' might be paraphrased as 'descriptions of behaviour'.

You've now worked out each word, but you can't stop here. Re-read the entire four-word phrase and then re-read the sentence. This might seem like a long, complicated process, but when you meet groups of words that present difficulties, you have to work logically through each word. Then you have to be *interactive* and to re-read the phrase and then the sentence and maybe the sentence before. If you don't do this, you might easily lose the thread of your comprehension.

Key points

- When you meet a word or phrase you don't understand, ask yourself if it is important. If you decide it is important, because of its position in the sentence, its frequent use or your purpose for reading, then try first to guess its meaning.

- To help you, use the context, familiar parts of the word and, if necessary, a dictionary. When you think you understand, re-read the entire sentence and, possibly, the sentence before it. Then, and only then, carry on reading.

ACTIVITY Try the same strategies with the following examples. Make sure you re-read the entire sentence and, at the end, see if you can paraphrase the underlined words. Don't worry if you cannot 'guess' the underlined words. For some of them, you will *need* to look in the dictionary.

1 The definition and measurement of effectiveness is even more <u>elusive</u>.

2 The <u>disparity</u> that our study highlighted has significant implications for future research.

3 <u>Psychometric</u> tests were rejected as it was decided that <u>qualitative data</u> were, at this point, more valuable.

4 <u>Intrinsically motivated, high-achieving managers</u> were asked to <u>disseminate</u> this information.

So far in this chapter we have looked at reading in general, reading for different purposes and some strategies for comprehension. I am asking you to think hard about something you normally take for granted and, now, to think particularly about reading purposes and reading processes.

In Reading appendix 1 at the back of this book is a text by Luthans entitled 'Successful versus effective real managers' (hereafter referred to as the Luthans text). You need to be very clear about my purposes for selecting this text. It is a difficult text. It is quite long and it contains complex ideas and concepts. It is possible that it is much more difficult than many of the texts you will encounter on initial management courses. However, I believe that if we work together on a difficult text, then a less demanding text will present fewer problems.

Have you ever followed an introductory guide or tutorial for a piece of computer software? You work easily through the tutorial and feel very pleased with yourself. Then you come to create your own file and suddenly you realise it's not quite as easy as the tutorial suggested. If the feeling is familiar, you will understand why I've gone for a 'deep-end' text rather than a 'shallow-end' text. It's as if, instead of teaching you to swim with a rubber ring, I'm trying to teach you to do without one from the beginning.

So, you need to stay calm. This text is difficult, but not impossible. You need to think about how *you* might apply the strategies we are going to practise here with other texts.

Defining purposes for reading

One of the purposes of reading the text on successful versus effective managers is to practise reading strategies. In a sense, this means that you will focus as much on the reading process as on content. However, in order to provide a practice situation, here is a sample task.

Task

You have been asked to read the Luthans text as part of your course reading. Additionally, a written assignment is based on the article, or parts of the article. The question you are ultimately required to answer, in writing, is:

'Managers can be successful and/or effective. Explain the distinction (with reference to Luthans' work) and decide if you fit into one of the categories. How might managers be both successful and effective? Relate your answer to your current work situation or to an organisation you know well.'

We are now in a position to define your purposes for reading the article.

ACTIVITY Write a list of three or four purposes now.

In order to proceed, I shall assume that your purposes are:

1 To read the Luthans article for information on successful versus effective managers.

2 To take notes/make summaries of main points from the article as part of the reading for the course.

3 To use the text to consider and practise your reading strategy.

4 To use the text for building confidence and as practice for other difficult texts that you may, occasionally, be required to study.

How you achieve your purposes will depend on the text and on your own preferred ways of working. Some managers read a text from start to finish and don't feel they can start looking for specific things until they've done this. Others search the text more strategically from the beginning. You must do whichever suits you. There is no right or wrong way. In the activities that follow I suggest one route that might help to achieve the purposes for reading. My advice is to follow my route and then to think about how else you could have got there. I include as many useful reading strategies as I can. You must learn to pick and choose from the appropriate strategies to suit your own purposes and preferred way of reading.

Reading is characterised by a series of hypotheses and hypothesis evaluations. If I tell you to read a text and I give you its title, then you can start immediately to make an intelligent guess, or hypothesis, about the text. In this way you start to get your head round the topic.

Getting your head round the topic – making initial hypotheses

Turn to the Luthans text and consider just the title. A distinction is made between successful and effective managers. Don't read anything else yet, just list any possible ways in which this distinction might be made.

You've already started to think about the topic. However, any initial hypothesis could be quite wrong or only partly right. We need to evaluate all hypotheses during reading by using the text to keep our ideas from running riot. When reading, you should use your own knowledge and ideas alongside, that is interactively with, the text information.

Using the text – checking hypotheses

Let's now look at the text. The *purpose*, at this point, is to find out the difference between an *effective* and a *successful* manager. To do this, you will use a *search strategy*, or, to use another term, a *scanning strategy*. You are scanning the text for a specific answer to a specific question. Try it now in order to complete the sentence below.

According to Luthans, successful managers _____

_____

whereas effective managers _____

_____

I've put:

> According to Luthans, successful managers are those who have been promoted quickly, whereas effective managers are those who have satisfied, committed subordinates and high-performing units.

I haven't, at this stage, paraphrased much information but I might now note:

Successful = Promotion related

Effective   = Work related

I shall try to keep these definitions in my head as I read the article.

Look back to your initial hypotheses on the differences between effective and successful managers. Were they confirmed by the text or do you have to reject them totally or in part? If they weren't confirmed, don't worry. You're not a thought reader and, simply from the title, you couldn't be at all sure about Luthans' distinction. However, the point is that you were *personally interacting* to seek information and you were *processing information interactively* to check the text information against your own ideas.

Now that we have a very general idea about the text topic, let's consider our wider *reading purposes*. Ultimately, we need to use the information in this text to answer a written assignment question. Initially, it is helpful to gain an appreciation of what the text is about. In order to do this it is useful to look through the text and to note any sub-headings the author uses. These might indicate what is to be discussed.

Using headings and sub-headings

Headings and sub-headings provide useful sign-posts for readers. Always note the sub-headings in the text. Sometimes when you're reading you will know exactly what information you are looking for. In this text you could, if you wanted to, start reading the 'Implications' section, which is at the end. Alternatively, if you were interested primarily in finding out how the author arrived at his distinctions between successful and effective managers, you might start at the section headed 'How the difference between successful and effective managers was determined'.

In all, there are nine sections to this text. I have included Endnotes as a section. The first section, after the title, is not given a sub-heading, but we can safely assume that it serves an introductory purpose. Even if you decide to ignore early sections of the texts you are considering, it is often a good idea to read the introduction to such texts.

Using introductions

Frequently introductions will 'set the scene' for readers. Often they will provide information on the following:

- the topic of the text
- why the topic is important or interesting

- what the text will be about – whether it covers the whole topic or only parts of it
- how the topic will be presented – the order of topics in the text.

Some texts have a summary instead of, or in addition to, an introduction. Do read this information as it will help to guide your searches and provide you with more information in which to 'set the scene' for the text.

ACTIVITY Read through the introduction to the Luthans text now and try to answer the questions below.

1 What is the topic of the text?

2 Why is this important or interesting (i.e. why was it written and why should I bother to read it)?

3 What is the text about? Does it cover the whole topic or only part of it?

4 How is the topic presented? What is the order of topics?

My answers were as follows:

1 *Successful versus effective managers.*

2 *Successful managers are often not effective managers. Can such a fact explain the performance problems currently facing American organisations? Perhaps this distinction might also help to explain performance problems in organisations in other countries.*

3 *The topic focuses on 'real managers' and finding solutions to performance problems in terms of first studying, and then promoting, effective managers.*

4 *Introduction: defines effective versus successful, and consequences of the distinction, outline of problem and suggested solution.*

In order to know the ordering of subject matter in this text we need to consult the sub-headings. When we have done this, then we can see the general order of the text.

Reading selectively

As well as looking at the introduction, it is often a good idea to read the 'conclusion' of a text before reading the entire text. In this text it's the 'Implications…' section that serves a concluding function. Read it now and see if it fits with any ideas you previously had about the text. Remember that reading a conclusion before reading the entire text will be a little like reading the end of a detective story without knowing the details of the crime and victims. You'll know the solution – in this case the author's suggestions – but you won't know how the author arrived at them. Sometimes you don't need any more than this so you would be unwise to waste time reading a text when the introduction and conclusion give you all you need. In this exercise, however, more understanding is required. By now you have a reasonable idea about the text. You know how long it is, you know a little about its contents and you know, in general terms, what the topic is about. Additionally, you know your purposes for reading and so, now, you should be able to plan your attack.

Sometimes you can use texts very selectively. A textbook index might indicate that there are four references to your topic. A chapter or article might contain only three or four points that are relevant to your information needs. Decisions about how much of a text you have to read can only be made when you have isolated your purposes for reading or when your tutor or the course material has provided specific instructions.

The Luthans article is to be read in order to inform a written answer and therefore I have decided that I need to read the whole text. I won't feel confident about summarising and explaining the distinction between successful and effective managers unless I have read everything in the text.

Highlighting main topics

In order to summarise the information content of the text, I am going to 'label' each main point, to give it a 'title', as I am reading. However, first I am going to read the whole text and highlight, or underline, the key points. Additionally, I will jot down any ideas or problems as I read and I will do this on the text itself.

My highlighting of paragraph 5 is shown below as an example – your highlighting will be quite different. That's fine, it's your reading.

And who are these managers? They are found at all levels and in all types of organisations with titles such as department head, general manager, store manager, marketing manager, office manager, agency chief, or district manager. In other words, maybe the answers to the performance problems facing organisations today can be found in their own backyards, in the managers themselves in their day-to-day activities.

ACTIVITY From your highlighting and, perhaps, from your jotting, make a list of the key points in the text by producing a label, or title, for each paragraph or main point of text.

I have completed the first three paragraphs as an example. Feel free to change my labels if you are not happy with them, and remember that one paragraph might contain more than one important point – if so, it will need more than one label.

Paragraph

1a	Definition - successful vs. effective
1b	Similarities effective and successful managers
2	Successful doesn't equal effective and vice versa
3a	Problem = performance problems of US organisations
3b	Possible solution/explanation – successful manager not effective

The full list of my labels is given at the end of this chapter in Appendix 3.1. Try not to look at these – your labels will be at least as good as mine. I've used the sub-headings provided by the author as further labels.

Using labels

You should now have a summary of the text in label form. The details and examples are not there but you know where to go to find them. If this were an important text in your studies you might want to store this list in a file with other similar records. However, our purposes for reading mean that we need to use this text to help us write an assignment.

Look back to the assignment question on page 65. Initially you need to explain the Luthans definitions. You can see where they occur and you should be able to do that now. Then you need to decide whether you are either successful or effective or, perhaps, whether you are a combination of both. Here, again, you are going to be *personally interactive*. You also need to explain combination managers but a quick look back to your labels should tell you where to look (looking at my list at the end of this chapter, it's in paragraphs 28 and 29).

Personal interaction

Spend five minutes thinking about you and the text now and, in addition to answering the question set, think about any problems you see in the Luthans article. Are his distinctions valid? Are his explanations adequate? If you are successful, effective or combining, then why is this? What has allowed, or encouraged, you to be like this at work? Does the Luthans article provide you with an adequate explanation or does it leave out important things?

I asked someone else – let's call him Mike – to read this article. Mike's comments on things that the article omitted included the following:

- any reference to contacts, 'old school tie' advantages, and being promoted – i.e. being successful as a result of these
- personality and its relationship to success/effectiveness/combination managers
- managers functioning as 'team-players' – successful versus effective roles as suggested/required by a company or organisation.

Jo, another reader, thought it possible that effective managers could spend too much time on communication and human resource management, and thereby lose sight of production objectives.

You have probably thought about other things and you may think Mike's and Jo's comments are irrelevant – that's fine. The point is you should, by now, have really become involved in the Luthans text. Your own ideas and experiences should have helped you to read the article critically and you should now be in a good position to start to answer the written assignment.

As far as answering the assignment is concerned, we've probably gone as far as we can. However, there are some important note-taking strategies for using information from texts in your written answers.

7 Note-taking strategies

If you are reading from your own course texts or from photocopied texts, then you will be able to highlight and annotate those texts as required. However, in order to work with borrowed books, or to take notes in order to 'learn' and to reinforce material, you will need to experiment with a variety of note-taking techniques before you know which you prefer to use.

Try to see note-taking as a learning strategy. Although you might, at the moment, feel confident that you'll remember the Luthans article, how much will you remember a month from now? Any note-taking activity should require you to process information. Do not be tempted to simply copy out key words and phrases in the order used by the writers of your texts. The more you play around with the ideas in a text the greater your chance of really understanding and learning the material. Of course, you will not be able to do this with every text you read so you should reserve most effort for the texts that you decide are most important.

You might like to use the flow-chart shown in Figure 3.1 below as a guide to your note-taking.

You may want to return to this flow chart after you have read the chapter and then modify it for your own use.

Figure 3.1

It takes time to make good notes. If a text is important you need to set aside enough time for note-taking. Don't be disheartened when you start studying. Your note-taking skills and the time you require to take notes will improve. Be patient with yourself. You'll get there in the end.

Basically, note-taking can be linear or non-linear. The labelling exercise you completed in the Activity on page 69 was linear. The example in Figure 3.2 below is non-linear or diagrammatic.

Figure 3.2

When should you use diagrammatic, non-linear notes and when should you use linear notes? Part of the answer depends on your personal preference. Perhaps you just can't 'see' things if they're noted diagrammatically. Don't worry, just stick to linear notes. However, the answer depends partly on the text and partly on the purpose for reading it and taking notes from it. The following examples illustrate a range of possibilities. You should try to experiment with each sort of note-taking and then you will be in a position to decide which serves your purposes and your preferences most effectively.

Annotating texts

As long as texts are your own, you can write notes and use underlining or highlighting to help. As always, devise a system of annotating that makes sense to you and be consistent.

Notebooks

You can summarise texts into a small notebook or personal organiser and keep this with you. You can revise your work from this book. If you buy a notebook get one that you can easily add to or delete from, in order to keep your notes up to date.

Using card indexes

You might want to summarise a text on a card and keep it, in a form you have devised, in a card index box. You should note the title, author(s), date of publication and source and a few sentences or key phrases or words that summarise the text.

For the Luthans article I would end up with a card like the one below.

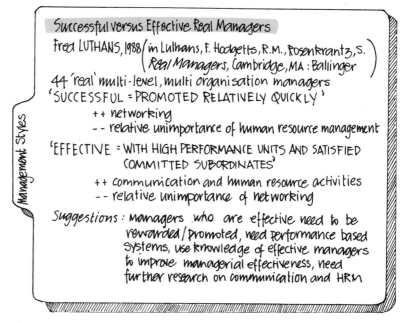

Figure 3.3

You will see that I've used quotation marks to indicate the writer's words and definitions. If you use the same words as the writer in your notes, always make sure you use quotation marks or some other notation to remind yourself that they are not your words. If you do this you will be able to acknowledge the original sources in your writing if you need to.

There is further guidance on using other writers' words in Chapter 5 'Writing assignments'.

ACTIVITY   Make your own card for the Luthans article in Reading appendix 1 *or* for the Germanity article in Reading appendix 2.

Tables

Tabular notes can be particularly useful if you're using a number of texts to take notes on one or two topics. Imagine you are using three texts, and that they are all related to effective management. The Luthans text you read earlier would be just one of the three. What you could do is to go through the labelling stage of the activities described above, and then, using those labels, start to build a table of information. From the Luthans text I might start a table like Figure 3.4 overleaf.

	Luthans	Smith	Jones
Details of Study	44 'real' managers 248 'real' managers		
Definitions	Successful = promoted Effective = get work done Combination = Eff + succ		
Characteristics	Succ = networkers Effective = Comm. & HRM		
Recommendations	Need to reward ie. promote effective managers so effective managers = successful managers		
Educational Background		MBA advantages	

Figure 3.4 Effective management

As you read more texts you may well need to adapt and add to your table. Subjects Luthans discusses might be ignored by other writers. This doesn't matter. Just leave the Luthans box empty if, for example, other writers talk about 'educational background' where the Luthans text does not.

ACTIVITY Using information from the Luthans article, complete Figure 3.5 to summarise the essential differences between Luthans', Fayol's, Mintzberg's and Kotter's views of managerial work.

	Fayol	Mintzberg	Kotter	Luthans
Observed managers	?	Yes	Yes	Yes
Details of study	?	5 CEOs and their mail	15 successful GMs	44, then 248
General findings	5 functions			
Managerial functions identified	Planning Organising Commanding Co-ordinating Controlling			

Figure 3.5

As you read more on your course you may find that tables you devise at the beginning of your studies need considerable addition; for example, you may think that a category in one table, such as 'managerial functions identified', requires a complete table to itself. You will find this easy to do as long as you don't see tables as final notes.

If you use tables like this you will find that, to design and complete them, you really have to get to grips with what you are reading. You will have to be *personally interactive* in your reading and, to understand what you are reading, you will also have to process interactively by using text information alongside the information already in your head.

Flow charts

Flow charts, another diagrammatic representation of texts, can be used effectively to summarise some parts of texts, or a process described in a text. You might usefully summarise the methods used in the Luthans article as follows:

Figure 3.6

ACTIVITY Complete the flow chart to finish the summary of the methods employed by Luthans and colleagues.

We've now gone through the most commonly used forms of notes. Ask your colleagues at work and on your course what they do. Swapping notes as a starting point for discussion can be a very beneficial exercise. Not only will you see other people's note-taking styles, but you will also have an opportunity to monitor your ability to spot the key points in texts. Sometimes what is 'key' for one manager may not be for another and a good discussion can follow. On other occasions, you may have spotted key points that a colleague has missed. So once again, collaboration can be both productive and stimulating. Try it.

Abbreviations and note-taking

In some of the examples above, you will have noted my use of abbreviations. No single set of abbreviations is better than any other and what you need to do is to devise your own form. Symbols can also help you to take notes, but make sure you use them consistently. Commonly used note-taking symbols and abbreviations include:

re	regarding	i.e.	that is
etc.	et cetera (and so on)	∴	therefore
>	bigger than	<	smaller than
→	leading to	∵	because

Additionally, you will probably need some symbols to register your personal reactions to texts. I use the following, but you should devise and use your own.

?	I don't understand this	Yes!	I agree
No!	I don't agree	λ	Something is missing
'Smith'	like Smith	NB	Note this – important.
✱✱	important		

Additionally, of course, you will use highlighting or underlining on some texts. This is also one of your note-taking techniques.

Key points

- Your notes are for you. It is you who must understand them, so develop a system of abbreviations and underlinings that works for you.

- In order to write good notes, you must read texts in an active, interactive way.

- Your notes should reflect what you want to remember and what you think is important.

We've now considered and practised different sorts of note-taking, but we need to take a little time to consider what to do with these notes once we've taken them.

8 Keeping notes

If taking notes is a way of extending your memory, then clearly you need to work out some kind of system for storing your notes where you can find them. To make a start, get hold of some folders and find shelf space, or some boxes, for storing them. You will then have to develop a filing system. It is very easy to end up with large piles of notes which are so disorganised that you can never face trying to find what you want. You will waste a lot of the time you invest in making notes if you don't also invest some time in working out a simple and effective system for filing them. Once you have stored your notes, what uses are you likely to put them to?

As you take your notes you might think, for instance, that one day you will sit down and read carefully through them all. Perhaps you will. But unfortunately there tends to be a shortage of suitable time for doing that. Your studies keep driving you forward into new areas and there is always something new to read, or another assignment to write. Going back over old notes is seldom as pressing, or as attractive, as going onwards to something new – unless, that is, you have a specific purpose, such as looking for material for an assignment, or pulling together ideas for an exam. So the fate of notes is often to accumulate dust on a shelf.

This means that there is little point in creating acres of wordage which faithfully cover all the main content of the course. Your notes are much more likely to be useful for reference purposes rather than as a source of extensive reading. You need to make them with this in mind. You need good questions, comments and summaries that will make sense when you come back to them. It doesn't necessarily matter if you never go back to a particular set of notes. The process of writing them is valuable enough in itself. However, if all your notes are very lengthy and unstructured you will find it difficult to make any future use of them.

Key points

Sometimes it is very useful to bring together the notes you have already made (e.g. while you were reading) and to make a new, very short, condensed version, that is, notes which summarise your earlier notes. This is a tremendous help to your learning because it makes your mind create orderliness at a higher level in your thinking – not 'perfect' orderliness, not something you would like to show to other people, but a lot better than no order at all.

As your course progresses you will need to update your filing system. If you are studying on a modular programme you might find that one file of photocopied texts and your notes will suffice for your first course or module. Later you may study other courses and may find that some of the material from the first course needs re-allocating to another file.

Key points

Study filing is not a waste of time. Revising your files is, in itself, a form of course revision – you should build it into your study plan.

Working out a filing system, as your course progresses, is an active study strategy. Again, you need a system that works for you. I use large A4 binders for different topics. I file each photocopied text and my notes from any text in the relevant topic file and give each a number. I number texts and notes in the order in which I read them, but then I might re-order them and keep an index at the beginning of each file. The Luthans article might be No. 23 in my 'Styles of Management' file. Let's imagine I have to write an assignment on 'An Effective Style of Management'. I have, say, a total of 10 photocopies and notes from texts that might help me in this assignment. I would look through my index – go to the texts and notes, and note any useful points for the assignment. I might end up with a list like the one below. Each key point on my notes is numbered (remember how we numbered the Luthans text?) and each set of notes also has a number. So my initial search of my texts/notes might give me the following list:

Paper	Point	
Luthans		
23	1	definition – successful vs. effective
	2	succ. = effective & v.v.
	9	Research context & methodology – 44/248
	27	synthesis of eff. vs succ.
	28	"Combination" real man.
	29a	only 10% high scoring succ. & eff. mans.
	29b	Bal. appr. of comb. mans
	30	Signif. disparity succ. & eff. mans.
Smith		
4	7	definition – effective manager
	8	research – 52
	11	re. Kotter's networking
	25	nec. conditions for eff. man.ment

The Smith text is fictional but this list gives you an example to try out. After this initial list I'd probably delete some of the points and then I'd order the points to look something like this:

Intro

Paper	Note No.	Connections
4	7	but NB
23	1	and
7	2	so
4	25	

Para 2 – Conditions & circumstances

6	3	similar to
4	25	

You will see that I've started to note the connections between points in the right-hand margin of my list. By the time I start writing, I'll have all of my notes or texts within reach and, although I'll probably need to re-read parts of the texts that I'm going to use, I'll only need to read the salient parts.

You might make notes of this kind as part of your revision for an exam (see Chapter 8). But it is also very useful to try to pull things together at other stages of the course, for example, when you have finished one topic and are about to move on to another.

When you have finished this chapter, you should be able to answer the following key questions about yourself as a reader of study materials. If you're not yet sure of some of the answers, then return to this section later.

1 Where do you read? Do you read different things best in different places?

2 For how long can you read an academic text without losing concentration?

3 Do you need to read an important text through once before highlighting, annotating or note-taking?

4 What sort of notes do you prefer to make – linear or non-linear? Describe your preferred note-taking methods and the reading tasks to which they are best suited.

5 Are you an active reader? Are you personally interactive and do you process interactively? Do you need to practise active reading?

9 Summary

Reading is an essential part of your study programme. As the course progresses, you will become a more efficient reader, but you should take action now to improve the reading strategies that will help you later.

To summarise, you should now understand that:

- Reading for study purposes will form an important component of your management education. You will need to read and understand a lot of material. You should start reading now in order to prepare yourself and to develop and practise good study reading and note-taking strategies.

- Reading is an active and interactive process.

- Good readers are personally involved with texts – reading requires *personal interaction.*

- Good readers can mesh what is already in their heads with what they read on a page – reading requires an interactive processing of information.

- Different texts and different tasks require you to read in different ways. If you try to read everything very thoroughly, and if you make full notes on every text you read, you will probably have no time to go to work. Good readers decide on their purposes for reading and then set themselves targets. Practise making study reading decisions.

- Your notes from texts will be important aids for your written assignments and examinations. Practise taking notes that work for you and use them as revision and consolidation aids throughout your course.

- Notes and annotated texts should be filed so that you can refer to them easily. Study filing should form a part of your study plan.

Appendix 3.1 Paragraph labels for Reading appendix 1

Paragraph

1a Definition – successful vs. effective

1b Similarities effective and successful managers

2 Successful doesn't equal effective and *vice versa*

3a Problem = performance problems of US organisations

3b Possible solution/explanation – successful manager not effective

4a Aim of article – examination of 'real' managers re: success and efficiency

4b Performance problem and solution

5 Study of real managers' day-to-day activities may provide solutions to performance problems

The current view of managerial work

6a Functions of managers – Fayol's 5 functions

6b Functions of managers – Mintzberg's challenge to Fayol's normative functions

7a Mintzberg's methodology

7b Mintzberg's view of managers in episodes inter and extra to organisation

7c Mintzberg's typology of 9 managerial roles – interpersonal information and decision-making

8a Kotter – challenge to Fayol – interaction of role of managers

8b Kotter – managers and network-building

Determining what real managers do

9 This research context and methodology – use of 44 'real' multi-level multi-organisation managers

10 Use of Delphi technique to form 12 descriptive behavioural categories of managerial activity to form eventual 4 way categorisation

11 Communication category – explanation and examples

12 Traditional Management category – explanation and examples

13 Human Resource Management category – explanation and examples

14 Networking category – explanation and examples

15a Comparison of this categorisation with Fayol, Mintzberg and Kotter

15b Superiority of this categorisation – comprehensiveness

16 Further methodology used to determine frequency of activities under 4 categories

How the difference between successful and effective managers was determined

17a Methodology used to determine effective versus successful manager's activities according to 4 categories

17b Determinants for success index

18 Determinants for effectiveness index

19 Limitations of determinants – methodology

What do successful real managers do?

20 Results of successful manager survey – significance of networking and relative unimportance of human resource management

21a Implications of successful manager results

21b Example of successful manager's views

22 Conclusion – networking as the key to success

What do effective real managers do?

23 Methodology for effective manager study – regardless of whether successful managers were also effective or ineffective

24 Results of effective manager study – significance of communication and human resource activities and relative unimportance of networking

25a Implications of effective manager's views

25b Example of effective manager's views

26 Conclusion – communication and human resource management as the key to effectiveness

27 Synthesis of effective versus successful manager activities

What do managers who are both successful and effective do?

28 Notion of 'combination' real manager – effective and successful

29a Small number of high scoring successful and effective managers: – 10%

29b Balanced approach of combination managers

30 Significance of disparity between successful and effective managers

Implications of the successful versus effective real managers findings

31 Suggestion – need to ensure effective managers are promoted/rewarded

32 Promotion may not be performance related but political/social skills related

33 Suggestion – managers who are effective need to be rewarded/promoted and organisations need to develop/encourage this performance based system

34 Suggestion – to use knowledge of effective managers in order to improve managerial effectiveness

35 Suggestion – to further research communication and HRM

Chapter 4 Effective writing

1 Introduction

As a manager, there will be occasions when you need to communicate effectively in writing. On some occasions, the successful transmission of your message will rely entirely on your ability to convey that message in writing. On other occasions, you will use both spoken and written communication in order to convey your message and then you will probably use a different, possibly more abbreviated, style of writing.

Whatever your message, and regardless of the way in which you are conveying that message, you will need to transmit information, instructions, enquiries, ideas and decisions in a written form that is appropriate to your audience and to your purpose.

You will also need to communicate effectively in writing on most management education courses. On some occasions, you will be writing for yourself, and no one else will need to understand your message. Note-taking and summaries are examples of such writing. These will help you to clarify your thoughts and to put complicated concepts and ideas into your own words as part of your learning process. At other times, you will be writing assignments for your tutors to read. On these occasions, your knowledge and understanding will be assessed on the basis of your written work. It is important that your writing does you justice and this chapter is intended to help you with the 'nuts and bolts' of effective writing.

If you are writing in English as a second, or foreign, language, then you will probably feel anxious about your writing. Take some time to work carefully through this chapter and also read Chapter 6 in order to practise writing before you start your management course.

In some of the Activities in this chapter, you will be asked to look at your own writing and/or the practice assignments in the next chapter. If you want to, work through this chapter with some of your own assignment-type writing in front of you; or you may prefer to work through the next chapter before this one – it's up to you.

If you read a management report with poor grammar and spelling mistakes, how do you feel? Do you take it as seriously as you might a better written report? Even experienced writers make mistakes but you, as a reader, probably never see them because experienced writers read their work and correct their mistakes.

When you are writing management assignments, you need to work hard to ensure your writing conveys your intended message. Tutors are human – they might 'switch off' if your writing is full of mistakes, if your message is confused or if your assignment is unclear or poorly structured. You will keep your tutors interested if you write logically, clearly and accurately.

Key points

Whatever you are writing, you must think about your audience. Good writers work hard to make their writing easy for their readers to understand.

In this chapter we will look at some potentially tricky issues and common worries in order to consider ways in which you, as a manager and student, can feel more confident that you have the requisite tools of written communication at your fingertips. Some of you will want to try most of the exercises and Activities in order to check which ones are of use to you. If, having finished them, you still have doubts about the issues raised, then go to a grammar book, a dictionary, a colleague or a tutor and pursue the issue until you are confident that you have understood it.

First of all, the chapter explores feelings about writing and asks you to think about the different sorts of writing that you do. We then look at some aspects of grammar that cause problems for some students. Each sentence you write needs to be effective but, in addition, each sentence you write needs to form part of the message, or part of the text, as a whole. Because of this we look briefly at sentence construction and ways of linking sentences to form paragraphs. After this we turn to spelling and punctuation. Finally in this chapter, we consider aspects of style in writing.

ACTIVITY   What is your aim in this chapter? How will you measure your success?

If you have no worries about the topics covered here, just move on to the next chapter.

2 Feelings about writing

Before we go any further, let's be honest. Writing is *not* easy. Very few people write easily and for most of us writing is one of the most demanding aspects of studying. Writing is time consuming and requires us to make difficult choices. Which word best conveys our message? How do the words work best together? How do we describe a complicated idea in only 100 words? How do we best order our knowledge and ideas?

Ask yourself at this stage how you feel about writing assignments. The best way to feel more positive about your writing is to write. One reason why managers panic when starting courses after a number of years away from study is that they are simply out of practice. You have time now before your course begins. Start writing but don't try to cover the exercises in this chapter in one evening – take it slowly and keep a note of how you are feeling as you progress. If you read the exercises and feel confident that you could complete them, then go on to the next chapter. However, you might still benefit from trying some of the Activities in this chapter in order to increase your confidence. Try not to make your first course assignment your first piece of writing for months – that will only add to the pressure!

ACTIVITY

1 List the three types of writing you most frequently undertake (e.g. letters, lists of 'things to do', reports) in column A below.

2 Note how you feel about these types of writing (e.g. 'necessary evil') in column B. Think about and include a note on how confident you feel about each type of writing (e.g. 'OK – no problems', or 'always have problems with completing these on time').

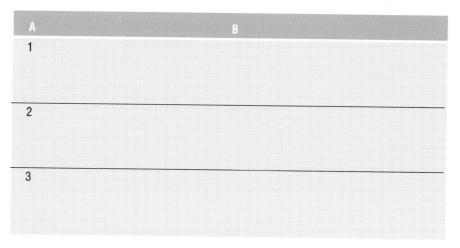

A	B
1	
2	
3	

3 Using the completed table above, write between 100 and 200 words entitled 'Writing and feelings about writing'. The first sentence of my paragraph is given below:

Writing is one of the most important aspects of my work.

You will notice that this sentence contains 11 words. If you reckon on 10 words per sentence, then you'll need only 10 sentences to complete this task.

Time your writing from the start of the Activity to the end.

4 Read through your paragraph and decide whether it conveys your intended meaning. Does it have a beginning and an ending? Are you confident that words are correctly spelled and that the grammar is correct? Do you want to make any changes?

5 Change anything and re-read your paragraph. Finally, make a note of the time now.

The task took me 18 minutes and I write every day. Even now I don't feel completely satisfied and, in order to produce a really good paragraph, I'd need another 10 or 15 minutes. What about you? How do you feel about what you've written? Make a note of your feelings by the side of your paragraph and, for the moment, leave it. Return to it later if you want to judge it afresh but now move on to some, or all, of the exercises. We will return to checking your writing at a later stage. The point for now is that you have broken the ice and started to consider your own writing.

3 Grammar

It is, of course, impossible to do more than highlight a few grammar topics in one chapter. What you will find here are some notes and exercises on topics of grammar that frequently cause difficulty. In order to write this section I asked tutors in the Open Business School to list errors that they frequently found in assignments they marked. I also asked individuals in business to list anxieties and errors they frequently saw. This section cannot explain grammatical rules in any great depth but it seeks to offer you guidance and rules of thumb for doubtful moments.

As with all parts of this chapter, do the exercises only if you think they might be useful to you. Most of us get stuck on just one or two grammatical points – try the first couple of questions in each exercise to check whether or not you need to go on. If you are perfectly happy about all of the topics covered in this section, do not waste your time here, and turn to the section on organising sentences.

Agreement

You should try to ensure consistency between tense, number and person.

Consistency of tense

Consider the following sentence:

> Simply checking in the dictionary helped him to make fewer spelling mistakes when he tries to communicate in writing.

You have probably spotted the error. The writer uses 'helped him' (past tense) and then 'he tries' (present tense). This is an inconsistent use of tenses. As for every instance of grammatical confusion, we need to think about what the writer was really trying to say. Consider the following correction:

> Simply checking in the dictionary helped him to make fewer spelling mistakes when he tried to communicate in writing.

Now change the sentence to the present tense:

> Simply checking in the dictionary is helping him to make fewer spelling mistakes when he is trying/he tries to communicate in writing.

Alternatively, you could have written:

> Simply checking in the dictionary helps him to make fewer spelling mistakes when he tries to communicate in writing.

Of course, at times you need to use two different tenses in a sentence. Consider the following sentence.

> She used to make frequent spelling mistakes but now she uses a dictionary and hardly ever loses marks for incorrect spelling.

Key points

As a rule of thumb, check that your tenses are consistent. If they are not, check whether you need a time 'switch' in the sentence – if so, that is fine. If not, make your tenses consistent.

ACTIVITY Look at the sentences below. If there is an inappropriate inconsistency, correct the sentence. Then try changing some of the tenses to see what effect that has. Note how changing tense can alter the meaning.

1 Good communicators understand that they had to think about their audience when writing.

2 Although improved grammar helped you to write better, it would not solve all of your problems.

3 Learning to correct the texts that you have written will mean that you are in greater control of your own writing.

Possible corrections

1a   Good communicators understand that they have to think about their
audience when writing.

or

1b   Good communicators understood that they had to think about their audience
when writing.

Note: *Either of the above is grammatically possible but note how the meaning*
changes according to the tenses used. 1a is in the simple present and refers to a
timeless general sense. 1b refers to a past sense. The choice is yours – but make
sure that you have made the choice and checked that it really conveys your
intended message.

2   Although improved grammar helped you to write better, it did not solve all of
your problems.

or   Although improved grammar can help you to write better, it will not solve all
of your problems.

or   Although improved grammar could help you to write better, it will not solve
all of your problems.

or   Although improved grammar would help you to write better, it would not
solve all of your problems.

3   Correction not necessary.

Some possible alternatives

Learning to correct the texts that you write will mean that you are in greater
control of your own writing.

or   Learning to correct the texts that you write means that you are in greater
control of your own writing.

Consistency of number and person

Consistency of 'number' refers to a consistent use of the plural or singular.
Checking that your sentences refer to the same person, or pronoun for that
person, is checking for consistency of person. Put simply, a pronoun is
something like 'he', 'she', 'they' or 'it', and is the word used for the person
or people referred to previously.
   Consider the following sentence:

   A good manager is aware of their strengths and weaknesses.

Correction

   Good managers are aware of their strengths and weaknesses.

   or

   A good manager is aware of his or her strengths and weaknesses.

ACTIVITY Now correct the two examples below and, where appropriate, play around with the language so that you can choose the one correction you prefer.

1 Managers need to develop excellent time-management skills so that he can make the best use of his available time.

2 One manager's approach to planning a report will not be the same as the approach of their colleagues.

Possible corrections

1 *Managers need to develop excellent time-management skills so that they can make the best use of their available time.*

or *A manager needs to develop excellent time-management skills so that s/he can make the best use of her or his available time.*

or *A manager needs to develop excellent time-management skills in order to make the best use of his or her time.*

Note: *To avoid falling into the trap of assigning either male or female gender to the manager in this example, you could use either 'he/she' (or 'she/he') or 's/he' or 'he or she' (or 'she or he') and 'his/her' (or 'her/his') or 'his or her' (or 'her or his'). Be consistent in both your use of the forms and the order they take, that is if you use 's/he' you should follow it, in the same sentence, with 'her or his'. However, using both 's/he' and then 'her/his' in the sentence above is rather awkward – in these cases it is advisable to use the plural forms so that, as in correction 1 above, you can use 'managers' and 'their time'.*

2 *One manager's approach to planning a report will not be the same as the approach of another manager.*

or *One manager's approach to planning a report will not be the same as the approach of his or her colleagues.*

When using pronouns it is important to avoid ambiguity. For example, these sentences are confusing:

Jones was a better salesman than Smith. He had worked for the company for only two years.

Tricky areas of consistency

There are some nouns that present particular problems. Generally referred to as 'collective' nouns, these are words that denote a plural meaning but take a singular form. Committee, company, family, jury, board, department and team are all collective nouns. Although the noun denotes a group of individuals, it follows the rules for singular nouns if the collective noun refers to the unit of individuals acting as one. Consider the following:

The senior team is meeting at this very moment.

The jury considered the case and arrived at its decision late yesterday evening.

The committee was unanimous.

However, if the collective noun is used in a sentence where the individuals are clearly *not* acting as a unified unit then use the plural. So, if the committee had not been unanimous in their decision you might write:

> The <u>committee</u> <u>were</u> not unanimous.

ACTIVITY In the following sentences decide, initially, whether the collective noun is being used to denote unified behaviour. If so, use the standard singular form for the verb. If unified behaviour is not denoted, use the plural form. The verb is given in its 'to' form, that is the infinitive (for example, to reach) – you are required to select the most appropriate form for each sentence.

1 We have just heard that the board (to reach) a unanimous decision after the longest board meeting in the history of the company.

2 The executive committee (to be) not of one mind concerning the question of sponsorship.

3 The improvement of writing skills (to depend) on the willingness of individuals to be self-critical.

Suggested answers

1 has reached

2 are or were

3 depends – the word 'improvement' (singular) and not 'writing skills' (plural) determines the verb form here. The collective noun decision is not actually relevant in this example.

If in doubt, do not use collective nouns. So, in examples 1 and 2 above, you could write the following:

1 We have just heard that the members of the board have reached a unanimous decision after the longest board meeting in the history of the company.

2 The executive committee members are not of one mind concerning the question of sponsorship.

Usage – a warning and a caution

Grammar can rarely provide us with hard and fast rules. The use of collective nouns is one such example. Frequently you will hear, or will read, instances where the guidelines above have not been followed. 'Parliament' and 'Police' are good examples and both of the following sentences are correct.

> Parliament have just voted on the XYZ Bill.

> Parliament has just voted on the XYZ Bill.

'Police', as in 'The police have just arrived at the scene' is always used with plural forms, regardless of any unity rule.

If in real doubt, avoid the collective noun. If something sounds very odd, such as 'the police has', follow your instincts and stick to what is common usage and, if you do use the collective noun, follow the unity rule until it sounds wrong – then the common usage rule of thumb applies.

Passive versus active

Some writing guides for managers suggest that you should always use an active rather than a passive voice in written sentences. I suggest you make your own decision. Some of you, however, may be constrained by a house style at work. If so, follow the house style guidelines.

Let's look at how you form the passive. Work your way through this section so that you are confident about using both passives and actives.

Forming the passive

To make an active sentence into a passive sentence, you need to use a form of 'to be' followed, almost always, by the past participle of a verb. So it looks like this:

Active: The IT manager *bought* three new computers.

Passive: Three new computers *were bought* by the IT manager.

or

Passive: Three new computers *were bought*.

You will see in the example above that the passive can be used when you do not want to name a person who would have been named in an active voice sentence. Again, however, you must be aware of the different effect this will have on your communication. Consider the following sentences:

Active: The managing director asked me to keep an eye on the new administrative assistant.

Passive: I was asked by the managing director to keep an eye on the new administrative assistant.

or

Passive: I was asked to keep an eye on the new administrative assistant.

You might have chosen the final example if you had wanted to suggest that you were keeping an eye on the administrative assistant but you did not want to say who had asked you to do this.

You may have been told that the passive voice should be used to convey thoughts and facts impersonally. The passive can frequently help you to do this but note that its use does change the emphasis of your sentence and, at worst, it can make your writing appear clumsy and pompous.

If you think of the passive as providing a way of de-personalising sentences and hence making them more objective, it should help you.

Consider the following sentences.

> I have asked the personnel department to reconsider its original proposal.

> The personnel department has been asked to reconsider its original proposal.

In this example the passive means that you need not use 'I' – this can be useful but, again, make sure you are choosing to use the passive voice and do not just use it without considering the choices.

Active versus passive choices can be particularly important when writing management reports. In some organisations the active is encouraged as part of the task-oriented culture and the passive would be criticised for sounding bureaucratic and lacking clarity or ownership. On the other hand, the active voice would seem strident and pushy in other organisations. Think about this in the context of your workplace. In your management assignments occasional use of the passive can help your writing to 'sound' more objective and less personal.

ACTIVITY In the two sentences below, change the active to passive or vice versa. When you have done this, decide what effects your changes have on your understanding of the sentences.

1 *Active*: John has suggested a number of ways of dealing with the new legislation.

2 *Passive*: Concern that Total Quality Management has not yet been adequately addressed by the group has been expressed by the Director.

Possible answers

1 *Passive: A number of ways of dealing with the new legislation has been suggested.*

2 *Active: The Director has expressed concern that Total Quality Management has not yet been adequately addressed by the group.*

Key points

The passive or active voice can alter the emphasis and focus of your message. Be prepared to play around with these forms until you are sure that the focus of your message is what you intend it to be.

Common errors

Opposite are some of the most common grammatical errors people make when writing. You will probably know many others. Read through the pairs of sentences and decide which is correct. Ask yourself how you would explain the 'rules' to colleagues.

ACTIVITY Underline the correct sentences.

1a New staff inevitably suffer initially with anxiety.

1b New staff inevitably suffer initially from anxiety.

2a It seemed as if the personnel director was not interested.

2b It seemed like the personnel director was not interested.

3a The ABC Company is different than XYZ because it remains open 365 days a year.

3b The ABC Company is different from XYZ because it remains open 365 days a year.

4a My new job is similar to the old Managing Director's job.

4b My new job is similar with the old Managing Director's job.

5a Responsibility for report writing has been given to my deputy and I.

5b Responsibility for report writing has been given to my deputy and me.

6a These arose because the Finance Director and me could not agree on target sales figures.

6b These arose because the Finance Director and I could not agree on target sales figures.

7a I lent the company report to my colleagues.

7b I borrowed the company report to my colleagues.

8a My colleagues lent the company report from me.

8b My colleagues borrowed the company report from me.

Correct answers

1b, 2a, 3b

Note. *Some people insist on 'different from' and say that 'different to' is incorrect. In fact, 'different to' can be used but unless you are prepared to explain it to critics, stick to 'different from'.*

4a, 5b, 6b

To decide whether to use 'me' or 'I', imagine the sentence without the other person/people. Another common error is to say 'between you and I' – it should be 'between you and me'.

7a, 8b.

Organising sentences

Let's define a sentence as any stretch of text starting with a capital letter and ending with a full stop. Almost every sentence you write must contain a subject and a verb. The subject is the topic, or the theme, of your sentence. It represents either the actor or the affected person or thing in the sentence. In the examples below it is underlined.

Managers from all over Europe met to discuss the proposals.

The managing director has responsibility for staff selection.

However, the company suffered major losses last year.

In declarative sentences the subject comes before the verb. Most of the sentences you write in your assignments will be declarative. If not, they will be interrogatives (questions), imperatives (instructions) or exclamatives (exclamations).

You also need a verb in each sentence. The verb is the part of the sentence that says what the subject is doing or being. In the examples below the verbs are in italics.

The managing director *is* a graduate of The Open University.

Every new manager *attends* an induction course.

Key points

- Check that every sentence you write has a verb, a doing or a being word, and a subject, the person or thing 'doing' or 'being'.

- If you are worried about recognising subjects and verbs you should consult a grammar book or ask someone for help.

See the end of the book for a suggested and supplementary reading list.

How much information we put into any one sentence will affect the ease with which our readers will be able to follow our writing. Good academic writing should not leave the reader with a headache because the sentences are long and convoluted.

Key points

As a rule of thumb, try to give one, and only one, new piece of information per sentence.

ACTIVITY The sentence below is too long. Break it down into two or more sentences in order to give the reader one piece of information at a time. You can, of course, use 'and' in the middle of a sentence to tie two related pieces of information together, but try to use this only when the information is related and fairly uncomplicated.

Because the training department has invested in the provision of language teaching, over 30% of the company's managers are now able to communicate at a survival level with their European counterparts in French or German and this has improved collaboration between the French, German and UK companies to such an extent that the training department has now been given a further £3,000 for additional language courses.

Possible correction

In this sentence, I'd either put a full stop after 'German' and start the second sentence with 'This has improved...' or I'd divide it into three or four even shorter sentences. It's up to you. I think you can get away with two sentences here, because the information is related. However, there is nothing wrong with short sentences.

What comes first in a sentence is important. You are immediately setting the tone of the sentence for your reader. You've already noted changes of emphasis in the passive versus active section. Let's look at some ways of starting sentences now.

Consider the following sentences. The first sentence is taken from a company report. Where companies and products were named in the original, they have been replaced with XYZ in order to preserve anonymity.

1 During the last five years, XYZ has spent over £1.5 billion on capital expenditure programmes to improve quality, boost production and increase efficiency.

2 XYZ has spent over £1.5 billion on capital expenditure programmes during the last five years to improve quality, boost production and increase efficiency.

Although the information contained in the two sentences is the same, you will have noticed that a given choice of ordering results in a different context in which the rest of the sentence is understood. In the first sentence, the context is the last five years and in the second example, it's XYZ, the name of the company.

ACTIVITY   Make two more sentences from the first sentence above and note the differences in effect. How would you decide which of the four sentences to use?

Look back to some of the writing you have produced recently. Would altering the order of information help you to communicate more effectively or are you generally satisfied with what you've written?

Linking sentences to form paragraphs

Having noted the need to check that every sentence has a verb and having seen the importance of selecting the order of elements in a sentence, we should now look at linking sentences to form paragraphs.

Each sentence you write should contain one, and preferably only one, point. Similarly, each paragraph you write should discuss or be concerned with one, and preferably only one, topic.

Let's look first at ways of linking sentences to form paragraphs. The words and phrases that help you to link sentences to, and indeed help to link phrases within, sentences are frequently called 'conjunctions'.

Conjunctions serve a number of different purposes, all of which should help readers to understand where you are going in your writing. Some of their main purposes plus examples are as follows:

Some of the words in this section are probably better classified as adverbs than as conjunctions. However, they can all serve a linking function so, to avoid complications, are included here.

■ to add information to what you have previously written
for example: in addition, additionally, and, furthermore, as well as, besides, moreover

■ to exemplify or develop what you have previously written
for example: in other words, an example of, for example, for instance, but

■ to provide an opposing or alternative view
for example: however, on the other hand, conversely, by contrast, nevertheless

■ to summarise or to conclude
for example: in conclusion, therefore, consequently, thus, for this/these reasons, as a result of, as shown above

■ to signal to the reader the order of your arguments/presentation of ideas
for example: initially, secondly, following this, after, finally, in conclusion, before discussing ….

As you will have seen from these examples, some conjunctions link ideas and information whereas some signal the direction of your writing to readers.

ACTIVITY Look at the introduction to this chapter. Before the first Activity you will find a short paragraph stating:

'First of all, the chapter explores feelings about writing and asks you to think about the different sorts of writing that you do. We then look at some aspects of grammar that cause problems for some students. Each sentence you write needs to be effective but, in addition, each sentence you write needs to form part of the message, or part of the text, as a whole. Because of this we look briefly at sentence construction and ways of linking sentences to form paragraphs. After this we turn to spelling and punctuation. Finally in this chapter, we consider aspects of style in writing.'

Underline or highlight the signalling phrases or words that link sentences and phrases within sentences.

You should have underlined 'first of all', 'and', 'then', 'after this', 'then', and 'Finally'.

In a long document such as a management report you may need to signal your text to your readers. However, you may find that a list of points, or in a long report, a contents page, is more appropriate. Similarly, you may use paragraph headings to signal to readers what is to follow. As always, follow house style at work and find out from your course tutors what is required.

Signalling words and phrases are important for the flow of your writing. Take a few minutes now to consider how using them can help to tie together your writing. Certain conjunctions can refer back and forwards. Consider the following:

A   **B**

… However, this does not always …

When you use 'however' you are implying that A is true, but that there is another argument or something else to consider – B. Make sure A and B relate to the same topic.

Similarly, if you use phrases such as 'in conclusion' and 'consequently' you need to make sure that your writing really does allow you, and your reader, to come to the conclusion or consequence you suggest. You must ask yourself whether you have written your argument or idea in such a way that your readers can follow your line of thought. There is more about this in the section 'Being logical' on page 106.

ACTIVITY   Make a list of advantages and disadvantages of examinations. Using your list, write a paragraph, or two, in which you present the arguments for and against examinations. Even better, think of a real 'pros and cons' situation at work and use that for this Activity. Try to present a balanced discussion but try to convince the reader to agree with your analysis. Do not list all of the advantages first and then all of the disadvantages but mix the 'pros and cons' as you go.

Key points

- An essential rule is to consider your audience – your reader(s).

- Good signalling will help your readers to follow your writing.

- Appropriate conjunctions will help your writing to flow – thus making it easier for your reader(s) to follow.

Being precise and giving enough information

You should note that the word 'evaluation' may be used differently in management education. This is a good example of the way in which different disciplines use the same words to mean different things.

Another important way in which you give the reader information can be classified under the heading of evaluation. For the moment, think of evaluation as a general umbrella term that covers ways of expressing your opinions, the extent of your information, the generality of your information and the applicability of your information. For example:

Managers study OBS management courses. (*No evaluation*)

Surely (*personal opinion*) managers studying OBS management courses benefit from an increased understanding of management principles.

A high percentage (*extent*) of managers studying OBS management courses benefit from an increased understanding of management principles.

Evaluation adds information to what we write. Read the following:

1 Managers from Europe study OBS management courses.

2 Accountants find the people-oriented aspects of management education difficult.

Neither sentence has much evaluation. After reading the first sentence you might say to yourself: 'So what? That's obvious.' Let's give it some evaluation in order to give more information and to avoid the 'so what?' question.

Managers from <u>all over</u> Europe study <u>a wide range of</u> OBS management courses.

The second sentence *does* provide more information *but is it true?* There is a section later on 'hedging your bets' but, for now, let's be more careful by adding evaluation to make the sentence read:

<u>Some</u> accountants find the people-oriented aspects of management education difficult.

ACTIVITY Add more evaluation to the following sentences:

1 Managers studying with English as a foreign language have problems with writing.

2 Writing is a skill required by managers.

3 Managers from the UK do not speak other languages.

My suggestions are given below.

1 *<u>Some</u> managers studying with English as a foreign language have problems with writing.*

2 *<u>Effective</u> writing is a skill required by <u>all</u> managers.*

3 *<u>A disturbingly high percentage</u> of managers from the UK do not speak other languages.*

When we write we often use evaluation without even thinking about it. We use it to strengthen our arguments (e.g. <u>all</u> managers) and to tone down our arguments (e.g. <u>some</u> managers). We use it to express certainty (e.g. <u>every</u> product <u>is</u>) and uncertainty (e.g. <u>some</u> products <u>might be</u>). Our choices of words and the order in which we use words will affect the message we give to the reader.

ACTIVITY Find a management report that is at least two sides of A4 paper in length. Try to identify the evaluation the writer uses. If the writer gives an opinion can you identify this? Can you differentiate fact from opinion? Do you agree with the writer?

Let's look now at an aspect of writing that is related to evaluation and the care and precision required when you write.

Hedging your bets

'Managwiz' is an
invented name.

The expression 'to hedge your bets' here means to be careful that you say nothing that could be refuted. For example, it would be foolish to write 'No manager has ever agreed completely with Managwiz.' How do you know? Can you be sure? If this is really your opinion you need to do two things. Firstly, you need to hedge your bets – try something like 'Few managers agree completely with Managwiz.' Secondly, you have to back up, to provide evidence for, your assertion.

Key points

Never assume that the reader of your writing is going to agree with you. Always ask yourself 'Can I prove it beyond doubt?' If you can, do so decisively, confidently and without hedging; if not, hedge your bets.

Always, then, ask yourself, 'Can I back this up with evidence and argument?' If not, hedge your bets even more or don't say it at all.

Some words leave no doubt: all, every, always, none, never. Other words, such as might, could, some, many, are less definite. Consider the following statement and note how, as it is altered, it becomes less and less 'definite'.

Every manager, the world over, needs a complete understanding of management theory.

Managers, the world over, need a complete understanding of management theory.

Managers, the world over, need an understanding of management theory.

Managers, the world over, would benefit from an understanding of management theory.

Managers, the world over, might benefit from some understanding of management theory.

ACTIVITY Look at some of your writing, or use a piece of writing from a company report. Have you or has the writer 'hedged bets' enough? Is the writing *too* tentative – is it over-hedged? Suggest changes as necessary.

We have now seen how language can be used in order to express ideas and facts with some precision.

Evaluation adds information and stops the reader saying 'so what?' Hedging your bets ensures that your writing cannot be challenged and, used appropriately, helps you to be precise.

4 Spelling

You probably know whether or not you are good at spelling. Even if you *are* good at it, there may well be some specific words that catch you out occasionally. Some rules of thumb can help but if in doubt check in the dictionary. Of course, to use the dictionary easily you often need a good idea of the word's spelling anyway, but get into the habit of some lateral thinking. If you do not find the word where you think it should be, try to think of a range of alternative spellings to look up.

Using the dictionary

Try to become familiar with a few useful spelling–sound correspondences. If you need to check a word that starts with the sound 'sigh' then try 'psy' as in: psychology, psychotic, psychometric, and then 'si' or 'cy' as in: siphon, cyclonic.

If there is an 'f' sound in the word, try 'f' or 'ph' as in: trifle, siphon, catastrophe, philosophy.

If the sound is 'or', try 'or', 'au', 'ou' or 'aw' as in: cortisone, fraught, ought, your, awesome, awful, trawl.

If the sound is 'ee', try 'ie', 'ea', 'ei' or 'e' as in: retrieve, preach, decrease, receive, preamble, decent.

For a 'sh' sound, try looking up 'sh', 'ss', 'sio', 'tia' or 'tio' as in: shambolic, reshuffle, passion, division, occupation, partial, recreation.

Homophones

Words such as 'principle' and 'principal' are known as homophones – they sound exactly the same but they mean different things.

ACTIVITY Use the correct homophone in the dotted spaces that have been left in the sentences below, and if in doubt check in the dictionary.

1 principle, principal

The .... remains the same – you should neither under- nor over-borrow.

The .... of the college has the final word; she decides whether you stay or go.

2 their, there, they're

.... are inadequate funds for this project.

.... understanding was not the same as mine.

.... not arriving until Tuesday so we have time to write a draft version before they come.

3 practise, practice

Many of you will need to .... your writing skills. The last decade has seen important research in the field of management ....s.

4   two, too, to

This section is designed .... improve your writing skills but it looks .... at reading skills because unless you use the .... skills together you will not be able to derive full benefit from these exercises.

5   know, no

I .... of .... better reason for improving writing skills than needing to write.

6   assent, ascent

If you .... you agree.

If you look at films of climbers on Mount Everest you will appreciate the difficulty of its ....

7   dessert, desert

If you .... the party you'll miss your ....

8   pole, poll

Talk of the latest .... on who will win the next election is driving me up the ....

9   effect, affect

The .... of monetarism has certainly ....ed the UK in the last few years.

10   compliment, complement

If you are frequently ....ed on your writing skills it may be that you do not need to do these exercises!

Good reading skills should .... good writing skills.

11   stationary, stationery

A .... vehicle is one that is not moving.

.... shops sell paper, pens, pencils, etc.

12   who's, whose

.... book is on the table?

.... coming to the meeting?

13   it's, its

.... a bad time for selling.

Put the computer back in .... case.

14   flout, flaunt

If you .... the rules you are expressing contempt for them.

If you .... yourself you display yourself and could be accused of showing off.

15   lead, led

This pipe is made of ....

She .... him to the door.

Answers

(1) principle, principal, (2) there, their, they're, (3) practise, practice, (4) to, too, two, (5) know, no, (6) assent, ascent, (7) desert, dessert, (8) poll, pole, (9) effect, affect, (10) compliment, complement, (11) stationary, stationery, (12) whose, who's, (13) it's, its, (14) flout, flaunt, (15) lead, led.

If you had problems with this Activity, try to devise 'memory aids' such as the one below for principal/principle.

The school princi<u>pal</u>'s a <u>pal</u> of mine.

ACTIVITY   Read the sentences below and pay particular attention to all underlined words. Some of them are spelled incorrectly and you should correct them or accept them according to the rules suggested earlier. Remember, if in doubt, use your dictionary.

1 Please keep till <u>receipts</u>.

2 There must be a simpler way of adding these <u>too</u> ingredients.

3 Counterfeit notes were circulating in the <u>two </u>biggest banks yesterday.

4 <u>There</u> journey to the <u>poll</u> was fraught with danger.

5 <u>Accomodation</u> will be provided.

Answers

(1) receipts, (2) two, (3) two, (4) their, Pole, (5) accommodation.

5 Punctuation

Sentences and full stops

In this section I have only included points about punctuation that frequently cause problems. If you are worried about other points – such as the use of colons and semi-colons – you should consult one of the books in the recommended reference section at the end of this book.

Let's keep to our definition of a sentence as the writing between a capital letter at the start of a section and the full stop at the end of a section. Unless the sentence is a question as in 'Can you arrange a meeting for next Wednesday?' or an exclamation as in 'The exhibition was a total waste of time!' all sentences end with a full stop. Thus, the only ending of a sentence not requiring a full stop is one where you have an exclamation mark (!) or a question mark (?).

Other uses of the full stop

If you use an abbreviated form of a word then put a full stop at the end of it unless the full version of the word ends in the same letter as the abbreviated version. So we have:

etc.	et cetera	Dr	Doctor
Dec.	December	Mr	Mister
c.	circa	Jnr	junior

When word groups such as the Department of Trade and Industry are abbreviated to the acronym D.T.I./DTI, some writers use full stops between each letter and some do not. Generally speaking, you do not have to use full stops, but the best thing to do is to decide on the form you prefer and be consistent with it. If the initial letters of a word group form a word such as NATO, UNICEF and UNISON then full stops are not normally used.

Be aware of your audience and, if you think there is any chance of misunderstanding, write the word group in full the first time it appears and put the abbreviated form immediately after it in brackets. You can thereafter use the abbreviated form knowing that readers can check back to see what the full form is if they wish. For example:

Take care when using acronyms and abbreviated or contracted forms with non-native speakers of English. In Spain, for example, NATO is OTAN.

> Charities subscribed to this year include the National Society for the Prevention of Cruelty to Children (NSPCC) and the Royal Society for the Prevention of Cruelty to Animals (RSPCA). We sent £4567 to the NSPCC in January, and ....

Commas

If you think of full stops as indicating the longest stretches of text in writing then you might think of commas as indicating the shortest stretches of writing *within* sentences.

The main, but not only, uses of the comma are described below.

When listing, for example:

> Recent purchases by ABC include XYZ holdings, the MNO Corporation, DEFG and the GHI Company.

Note that the last item on the list comes after 'and' and, generally speaking, no comma is added before 'and'. However, if a comma would prevent ambiguity, then add it at the end of a list. So, in the example below, a comma helps to keep the names Taylor and Smith apart, telling us that, unlike James and Jones, Taylor and Smith were not presenting together.

> Recent reports on the topic have been presented by James and Jones, Hudson and Black, Taylor, and Smith.

A common error is to insert commas whenever you use a long sentence. You should use them only when they are required to clarify your message.

ACTIVITY Punctuate the following sentence in two different ways to form two sentences with the same words but different meanings.

> It is usually the senior managers who are required to write company reports who ask for additional input on the Managing Communication Skills course.

It could read:

> *It is usually the senior managers, who are required to write company reports, who ask for additional input on the Managing Communication Skills course.*

By implication the use of commas in this sentence suggests that all senior managers have to write company reports and thus all senior managers, as opposed to middle/junior managers, will ask for additional input.

or

> *It is usually the senior managers who are required to write company reports who ask for additional input on the Managing Communication Skills course.*

Without the commas the sentence suggests that it is the senior managers who write company reports who want additional input. In this sentence the implication is that not all senior managers are required to write company reports.

The apostrophe (')

The apostrophe is used to show that a letter, or letters, are missing from a word or alternatively to show possession.

In the following examples, the apostrophe is used to denote omission.

There shouldn't be any need to spend too long on this.

If you're not able to attend please let my secretary know.

Note that the apostrophe is inserted in the space where the letter is missing.

ACTIVITY Insert the apostrophes in the correct place in the words below and note the letter or letter that is missing beside each word.

1 wouldnt	4 were
2 dont	5 Ill
3 theyre	6 shes
	7 Im

Answers

1 *wouldn't* *o*	4 *we're* *a*
2 *don't* *o*	5 *I'll* *wi*
3 *they're* *a*	6 *she's* *i*
	7 *I'm* *a*

The apostrophe is used to denote possession in the following examples:

1 The manager's chief role is to ………

2 Employees' rights have improved considerably since ………

3 This employee's complaint is apparently justified.

Note: the apostrophe denoting possession goes after the relevant noun. If it's a plural noun, as in example 2, you write 'employees'' but if it's a

2singular noun, as in example 3, you write 'employee's'. The singular noun's possessive is formed by 's, whereas the plural noun's possessive is formed by s'.

Pronouns such as 'its', 'hers', 'yours', 'theirs' and 'ours' do not use the apostrophe. Remember it's with an apostrophe always means 'it is'.

ACTIVITY The most common mistakes of apostrophe use that I come across seem to be in shops. The following are all authentic examples of incorrectly used apostrophes. Correct them and as you are doing so think how you would explain your corrections to a colleague:

POTATOE'S 15p @ lb.

ENGLISH TOMATO'S NOW IN!

ITS' A BARGAIN!

YOU'RE CHANCE TO WIN A DREAM HOUSE

You may think these examples have nothing to do with management. That's true – in a sense – but their frequent occurrence can lead to confusion and misuse by all of us. We get so used to seeing incorrect forms that we have to guard against copying them.

Corrections

POTATOES 15p A LB

ENGLISH TOMATOES NOW IN!

IT'S A BARGAIN!

YOUR CHANCE TO WIN A DREAM HOUSE

Additional uses of the apostrophe

In the examples below the apostrophe still denotes that something is missing but, as it is missing from the front of the word or number, the apostrophe is put there.

The figures for '93 are now available.

If you need to use the 'phone please try to wait until after 1 pm.

6 Style

'I' or 'we'

You may have been told that good academic writing is impersonal and that, therefore, the use of the first person, I or *we*, should be avoided. To the extent that your written assignments should be objective and not merely anecdotes phrased in narrative style, this is true. However, use of the first person *is* allowed, especially in cases where not using it would involve creating long, tortuous sentences. When called upon to state your own opinions or experiences, you need to make it clear that it is your opinion that you are referring to. Let's consider some examples.

Finally, the report concludes with an appropriate action plan.

In this example no personal pronoun is used and 'the report' functions as the grammatical subject, or topic, of the sentence.

> The writer, who is presently undertaking a management course, believes that such a decision is inappropriate and advocates that the investigation should be allowed to continue. Certain other courses of action are, however, advocated.

In this example 'the writer' is the manager writing the assignment. Presumably worried that an assignment should avoid the use of the first person, this writer tries to distance himself from the belief mentioned. However, the result is rather tortuous and, I would say, rather pompous. I'd have preferred the following:

> I believe that such a decision is inappropriate and advocate that the investigation should be allowed to continue.

The writer could then back up his argument and explain why such a decision is inappropriate. I don't think we need to know that the writer is studying on a management course – a tutor would already know that. Look at another example:

> This report, written by the Projects Controller, XYZ Services, attempts to form a judgement as to the present strategic position of the department and the company, together with a likely future scenario.

I think this reads very strangely. Although using 'this report' or 'this assignment' are useful ways of depersonalising your writing, I think you need to take care that you do not make reports and assignments sound too much like human beings. Can a report attempt to form a judgement? No, of course not – it's the writer who does.

As a rule of thumb you can use the first person if you want to make it clear that 'this is *my* opinion or experience' or if, to avoid the first person, your sentence ends up being pompous and difficult to read. Useful alternatives to the first person, especially in grammatical subject position, are 'this report' and 'this assignment'.

Key points

Good writing should read smoothly and fluently. Good assignment writers express their ideas and convey their knowledge in a way that makes it easy for their tutors to read their writing. Avoid pompous, long-winded words and sentences. You are writing assignments in order to convey your understanding of management topics – not in order to show your tutors how many long words you know.

Avoiding colloquialisms and spoken forms

When we talk to people we use forms of language that may be inappropriate when we write. The Activity below asks you to read the spoken forms and to transform the underlined words and phrases into acceptable written, academic forms. The first sentence has been completed as an example. In some of the examples below you may need to invent information and in other examples you may be unable to think of a suitable alternative. There is often no way of transforming what might be acceptable in conversation into good academic writing. You need to remember this when you are writing assignments. Don't try to write as you speak – it won't work!

ACTIVITY

1 We need to <u>take this on board</u> now! *This must be considered now.*

2 XYZ's a market leader but that doesn't mean we can <u>just rest on our laurels</u> – <u>our tail's being chased</u> and, for example, ABC's <u>coming up fast behind us</u> with <u>this</u> new SuperCar.

3 Sales figures have <u>boomed, I'm glad to say</u> but there are signs that <u>the bottom's falling out of the market</u> and what we have to do is to <u>get our thinking caps on, stir up the old grey matter</u> and think up a new, exciting marketing ploy.

Read through your written sentences and see if you managed to capture the flavour of the originals. In some sentences, especially sentence 3, this is virtually impossible because the message is too involved and subjective to be transformed exactly into a clear writing style without substantial rewriting.

Consistency in writing

Just as you need to be consistent in your selection of tenses and people in sentences, so too you need to be consistent in the overall organisation and structure of your writing.

Always keep your audience in mind. If you are writing an assignment for a tutor, remember *why* you are writing. You need to be objective and to guard against changing your tone of voice.

See Chapter 5 for more on assignment writing.

If I gave you a management report, a letter from my bank, an advertisement and a personal letter from a friend, and if I had typed out each of these four texts using the same typeface and format, you would still, almost immediately, be able to tell me what they were. Look back to the second Activity you completed in this chapter and note the different types of writing you undertake. Almost certainly you will be able to think of differences (and similarities) between these types of writing. This is because types of communication – often called genres – are recognisable to users of those genres and they have certain conventions. When you start to write assignments for your management course you may not, initially, know the conventions of assignments, but you need to find out. Once you know what is required then you will be able to work towards a consistent 'style' of writing. For example, if you are asked to write an assignment in report format then it would be inconsistent, and quite inappropriate, to write a long, wordy essay-type introduction – a list of contents would probably work much better. Similarly, if asked to write an analytical assignment then it would be inconsistent to start off by analysing your company's organisational structure and follow this by an emotional diatribe on the ways in which the organisation is going wrong – from your point of view. Analysis is objective – your opinion will be required but it must be written in a consistent and hence an objective, well reasoned manner.

Key points

- Be conscious of the genre of text you are producing when you write.
- Be consistent and conform to the conventions of the genre.

Writing enough but not too much

You may have been told that good management writing style is brief and to the point. That's absolutely right. However, I'd add that a*ny* piece of writing needs to keep to the point and not repeat things for the sake of it.

ACTIVITY Re-read some of your own writing. Are you guilty of labouring the point? Do you include unnecessary repetition? On the other hand, are you guilty of providing inadequate information?

Try to read your writing afresh. Leave a day or two between writing and correcting and during your correction phase try to assume the role of a tutor. Correct your own difficulties *before* submitting your work.

Finally, in this chapter, we will look at being logical when you are writing.

Being logical

Remember that *before* you start writing you should have all of the required tools available. You should have made a plan and this plan should be logically ordered. However, just because you know the logical links between sentences and paragraphs you should not presume that these are immediately apparent to anyone reading your text.

A useful exercise is to go through your text and to highlight every point you make. Then see if you've argued logically or if you're assuming the reader will accept what you've written. The rule is *make your logic explicit.*

Consider the following sentences:

All managers have some responsibility for people.

Being responsible for people demands an understanding of people.

One demand upon managers is that they understand the people for whom they are responsible.

This is a very artificial example, but it does show logical arrival at a conclusion. To develop this point, consider a second artificial example in which the concluding, third sentence, does *not* follow logically from what's gone before.

> Most managers would benefit from a course in human resource management.
>
> The OBS runs courses in human resource management.
>
> Most managers would benefit from a course with the OBS.

All of the sentences above may or may not be true and you may or may not agree with them. However, the conclusion in the third sentence is *not* logically argued. Other educational establishments run courses in human resource management. Following from the first sentence, all we can say is that *any* course in human resource management would be beneficial. Additionally, the third sentence doesn't refer to human resource management at all – would *any* course be beneficial? It might be but that's not the point of the argument. Let's try to make it logical by asking what we are trying to 'prove'. Assume we're trying to show that human resource management is beneficial for managers, that the OBS runs a human resource management course, and that *therefore* managers would find this beneficial.

> Most managers would benefit from a course in human resource management.
>
> The OBS runs courses in human resource management.
>
> Most managers would benefit from the OBS course in human resource management.

Now, if we want to be more evaluative and to really 'sell' the OBS course we could add more evaluation to the argument and write:

> Most managers would benefit from a good course in human resource management.
>
> The OBS runs a good course in human resource management.
>
> Most managers would benefit from the OBS course in human resource management.

ACTIVITY The following examples require the addition, or alteration, of information in order that they read logically. Alter them as appropriate. Add a fourth or fifth sentence where this helps.

Example 1

Every individual joining a new organisation will have a particular set of needs. These needs must be fulfilled before individuals can begin to feel comfortable and to operate effectively. Therefore the induction period is vital if new employees are to operate effectively.

Example 2

The size of groups can have a significant effect on the performance of group tasks. As a result we should ensure that no group should have more than 10 members.

My responses are given below. Yours may be very different. Just make sure your responses are logically argued. I have underlined the additions I have made.

Example 1

Every individual joining a new organisation will have a particular set of needs. These needs must be fulfilled before individuals can begin to feel comfortable and to operate effectively. <u>Such needs can be discussed and at least partly fulfilled during a period of induction.</u> Therefore, the induction period is vital if new employees are to operate effectively.

Example 2

The size of groups can have a significant effect on the performance of group tasks. As a <u>group increases beyond, say, 10 or 12 people, it may become less effective for certain tasks. It is important, therefore, to identify tasks that are most effectively completed by less than, say, 10 people.</u> As a result we should ensure that <u>these tasks are only allocated to groups with less than 10 members.</u>

ACTIVITY Go back to some of your writing and/or go back through this section when you have written the practice assignments in Chapter 5. Are your arguments logical? Add information and make alterations as necessary.

7 Summary

When you have finished working through this chapter you should feel more confident about some of the 'nuts and bolts' of writing and you should be in a better position to act as a marker and a corrector of your own writing. You should be able to read through your writing and check it before sending it, or giving it, to your tutor.

You might like to use the following checklist to help your marking.

Checklist

1   Have you kept your audience in mind throughout your text?

2   Have you said what you meant to say? Does your writing convey your intended message?

3   Have you been consistent and followed the conventions of the genre in which you are writing?

4   Have you signalled the organisation of your text in the most appropriate way?

5   Have you given your writing to anyone else to read in order to make sure they understand it?

6   Are your arguments logical?

7   Have you 'hedged your bets' when necessary?

8   Have you used enough evaluation? Is your evaluation careful and precise?

9   If you know you have trouble with some grammatical points, have you checked these?

10   Has every sentence got a subject and a verb?

11   Do your verbs agree with your subjects?

12   Do your sentences have agreement of tense, number and person?

13   Have you checked your spelling? If you have used a word-processing spelling checker, have you then checked your spelling yourself?

14   Have you checked your punctuation?

Finally, you can learn a lot about good writing from studying writing. Take some time to analyse what makes texts good and bad.

Appendix 4.1 Some rules of thumb for spelling

1   'i' before 'e' except after 'c'

So we have:
friend, receive, brief, receipt, achieve

However, there are exceptions:
neither, weight, seize, weird, counterfeit

Check in the dictionary when in doubt.

2   Verbs ending with one 'l' double the final 'l'.

So we have:
model, modelling, modelled
compel, compelling, compelled
propel, propelling, propeller

3   Comparatives and superlatives.
NB: 'better' (than that) is a comparative and 'best' is a superlative.
Add 'er' and 'est' to one syllable words.

So:
fast, faster, fastest
slow, slower, slowest.

Add 'i' and drop 'y' of words ending in 'y'.

So:
lucky, luckier, luckiest
easy, easier, easiest
lazy, lazier, laziest.
Words ending in 'e' drop the 'e'.

So:
late, later, latest
simple, simpler, simplest
large, larger, largest.

Double the last letter of words ending in a single vowel followed by a single consonant (except 'w' and 'l').

So:
hot, hotter, hottest
fat, fatter, fattest
big, bigger, biggest

but slow, slower, slowest
     cool, cooler, coolest.

4   Past tenses and past participles.
Words ending in 'e' add 'd'.

So:
live, lived
save, saved.
'y' ending words drop the 'y' and add 'ied'.

So:
hurry, hurried
cry, cried.

But take care, there are many irregularities – again, use your dictionary.

Chapter 5 Writing assignments

1 Introduction

By written assignment we mean an extended piece of writing such as a report or 'essay' which is part of course assessment.

This chapter goes beyond the nuts and bolts of writing, which we looked at in Chapter 4, and starts off by considering the purposes of assignment writing. This is followed by a section on answering the question set. Then we look briefly at writing tools and the use of computers and word-processing packages. Two practice assignments are then provided and assignments in the form of management reports are discussed. Finally, the characteristics of good management assignments are discussed.

ACTIVITY   How do you feel about the prospect of assignment writing? What is your aim in this chapter? How will you evaluate your success?

Remember to look back to this Activity when you have completed this chapter.

2 The purpose of assignments

Most management courses will require you to write assignments. Why do you think this is?

ACTIVITY Jot down four or five purposes of assignments.

My list includes the following purposes:

To reinforce and consolidate learning

Writing forces you to consider what you have been learning. Additionally, the very act of writing helps to reinforce concepts and serves a useful learning purpose. Often I am unable to get to grips with something until I have written about it. Like many of you, perhaps, I dread having to face the empty screen or blank page – I know that once I do so I will really have to sort out what I know and what I don't know and I will be forced to re-consider what I have learned and what I still need to learn. Writing forces me into a discipline that is vital for learning – for that reason it is a necessary evil.

To evaluate learning

Your tutors will use your writing to assess whether or not you have understood what has been covered on your course. Gaps in your understanding, or any confusions you may have, might become evident only when your tutor reads your written assignments. Don't be unduly disturbed by this. Your assignments provide you with the opportunity to check on your progress. I'd prefer a tutor to read an assignment and tell me I'd misunderstood something before I had to apply it in practice or write an examination, wouldn't you? Thus assignments are useful 'progress indicators' for your tutors *and* for you.

To demonstrate knowledge and understanding

This relates to the points above but, on a positive note, assignments provide you with the chance to demonstrate that you have understood concepts and theories taught on your course and can apply them to the real situation. Your tutors will be pleased that you demonstrate understanding and they will judge this to be a success. They will not be trying to trip you up and they will not just be looking for things you have omitted or misunderstood. Your tutors will share your pleasure when you demonstrate understanding – remember this when you are worrying about writing your first assignment.

Assignments give you an opportunity to practise the art of communicating points and presenting arguments. In this respect they provide you with a chance to practise skills that you use at work when explaining and presenting to subordinates, to colleagues, and to those senior to you.

To apply theoretical concepts to the 'real' world

I'll say more about this later but just stop to think for a moment. Are you one of those managers who says 'I do my job perfectly well and I don't need fancy words and theories to describe what I do. Theories are for academics – I need to get on with my job'? Does this sound familiar?

A management course provides you with an opportunity to reflect on, and to develop, your skills. A group of managers who recently completed courses offered by the Open Business School were asked about the benefits of their programme. 'Increased confidence' was an answer many of them gave. Many also wrote things like 'I now have a wider understanding of management issues' and 'Good job satisfaction and feeling of achievement'. What, you may ask, has this to do with writing assignments? I think it is an important reminder that your management course will be closely related to what you, as a manager, do at work.

You may be an 'expert' already and the theories and the concepts you study will enable you to reflect on your expertise and on your existing knowledge and practices. Indeed, if you do not relate course concepts to the workplace, you will get less value from them. Your studies should extend or develop your expertise and ideally you will be open-minded enough to use the course as an opportunity for critical reflection in the light of your increased knowledge and awareness.

In your assignments you will *have* to relate course concepts to your own or others' work practices and experiences. In this way I believe assignments give you the chance to relate theory to practice and to see for yourself the relevance and application of what you have been studying. Of course, your reading will have suggested that you make these relationships, but your writing is a further opportunity to do so. Use the opportunity.

If you are not able to apply course concepts directly to the workplace, draw on core study materials, course examples, work in voluntary jobs and so on. The key point is that management is about practice.

The advice given here is certainly true for Open Business School courses offered by the Open University. If you are studying with another institution, check with your tutors.

Key points

Writing assignments will help you to learn and to develop communication skills that are useful in management.

3 Answering the question

Good assignments fulfil a number of criteria. First, and foremost, a good assignment *answers the question*. It's no good writing an excellent answer to a question that wasn't set or writing an answer to only part of the question. Straying from the point, however interesting and well written your answer, will earn you no marks at all. You must, therefore, take time to analyse the question. Read and re-read it and, at every stage in your assignment planning, go back to remind yourself of the precise wording of the question. Print out or write out a copy of the question, and stick it above your desk. If you know you're someone who has a tendency to stray from the point this might help to discipline you.

Analysing questions depends on your understanding of key instructions. In management education you are frequently asked to write assignments in report format and I look at this type of assignment later in this chapter. Sometimes, however, you will meet words such as 'discuss', 'evaluate' and 'analyse'. You may be happy with these key instructions – if not, complete the Activity below and check your answers.

ACTIVITY In this Activity you are given a list of key instructions and another list of explanations for these instructions. Read through the key instruction words and note what you think each means. Then read through the explanations and assign one explanation to each of the instructions.

(1) compare, (2) contrast, (3) criticise, (4) define, (5) describe, (6) discuss, (7) evaluate, (8) explain, (9) illustrate, (10) interpret.

A Give your judgement about the merit of theories and opinions, or about the truth of facts; back your judgement by a discussion of evidence or of the reasoning involved.

This section draws on The Open University's Open Teaching Toolkit: Analysing Essay Titles.

B Investigate or examine by argument; sift and debate; give reasons for and against.

C Look for similarities and differences and perhaps reach a conclusion about which is preferable.

D Use a figure or diagram to explain or clarify, or make clear by the use of concrete examples.

E Set down the precise meaning of a word or phrase; in some cases it may be necessary or desirable to examine different possible or often-used definitions.

F Make an appraisal of the worth of something.

G Set in opposition in order to bring out differences.

H Give a detailed or graphic account.

I Expound the meaning of; make clear and explicit, usually giving your judgement as well.

J Make plain; interpret and account for; give reasons.

Answers

(1) C, (2) G, (3) A, (4) E, (5) H, (6) B, (7) F, (8) J, (9) D, (10) I.

If a question has three parts then you must answer three parts. Sometimes you will be told how many marks each part of an assignment is worth. Use this to guide the amount of effort, time, and space you devote to each section. If Section 1 is worth 5 points and Section 3 is worth 10 points then, logically, your response to Section 3 should be roughly twice as long and twice as detailed as your response to Section 1. Thus, when you start to look at an assignment question you need to do the following:

- Read and re-read the question.
- Summarise the question and its parts.
- Allocate an approximate space/word allowance to each part of the question on the basis of sections and any guidance given, such as the distribution of available marks.
- Re-read the question frequently throughout the planning and writing stage.

4 Writing tools

Some of you will write your assignments on word processors or computers, whilst some of you will use pen and paper. In this section I will first outline some points about using computers to write assignments.

The first decision to be taken concerns the point at which you start working on the computer. Some people plan on paper and then turn to the computer, whilst others use the computer from the beginning. You may have a word-processing package with a 'planner' or 'outliner' and, if so, you may find it useful to use this in the planning stage. You will need to experiment to find out at which stage you prefer to start word processing. Some of you won't want to start word processing until you have a final draft version of your whole assignment written by hand. However, to those of you writing with a word-processing package, the following points are worth considering.

You can use your word processor to help you to build, or to 'grow', your assignment. If you do this, you can type in the skeleton and gradually add words, phrases and sentences to it. The editing facility will allow you to move sentences and sections around and you will probably benefit from experimenting with different sequences. Personally, I find it difficult to correct my writing on the screen and so I print out my work and correct hard-copy drafts. I also like to use double spacing as this allows me to make corrections more easily. Again, find out how you work best.

Another editing facility that can be useful is to copy previous files, or parts of files, into an assignment document. If you have a package that allows you to manipulate documents, you might, for example, pull in your notes on the assignment topic and then revise them as necessary for the current assignment.

If your package has a word counter this can be very useful. Your plan will tell you how many words any section should contain and by using a word counter you can regularly monitor your progress. Spelling checkers are also very useful, but remember to proof-read your work, as a spelling checker won't pick up mistakes that are in themselves correct words but aren't what you want to say in the context (for example, I *reed* every day).

Finally, do remember that your course may require you to write examination answers by hand. If this is the case, you *must* practise hand-written assignments at some stage – if not, you will be in trouble at exam time.

5 Practice assignments

In this section I will look at two practice assignments. In these assignments two basic ways of approaching assignment writing are suggested.

If you are not sure how best to approach written assignments, work through the examples given here and decide which approach you find best. As your course progresses, you should develop your own preferred approach. This may be a mixture of the suggestions made here. In the next section I look at assignments in report format.

Key points

We all write in different ways, and one person's approach to assignment planning and writing will probably not be the same as another person's. You need to develop an approach that works for you.

Consider the following assignment questions. They are very general because you may not have started your management course. They serve as examples for thinking about *how* to write assignments rather than as examples of *what* to write. Your first course assignment will probably not be as difficult as the examples below. You should not be discouraged by the difficulty of these assignments, which have been carefully chosen to show you how to cope.

Practice assignment 1

'A good manager is born and not made.'

Discuss this idea with reference to your own experience. Consider the role of management education in improving management performance. What pre-service and in-service training have you and/ or your fellow managers received? Was the training in-house or external? Evaluate any such informal or formal management education that you have received and make suggestions for future training that would be beneficial. Your answer should provide sufficient information on your work context for your tutor to understand the situation you describe. Write about 500 words.

I've kept to 500 words for this first practice assignment. Your actual course assignments will probably be longer than this.

This assignment provides no explicit guidance on how marks will be allocated but there are clues if we look more closely. The key instruction words in this question are 'discuss', 'with reference to', 'consider', 'what', 'was', 'evaluate', 'make suggestions' and 'provide information'. These words, and your understanding of them, are crucial and you might want to highlight these key instructions on assignments you undertake.

In the following three Activities you are led through one approach to assignment planning. As you work through them note any changes, additions and extra steps you might use. The Activities are here for you to use in an experimental way.

ACTIVITY **Stage 1** Break the question down into a series of parts by underlining the key instructions and information the question requires. Alternatively, sketch out a diagram of the main points in the question.

I've done this in linear form, using highlighting and breaking the question up into five parts. Compare your underlinings and notes with mine. Don't change your notes unless you have missed something that you now think is important.

1 'A good manager is born and not made.'

Discuss this idea with reference to your own experience.

2 Consider the role of management education in improving management performance.

What pre-service and in-service training have you and/or your fellow managers received?

3 Was the training in-house or external?

4 Evaluate any such informal or formal management education that you have received and make suggestions for future training that would be beneficial.

5 Your answer should provide sufficient information on your work context for your tutor to understand the situation you describe.

Sketching a diagram, making a non-linear plan, is another possibility for question analysis. I've done this below in Figure 5.1. Try drawing your own question plan before looking at mine.

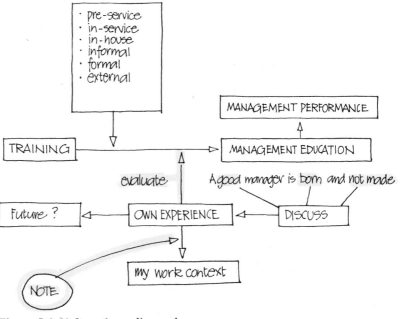

Figure 5.1 *A Stage 1 non-linear plan*

If you've drawn a diagram it is probably very different from mine. That's as it should be. If you haven't sketched a diagram you could try to do so now or do so with the next practice assignment. Experiment until you can decide whether you prefer a linear or diagrammatic question plan.

In the next few paragraphs I've written my thoughts about how I'd tackle this assignment. You might like to read my thoughts and then think about what you would have written. Better still, work out your own plan first and then read my notes. Again, I have used two different approaches. At this stage I prefer to 'brainstorm' and make a note of key points. I don't worry about ordering the points and I just write them down as I think of them. Then I try to develop a structured list of points by going back to the question to help me to sort out my ideas.

Having broken the assignment down into five parts, I now feel better able to think about it. Part 5 looks as if it should come first. If it's to help the tutor understand my work context then I don't want to leave it until the end of the assignment.

The 'Discuss this idea' section seems to be an overall requirement – I'm going to keep it in mind in each section and discuss it initially and then, as a result of what I write in other sections, discuss it again in the conclusion of my assignment.

The question in itself also gives me some clues as to how I might break down or structure my answer. Distinctions are made in the question between *in-house* and *external courses* and between *formal* and *informal training*. I need to think about these distinctions and to use them to plan my answer.

I also notice that both *management education* and *training* are used in the question. I know there's a difference between education and training and I'll have to decide whether to make and use the distinction. It doesn't really matter at this stage in my course, but I must be consistent and tell the tutor what I'm doing.

The next thing to do is to allocate space or words to each section and to get some sort of order. The assignment needs to be about 500 words. I'll plan for 450 because I know I have a tendency to write more than I should – I'll almost certainly have to cut some of it later. If you have the opposite problem, plan for 550 words at this stage. I also need to break the sections down a little more.

ACTIVITY **Stage 2** Using your linear or diagrammatic sketch from Stage 1, brainstorm further ideas on the question.

I've done this by drawing another diagram (see Figure 5.2). This helped to refine my thoughts about the question.

ACTIVITY **Stage 3** Using your own linear or non-linear Stage 2 breakdown of the assignment question, start to provide more details of what you will write in your assignment. Include 'Introduction' and 'Conclusion' sections.

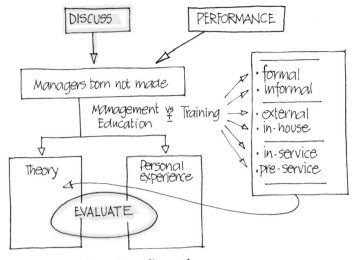

Figure 5.2 *A Stage 2 non-linear plan*

This takes time but it is time well spent. It is all too easy to write an excellent assignment and then just finish abruptly, without a conclusion, because you've used up your word allocation. My Stage 3 linear plan is shown below. Compare my plan with yours but don't be too influenced by mine as we will all write different answers. At this point I haven't included my non-linear diagram because it looks very complicated and is probably understood by me alone. Personally, I like to plan at Stage 3 by returning to the sort of linear plan I've used here. I do this after adding word counts and ordering numbers to my non-linear plan. Again, experiment and try using a mixture of linear and non-linear plans as part of this experimentation.

As you will see from my Stage 3 notes, I'm writing my thoughts for my own use. For example, I tell myself 'so need to', 'and then to', etc. 'Man.' refers to management or manager and 'Ed.' to education. In your plans use any abbreviations that make sense to you.

I've only provided the introduction, one paragraph, and the conclusion from my plan.

Stage 3 linear plan

Para 1 Introduction

'A good manager is born and not made' will be discussed with reference to my own experience

so need to

provide information on work context and then to outline types of Man. Ed. (say Ed. & Training used interchangeably here)

outline Man. Ed. & improved Man. performance and

outline different types of course & relative benefits to company to individuals (me & others)

outline reconsideration of opening statement saying that If Man. Ed. meets said criteria it CAN improve Man. Perf. & thus make good AND bad mans. better

60 words

Para 3 'A good manager is born and not made'

Discussed briefly — probably true in general but good and bad managers can become even better with good Man. Ed.

20 words

What is GOOD Man. Ed.? — relevant, immediately transferable/usable, at right level, as part of organisation's overall management development programme, supported by superiors, adequately resourced — staffed, sponsored, time allocated for courses & preparation — who does my job if I'm away? — do I have a horrendous back-log when I get back?

What benefits does a manager need to derive from it? — motivation, interest (perceived relevance/importance — see above); time, rewards? — why do it?

What does the organisation need to do? see resourcing above

40 words (I'll need to select most important points here.)

Para 10 Conclusion: 'A good manager is born and not made'

re-evaluate — discuss now in light of answers and e.g.s from above

50 words

My Stage 3 plan will need 'cutting' because if not I will exceed the allocated number of words. I now need to go back and decide what is important and to cut parts I can do without. Have you done this with your plan?

Try not to see this exercise as a waste of time. Assignment planning involves analysing the question and then thinking about it. When you are thinking about it then it's probably helpful to note anything that comes into your head. After that you go back to the question and decide which of your thoughts are relevant and which will help you answer the question.

Figure 5.3 below illustrates the process.

In this diagram 'understood & known' refers to questions you should ask yourself about the question. (a) Do you understand the question? and (b) Do you know how to answer the question?

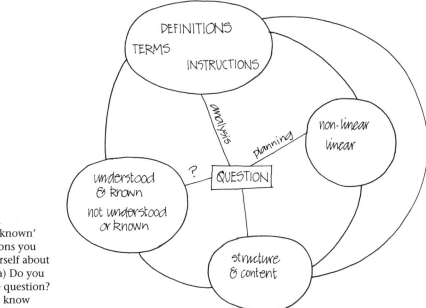

Figure 5.3 *The process of assignment planning*

Key points

■ Good planning helps to ensure you answer the question that is set.

■ It also helps to ensure you answer all parts of the question set.

Here is another type of assignment question. For the moment, leave the last assignment planning and look at Practice assignment 2 below.

Practice assignment 2

Part 1

Describe the company/organisation that you work in, or have previously worked for. Include the name of your organisation, the sector (private, public, non-profit/voluntary), its size, its turnover/budget, its product/s or function/s, and your role within it. (10%)

Part 2

Explain and analyse the way in which the organisation is managed. Is there a clear hierarchy of management – a chain of command – or is it managed in some other way? Consider who you answer to and who answers to you. Where do you fit in the management structure? (10%)

Part 3

Outline the main channels (paths) and modes (methods) of communication in your organisation and relate these, where appropriate, to the management structure you have analysed in Part 2. Consider both formal communications (e.g. company reports, formal meetings) and informal communication (e.g. coffee-break chats, corridor exchanges). (40%)

Evaluate your own pattern and methods of communication within the organisation and relate this to the structure of the organisation. Within the existing management structure could you be more effective? If the management structure were different would this enable you and your fellow managers to be more effective? (40%)

Write about 1200 words.

In Practice assignment 2 you are given a very clear indication about how marks will be allocated.

ACTIVITY   Following the examples from Practice assignment 1, complete Stages 1 to 3 of assignment planning for Practice assignment 2. Use whichever approach – linear or non-linear or a mixture of the two – you feel suits you best.

You should now have at least one assignment plan that is based on a good understanding of the question. Now you can start writing.

Your practice assignment answers will provide data for Activities in section 7 of this chapter.

ACTIVITY Write Assignment 1 now and Assignment 2 in the next week or so. Remember you must not write more than 500 words for Assignment 1 and 1200 words for Assignment 2 and you *must* try to follow the question. Don't worry that you have no references or course information to draw upon. At this stage, we are practising the planning and initial drafting of an assignment. It is worth taking a few hours to write these practice assignments as I will draw on them later in this chapter. Moreover, the sooner you start writing, the less daunting the task will be. Remember to return to the assignment question throughout – this will help you to keep to the point.

Having considered two assignments we shall now look at reports as a special type of assignment writing.

6 Report writing

This section complements the guidance on good writing given in this chapter and in Chapter 4. Here I shall concentrate on report writing and, after a brief introduction, I shall focus on the following three key areas:

- structure, format and style
- making recommendations
- concise writing.

Introduction: real reports and assignment reports

When an assignment question requires you to write a report many of the issues are much the same as for writing a report at work.

A good, practical, management report will be written to achieve specific objectives (usually to give information, to persuade, or to bring about some action). The writer will carefully consider the people who will read the report and tailor the content to their needs. The document will have a clear structure, with headings and sub-headings to guide the reader through the content. Care will be taken over the presentation of the report: spelling and grammar will be checked and it will look good, that is to say first impressions will be positive.

Not all management reports are like that but those that are will be more effective.

ACTIVITY The points in the left-hand column in the table opposite are taken from the description of good management reports we have just considered. In the second column mark up whether or not these points also apply to reports written for assignment purposes. The end column is for any notes you wish to make. The exercise is quite simple – though the point of it is an important one.

Element of report writing	Does this also apply to reports written as a course assignment?	Other comments
Clear purpose(s) in writing the document		
Must recognise the needs of the likely reader		
A clear structure		
Use headings as signposts for the reader		
Care with spelling, punctuation, etc.		
Importance of initial impact		

It seems to me that similar things are important both in reports for the workplace and in assignment reports. Even the ambiguity of writing an assignment report addressed to your manager, but using course concepts and knowing that your real reader is your tutor, reflects the work situation. After all, in the workplace a single report may well be read by, and have to convince, a number of readers with quite diverse requirements. Thus report writing for assignments is a valuable opportunity for developing important practical management skills.

Key points

The importance of the *purpose* of your report and the *needs of your readers* should be kept in mind throughout.

I shall now go on to consider some key aspects of writing management reports.

Reports: style, structure and format

Style

There is no one right style for reports. The report with its separate title page, contents list, acknowledgements and detailed paragraph numbering might be seen as excellent in one organisation, but may be thought to be long and cumbersome in another context. You may work for an organisation that has a defined 'house style' – if so, you should follow this at work and ask yourself if this style is appropriate for an assignment.

Within the confines of style, there are some basic requirements that must be met. For example, a basic minimum of information needs to be provided at the start of a report. Figure 5.4 overleaf illustrates two ways of giving this information.

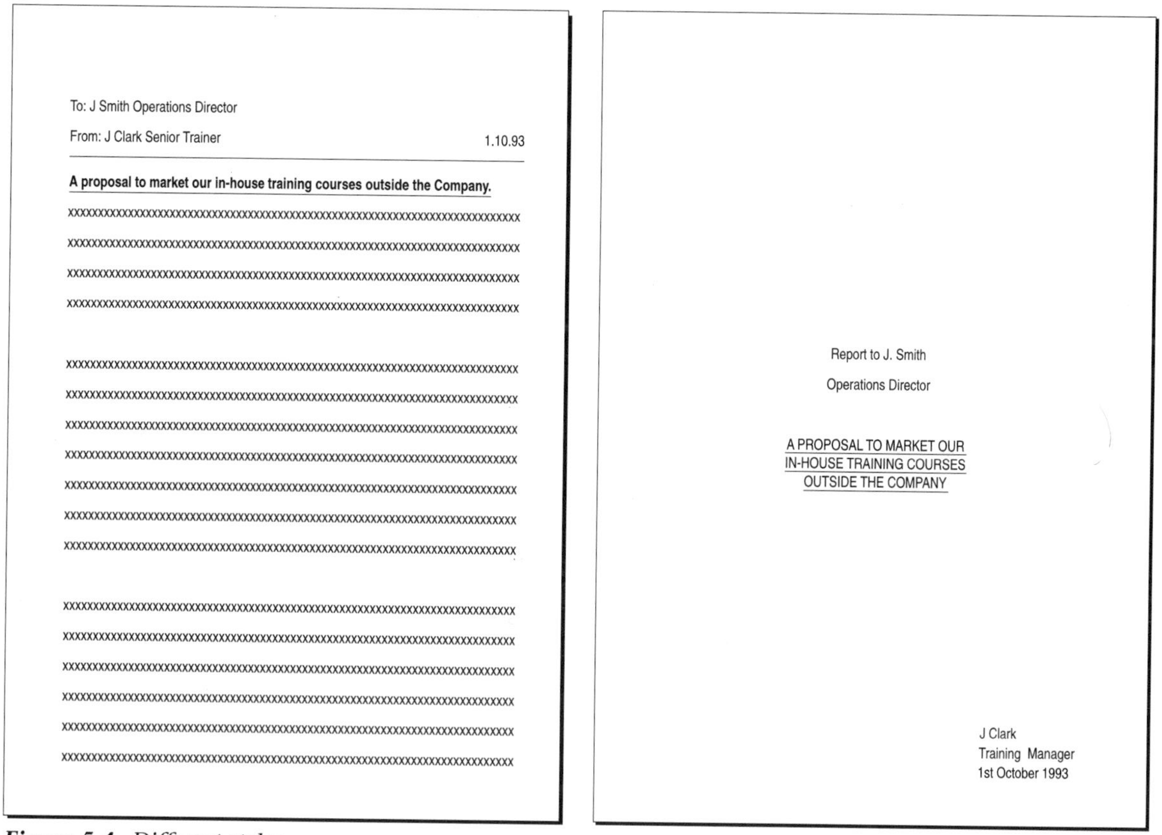

To: J Smith Operations Director

From: J Clark Senior Trainer   1.10.93

A proposal to market our in-house training courses outside the Company.

xxxxxxxxxxxxxxxxxxxxxxxxxxxxxxxxxxxxxxxxxxxxxxxxxxxxxxxxxxxxxxxxxx
xxxxxxxxxxxxxxxxxxxxxxxxxxxxxxxxxxxxxxxxxxxxxxxxxxxxxxxxxxxxxxxxxx
xxxxxxxxxxxxxxxxxxxxxxxxxxxxxxxxxxxxxxxxxxxxxxxxxxxxxxxxxxxxxxxxxx
xxxxxxxxxxxxxxxxxxxxxxxxxxxxxxxxxxxxxxxxxxxxxxxxxxxxxxxxxxxxxxxxxx

xxxxxxxxxxxxxxxxxxxxxxxxxxxxxxxxxxxxxxxxxxxxxxxxxxxxxxxxxxxxxxxxxx
xxxxxxxxxxxxxxxxxxxxxxxxxxxxxxxxxxxxxxxxxxxxxxxxxxxxxxxxxxxxxxxxxx
xxxxxxxxxxxxxxxxxxxxxxxxxxxxxxxxxxxxxxxxxxxxxxxxxxxxxxxxxxxxxxxxxx
xxxxxxxxxxxxxxxxxxxxxxxxxxxxxxxxxxxxxxxxxxxxxxxxxxxxxxxxxxxxxxxxxx
xxxxxxxxxxxxxxxxxxxxxxxxxxxxxxxxxxxxxxxxxxxxxxxxxxxxxxxxxxxxxxxxxx
xxxxxxxxxxxxxxxxxxxxxxxxxxxxxxxxxxxxxxxxxxxxxxxxxxxxxxxxxxxxxxxxxx
xxxxxxxxxxxxxxxxxxxxxxxxxxxxxxxxxxxxxxxxxxxxxxxxxxxxxxxxxxxxxxxxxx

xxxxxxxxxxxxxxxxxxxxxxxxxxxxxxxxxxxxxxxxxxxxxxxxxxxxxxxxxxxxxxxxxx
xxxxxxxxxxxxxxxxxxxxxxxxxxxxxxxxxxxxxxxxxxxxxxxxxxxxxxxxxxxxxxxxxx
xxxxxxxxxxxxxxxxxxxxxxxxxxxxxxxxxxxxxxxxxxxxxxxxxxxxxxxxxxxxxxxxxx
xxxxxxxxxxxxxxxxxxxxxxxxxxxxxxxxxxxxxxxxxxxxxxxxxxxxxxxxxxxxxxxxxx
xxxxxxxxxxxxxxxxxxxxxxxxxxxxxxxxxxxxxxxxxxxxxxxxxxxxxxxxxxxxxxxxxx
xxxxxxxxxxxxxxxxxxxxxxxxxxxxxxxxxxxxxxxxxxxxxxxxxxxxxxxxxxxxxxxxxx

Report to J. Smith

Operations Director

A PROPOSAL TO MARKET OUR
IN-HOUSE TRAINING COURSES
OUTSIDE THE COMPANY

J Clark
Training Manager
1st October 1993

Figure 5.4 *Different styles*

Both approaches give the same information. Some people would see the one on the right as the more professional of the two; others would see it as wasteful of paper and space. When you write reports you need to find out what is preferred by your organisation and/or your tutor.

Structure and format

In the workplace there are factors which help you to decide on an appropriate structure – not least of which may be the preferences of your likely readers. Some possible basic structures are:

- chronological – the order in which things or processes happened
- problem statement, analysis of options, recommendations
- proposal – 'pros and cons', recommended action.

The example question is an amended version of part of Assignment 03 in the Open University Course B789 *Managing Voluntary and Nonprofit Enterprises.*

You may well feel these structures could suit your purposes in an assignment, but other issues will affect your choice as well. In particular, you need to address all parts of the question as well as gaining good marks and learning from the process. Let's consider an example question:

Choose a group or team at work of which you are a member. Write a report for an appropriate person on its performance covering:

(a) A brief description of the group, its purpose, function(s) and relationship to the wider organisation. (20%)

(b) An analysis of how the group/team works, highlighting any important strengths and weaknesses. (40%)

(c) Recommendations for how the group/team's performance could be improved in the future. (30%)

Students must use ideas from the relevant section of the course materials. The remaining 10% of the marks will be for report structure and presentation. The answer should not exceed 1000 words.

It might seem common sense to use a structure that, after a brief introduction, gives an analysis of the group's problems followed by recommendations. The difficulty is that it would probably not do justice to Section (a) of the question. The point I am trying to make may seem obvious, but is overlooked by many students. As I stressed in the earlier practice assignment notes, you must use the sections of the question to help structure your answer. Thus the sections of your answer could mirror the sections of the question. However, the question may not be split in the way shown above. Or, you may prefer a structure that doesn't follow the shape of the question if you are confident that you can still address all of its parts.

Before returning to the example question I shall deal with one more aspect of structure: the various sections that could go into a report.

Simple reports may include the following:

Some reports start with recommendations. This can be especially useful if the report is very long and complicated.

- Title, author, date, etc.
- Contents page
- Executive summary
- Introduction
- Main text:
  Subject 1
  Subject 2
  Subject 3 (etc.)
- Conclusions
- Recommendations
- Appendices.

This list is best seen as a sort of menu from which to choose options according to the needs of the particular report. If an assignment requires a report of 750 words, then a summary is not really necessary. On the other hand, if you were writing an MBA assignment of 3500 words, a contents page and management summary would probably help your reader.

There are various conventions for numbering the sections of a report. The golden rule is 'be consistent'. One way is to number the main sections 1, 2, 3, and so on. Then, within Section 1, the sub-sections would be numbered 1.1, 1.2, 1.3 etc. In Section 2 they would be 2.1, 2.2, 2.3, and so on. Another approach is to label the sections A, B, C, etc.

In Figures 5.5 and 5.6 opposite the dotted lines represent text.

Staff Training and Development in A.B.C. Department.

1. INTRODUCTION

....

....

2. The present state of affairs is ....

.... and within this the problems are

A) ....   B) ....   C) ....

3. Conclusions

A) ....

B) ....

C) ....

4. Recommendations

4.1 ....

4.2 ....

4.3 ....

STAFF TRAINING AND DEVELOPMENT IN ABC DEPARTMENT

1.   INTRODUCTION

     ....

     ....

     ....

     ....

2.   FINDINGS

2.1   Current Situation

     ....

     ....

     ....

2.2   Problems Encountered

2.2.1   ....   (OR USE 'BULLET' POINTS)

2.2.2   ....   •   ....

2.2.3   ....   •   ....

3.   CONCLUSIONS

3.1   ....

3.2   ....

3.3   ....

4.   RECOMMENDATIONS

4.1   ....

4.2   ....

4.3   ....

Figure 5.5 *Inconsistent numbering*   **Figure 5.6** *A consistent approach*

In Figure 5.5 sections are identified with a mixture of letters and numbers; headings are not consistent in the use of lower case, capitals and underlining. Figure 5.6, whilst not perfect, at least shows a reasonably consistent approach to numbering and presentation of headings.

Again, there are issues of judgement and style here. In a report of 750 words, it would seem rather cumbersome to use 2.1.1, 2.1.2 etc. for sub-headings. For a document of that length it would probably be sufficient simply to number the main sections 1, 2, 3, etc. In Figure 5.6 note the possibility of using bullet points to separate items without using complex numbering systems.

ACTIVITY Look back to the example question opposite on page 124. Imagine you are going to answer that question and then draft out:

- the initial report headings (title, who the report is to, author and date)

- headings for each main section

- sub-headings if appropriate; in section (b) you may wish to consider key aspects of the team as separate sub-sections

- number the sections to the extent you feel appropriate for a report of 1000 words.

Variations in style are permissible. Don't worry too much if your answer differs from mine, especially on the basis of 'In our company we number sections this way', or similar.

To: A. Brown
From: B. Brooks   21 October 1993

The Marketing Team - Performance & Development

- -

1. Introduction   (75 words)

2. Description of the Team
    General
    Functions
    Purposes   (175 words)

3. Team Work: Strengths & Weaknesses

 * General
 * Are we a team ?
 * Strengths
 * Weaknesses   (375 words)

4. Recommendations
                                   (275 words)

Figure 5.7

This advice on conclusions is only for reports. Essay-type assignments need conclusions.

In Figure 5.7 I've added a rough estimate of words for each section to match the marking scheme. Do you think a 'conclusions' section is necessary? My view is that as conclusions, by definition, don't say anything new, then the words could be used better to gain marks elsewhere, but this is a matter of opinion.

The level of numbering is limited. This seems appropriate to a 1000-word report, but if you feel a fuller numbering is needed, that's fine. Note how the sub-sections use words from the question. This helps focus your writing on what the question is seeking.

A general rule of thumb for appendices is that if the item (a chart or table of figures perhaps) is essential to the understanding of your case, then put it in the main body of the text. If the item is of interest, but not essential, or it is supporting information, then put it in an appendix and make sure you refer to the appendix in your text.

Writing recommendations

Outlined below are some key points to bear in mind when making recommendations:

- *Recommendations should flow from the preceding content.* If your report has analysed a situation, then the recommendations should arise out of that analysis. You may introduce new theoretical concepts in a recommendations section, but the issues must have already been discussed.

- *Recommendations should be proposals for action.* Recommendations are not a discussion of the issues, or statements of the ideal situation; they are specific proposals for action. Imagine your reader saying, 'Yes, I'm convinced about the problem but how do I tackle it?' They should be able to turn to your recommendations for realistic proposals about what to do.

- *Recommendations should stand out and propose clear, specific actions for the reader.* Imagine your reader saying 'I know what the problem is but what are the solutions?' Can they find your recommendations easily? Is the section clearly headed? Does each item stand out? Use of bullet points or numbered paragraphs with space between each point helps here.

- *Ensure that your proposals are sensible and realistic.* Avoid recommendations which solve the problem 'at a stroke' or which project all the difficulties on to senior management. Acknowledge any possible opposition and cost implications.

Concise writing in reports

Word limits on assignments are often challenging, but then so are the demands of senior managers. 'I want it on one side of A4' is a demand you may recognise. One way to reduce the number of words used, and to give impact to what you say, is to *use bullet points*. I shall use that format here:

- Only include material that is relevant to your purpose and to your reader.

- Use the categories 'must know', 'should know', 'nice to know' to sort your material.

- At the draft stage, see whether you are saying the same thing twice; if so, eliminate one reference.

- Cut out words and phrases that are 'padding'. In reports, most uses of 'however' can be removed; 'at the present time' can generally be replaced by 'now' and 'in the near future' by 'soon'.

- Avoid phrases that take two words to say what is already said with one word, such as (totally) unique, (new) innovation, (mutual) co-operation, (unfilled) vacancy.

The material in Chapter 7 might be helpful here.
- Use diagrams and tables if you are able to do so. They can be valuable in expressing a lot of information in a concise way.

- Restrict the introduction to a brief statement of your purpose, the shape of your report and, if necessary, brief details about the context.

- Keep the detail of necessary examples to the bare minimum.

- Avoid the written style you would use to 'discuss' or 'compare and contrast'; report style is more direct and generally avoids discussion.

Key points

- Always keep your reader's needs in mind.

- Keep your purpose(s) in mind.

- Use the assignment question to help structure the answer.

- Make sure your report answers the question and that it addresses *all* of the question.

- Use headings and sub-headings to signpost the reader through the content.

- Recommendations are exactly that – specific proposals for action arising from your analysis.

- Take trouble over the visual impact and the detail – proof-reading is important.

7 Characteristics of good management assignments

In this section 'Key points' come before the text where those points are outlined.

Look back to your own list of purposes for assignments and revise it if appropriate in the light of what you've read and/or done. I'm sure you will have thought of other purposes for assignment writing. Look at your list again before and after writing your first, or next, assignment.

Good management education assignments have the following characteristics:

- They answer the question.

- They keep to the point and are concerned only with relevant information and details.

- They draw upon and make explicit reference to relevant course concepts.

- They are properly referenced – sources are fully acknowledged.

- They draw upon and make explicit reference to the 'real world' – to your work environment and situation.

- They are objective and analytical – they are not subjective and neither are they unduly biased.

- They are a synthesis of theory, practice, and common sense.

- They are well written – they are comprehensible to the reader.

- They are appropriately and clearly structured.

Let's take each of the above in turn and use examples to help. The examples given here are mostly taken from managers' assignments written during their studies with the Open Business School. The 'rules' look straightforward but, in fact, demand practice and revision. I've put the first two 'rules' together.

Key points

A good assignment answers the question, keeps to the point and is concerned only with relevant information and details.

The comments below were written by tutors marking managers' assignments. Read through them and then see if they could apply to the assignment you've just written.

'Whilst you started off with a clear structure, you took a long time to start tackling the question head on. The balance across the three parts of the question was heavily skewed towards the first section – and yet this was your worst section. Quantity does not mean quality!'

'You describe when you were asked to analyse. No marks for pure description.'

'Your description was long and your critical analysis short. It should have been the other way round!'

'In conclusion, you gave a very good historical analysis of how you got to where you are but no direction for the future – and the future is what the question is all about.'

'As with the last assignment your answer is well over the required length and as a result a lot of marks were lost.'

All company details and names have been removed and, in order to further preserve anonymity, some further, minor alterations have been made. Company names are usually changed to XYZ. Named products have been changed, where necessary, to A, B or C.

ACTIVITY Could a tutor write similar comments on your assignment? If so, make a note on your assignment. In this Activity I am asking you to start monitoring or 'marking' your own assignments. This is a very useful skill to practise as it helps you to feel more in control of your writing.

Re-read the question. Have you followed the key instructions? Have you, for example, evaluated and been critical where required or have you simply described? Have you allocated appropriate effort, and words, to specific sections of your answer (especially when you are guided as in Practice assignment 2)?

Key points

Good assignments draw upon and make explicit reference to relevant course concepts.

You have probably not yet started your course and so can't really evaluate this aspect of your writing. A set of tutors' comments, both positive and negative, are shown with extracts from the assignments. Don't worry about the content of the examples – they were written by managers who had been studying for at least a year. You should focus on the tutor's comments and note what is and what is not acceptable. The examples cannot reflect the whole of the assignment but they give an idea of the writing.

Good example

Again using the terminology of the course, the company generates its own hostile environment and therefore will tend to centralise.

Tutor: I thought your use of course concepts was confidently and effectively done and you demonstrated to me that you were able to order your thinking and develop your analysis using these tools.

Good example

XYZ's culture, using Kakabadse's analysis, is primarily task-oriented with many project groups working together for the duration of the project. Many departments are also heavily project focused, but this can lead to problems; such departments do not identify strongly with the aims of the organisation because of their strong identification with their immediate work group.

The manager referred to above names people but doesn't reference completely (see key points below). I assume that s/he has already referred to the people and provided dates of their work at an earlier stage.

Tutor: Good use of academic source.

An important question for you when you start to write course assignments is 'Could I have written this without doing the course?' If the answer is 'Yes' then you need to re-draft your assignment. It's not enough to understand – you have to *demonstrate* that you understand in order to avoid tutor comments like the following.

Tutor: Apart from one early use of Porter's model of the market (which was fine) you did not make use of any other material from the course. From page 3 onwards you could have written the same answer without having taken this course. This means that your analysis is very limited. You provide bland descriptions rather than focus on the strengths and weaknesses of the processes as you were asked to.

Poor example

… the re-organisation was poorly handled. Most staff were formally notified only one week before the new staff member was due to arrive …. When X complained to him about the lack of consultation and consequent staff demoralisation, the Personnel Officer seemed genuinely surprised that there was any cause for complaint. In his view, staff needed to know only after cut and dried decisions had been taken.

Tutor: What would you call this style of management? I am sure from your contribution at the last tutorial that you have fully understood the course material but your assignment shows no indication of this. I much regret that I am obliged to award such a low mark as I am working to a strict marking schedule.

Key points

Good assignments are properly referenced. Sources are fully and explicitly acknowledged.

Not only do you have to refer to and use course concepts in your assignments but you *must* acknowledge your use of sources. It's useless to copy paragraphs from books and articles. Your tutor will almost certainly recognise them and anyway the point is that you need to demonstrate your understanding of sources and not your ability to copy. In the examples below managers have referred to people but they haven't referenced them properly:

Example

Following Porter, I am going to attempt a brief analysis of the 'industry'.

Tutor: Which Porter book/paper?

Example

I have used one of the models in the course book to analyse the IT industry.

Tutor: Reference, please! Which model?

I've suggested that you should *always* provide full references for your sources. However, it is possible that specific courses you take will have different approaches. In just the same way that you should always follow house style when writing reports and documents at work, you should follow your 'course style'. Make sure you find out what your courses and tutors require and always follow the advice given. For example, there are some courses that do not require academic references. Similarly, a report is unlikely to contain *any* references.

Whenever you refer to anyone's ideas or theories you should give a full reference to that person. There are a number of ways of doing this and these are shown below. Ask your tutor for guidance if you are unsure. I prefer the first method where I'm given the name and the date of the work – other tutors might prefer other ways. Additionally, if you do use a sentence or two directly from someone else, then acknowledge this as shown in the second example below.

Examples

1 Following Smith (1987) and Williams (1992) I will use the ….

2 As noted by Jones (1993, p. 18) 'no style theory explains this managerial problem'.

3 Following Smith (1) I will use the ….

4 According to some theorists (3, 5, 8) there is ….

At the end of your assignment you would have a 'References' section giving full details. For examples 1 and 2 above these references would be in alphabetical order as below:

Jones, J.	1993	*The Psychology of Organisational Behaviour*, Camford: Cram Holm.
Smith, T. E.	1987	'Managers in Crisis' in H. Drift and L. Wood (eds), *Models of Management*, London: Link Press.
Williams, B. L.	1992	'Managing Change: Implications for Communication' in *Journal of Occupational Communications*, Vol. XXI, pp. 56–74.

These references are fakes.

The title of the book or the journal is shown in italics (you could use **bold** instead) and the title of a book chapter or paper in a journal is shown in quotation marks. The place of publication is shown before the publisher (London: Link Press). If the book you are referring to has been edited, and not entirely written by someone then you indicate this by '(eds)' as in the Smith (Drift and Wood) example.

Writers' initials are important. How many Smiths are there in the UK? If you are referring to articles in journals follow the format above, giving the date and volume number of the publication and using 'pp.' to indicate the page numbers of the article.

If you use a numerical reference system then you write your references in the order in which they occur in your text, as follows:

1 Smith, T. E. 1987 'Managers in Crisis' in H. Drift and L. Wood (eds), *Models of Management*, London: Link Press

2 Jones, J. 1993 *The Psychology of Organisational Behaviour*, Camford: Cram Holm.

If you are hand-writing assignments, then bold and italics are not available. Check with your tutor but you could underline rather than use italics and you could use capital letters rather than bold.

Key points

Good assignments draw upon and make explicit reference to the 'real world' – to the work environment and situation.

You can read your assignment and evaluate your success on this 'rule'. In addition to blending theory and practice, you need to provide specific examples of connections between course concepts and the real world. Read the extracts from managers' assignments and the accompanying tutor comments below.

Examples

The strategy currently developed by the company is to maintain an advantage over its competitors.

Tutor: How? Cost, quality, niche? What is your distinctive edge versus the competition?

People are, therefore, largely ignored in strategy formulation and, consequently, morale and commitment fall.

Tutor: Which people? Strategy for what?

Changed behaviour must be reinforced or those who find change a struggle will be tempted to resume their old ways. Managers should examine the reward system to see if it is consistent with the change being sought. Rewards need not be monetary to be effective. (Salter, 1973, Unit 11, pp. 82–3)

Tutor: What has your organisation done in this area?

You will have seen that not only do you need to use course concepts but in most management education courses you need to apply them to specific examples in the real world. The last writer above summarises and references course learning but omits to say what has happened in his or her organisation when the assignment apparently required this. Making links between theory and practice is your responsibility in writing assignments and you need to be specific and explicit.

ACTIVITY Re-read your practice assignments. Could more specific examples help to illustrate your points? If so, note where you might insert them.

Key points

Good assignments are objective and analytical. They are not subjective and neither are they unduly biased.

One of the difficulties of writing about your work context is that it is very familiar to you and you may have very strong feelings about it. If you have been learning about styles of management on your course you may, for example, have come to think that your own superiors are adopting a less than effective management style. You might have thought this before but now you have the appropriate knowledge and terminology with which to describe it. Be careful! You must try to distance yourself emotionally from your situation and to maintain an objective and analytical stance. This is not always very easy. Look at the following tutor comments.

Tutor: A common-sense narrative with a semi-personalised approach is not appropriate for this assignment. You must force yourself to a disciplined use of course concepts. You should analyse situations and draw your conclusions. You must show a dispassionate, ruthless objectivity to your analysis before introducing any personal opinions.

Example: *ABC [a process] has, over the last 5 years, declined but should be encouraged as a means of a lead in to the aforementioned work.*

Tutor: To improve this we would need to know why it should be encouraged. Do you have a vested interest? Has it really declined? – figures, etc., would help. Also it is not clear what 'as a means of a lead in' means.

Example: *XYZ is still a costly, paternalistic organisation where job security is considered to be high and the tasks are largely bureaucratic. The elected members are viewed as stakeholders who disrupt the actual work of ABCs rather than contribute to or complement their work. The staff are committed and hardworking but not always viewed as efficient.*

Tutor: Is this a biased view? You should have provided examples of, for instance, bureaucratic tasks and the time spent on them and specific examples of disruptions by elected members. Try to avoid an over-emotional reaction.

Example: *The process of management accounting, with its lack of IT networking, low paid and basically untrained staff (in constant change) is grossly inefficient .... Changes to suit managers' needs and improve their efficiency are almost impossible to achieve. In consequence, department heads are working totally in the dark ....*

Tutor: Write three positive things about XYZ. This assignment has been a stream of negatives so far. Your personal disenchantment is coming through and the tone is less than professional and detached.

ACTIVITY   Re-consider your practice assignments. Have you been analytical and objective or are you 'too close' to the subject? If you've made negative or positive statements have you backed them up with facts and figures? Underline any emotional parts of your writing. Go back and try to be more objective. This is sometimes difficult but always essential.

Key points

A good assignment is a synthesis of theory, practice and common sense.

This really puts everything that's been said before into one 'rule'. Probably the most demanding aspect of good management assignments, this will take time to learn. Don't expect to get this synthesis right at your first attempt. However, if you try to visualise an assignment as a sandwich of many layers this might help.

Key points

When you've made a plan, and then again when you read through your first draft, ask yourself these six questions.

- Have I used course concepts at every point?

- Have I referenced the use of concepts and theories?

- Have I related the concepts and theories to the workplace?

- Have I related the workplace to concepts and theories?

- Have I provided specific examples from the workplace?

- Have I used common sense to order, to synthesise and to critically evaluate my own writing?

ACTIVITY   Look back to your practice assignment and ask yourself the six questions above for each point you make. If you can answer 'yes' all the way through, then congratulate yourself! If not, note any additions or alterations you should make.

Key points

Good assignments are well written and comprehensible to the reader.

Write as though you are writing for an intelligent but relatively uninformed person. Introduce and explain new concepts and ideas.

As noted in the previous chapter, you need to become skilled at reading and correcting your own writing. Never assume that your tutor will be able to read your mind; don't take too much for granted. For example, just because you know how a course concept relates to an example you use, you must not assume this will be obvious to the tutor.

Good assignments are appropriately and clearly structured.

This rule refers to answering the question and providing clear signals or 'signposts' for your tutor about the direction of your assignment. If you are asked to write in report style, then you need to do just that. Divide your assignments into logical sections, provide sections with headings or titles, and give these section details at the start of your report. Similarly, if you are asked to 'list' something, then don't write in paragraphs.

Clear structuring will help you to write your assignment but, additionally, it will help your tutor to read and to follow your thinking and writing. All assignments should have an introduction. If you are writing an essay-type assignment, this might take one or, at the most, two paragraphs. You will need to outline the topic you are writing about and to say, briefly, where your assignment is going. Think of the introduction as a map for a walker. You say which direction you're taking, in which order, and then you do actually follow the directions given so that the walker doesn't get lost. Read through the following examples of good signposting.

> 'This assignment assesses XYZ's fit with the external environment, utilising some of the concepts in units 3 to 7.'

> 'The purpose of this assignment is to consider and provide information on XYZ's present and future communications policy.'

> 'This report is an appraisal of strategic management at XYZ. The introduction will give a brief description of the organisation and of the level of analysis undertaken in this report. The second part will be an assessment of the organisation's fit to its environment and will comprise an analysis of the environment, an analysis of the organisation's resources and its distinctive competencies, a description of its chosen strategy, and a comment on the suitability and efficacy of that strategy. The third part will describe the existing strategic management processes of the organisation; how strategy is formulated, how decisions are made, and which individuals and groups contribute to them. The final part of the report evaluates how the organisation manages strategic change, and assesses power, structure and control within the organisation.'

Your assignments may not need the detail given in the last example above but, in the case of a 2000-word report, such a format signposts a very clear direction for the reader to follow.

I always leave my final version of the introduction until I've written a text. I start off with a draft and keep a skeleton of the assignment to hand but, until I've drafted and redrafted, I leave the actual introduction. Experiment to see when you prefer to write your introduction but remember you must write what you say you are going to write.

Finally, in this section, do remember that the Conclusion is as important as the Introduction. It's tempting to get to the end of an assignment, put the pen down or switch off the computer, feeling instant relief that you've finished. Don't fall into the trap of trailing off and losing the opportunity to tie together the points you have spent so long making. Look at the tutor's comment below:

> **Tutor:** My only concern is the way it fades out. You have an extraordinarily forceful summary at the beginning and a rather feeble conclusion.

Learning from assignments

As noted at the beginning of this chapter, assignments are an important means of consolidating and evaluating learning. When your tutor returns your assignment to you, take time to read the comments. These should help you to know where you went wrong, where you could have done better and what you did well. If you are disappointed by the grade on your first assignment, try not to let this have a negative effect on your studies. Use feedback from your tutor to help you to write future assignments. If you are unclear or confused by your tutor's comments, then make sure you seek clarification and explanation. You need to understand why and where you went wrong and to feel confident that you know how to approach your next assignment. Similarly, you need to build upon what you did right and to use this in the future.

8 Summary

When you have worked through this chapter, you should have a good idea about the purposes of assignment writing. Moreover, you should be in a position to work towards writing good assignments because you should be aware of the major characteristics of good assignments. Try to become self critical in a positive way. Read your assignments carefully and, using sections of this chapter and Chapter 4 to help you, become an evaluator of your own work.

Chapter 6   Studying with English as a foreign language

1   Introduction

If this is the first chapter you have turned to in this book, then it is probably because English is not your first language, not the language you use most frequently in work, or at home, or not the first language you learned as a child. Alternatively, English may be your first language and you want to see if the chapter contains any general advice that might be of use – in particular, you may read Section 3 on active learning. Look through the chapter's contents and dip in to explore whatever looks interesting and useful.

The longest sections of this chapter are on feelings about using English as a study language, and on reading. The comparative length of these two sections reflects the need for learners to feel in control of their learning and the important role of reading in most management education courses.

In Section 7 of this chapter you will find an Activity that asks you to provide titles for information in paragraphs of a text. There is a similar Activity, using a different text, in Chapter 3.

Some of the material in this chapter is repeated, using different examples, in other chapters. This is because I wanted to give you two opportunities to practise specific study tasks. Additionally, I felt that it would be useful to keep all key aspects of study together in one chapter for readers who opted to read this chapter before anything else in the book.

To 'cope', in this context, means to manage effectively.

You are either soon to start, or are already studying, a management course using English. If you were about to start a management course using your first language, you would probably be looking forward to it, although you might still be asking yourself if you would be able to cope. Whatever their first language, most people question their ability to cope with a course before it starts. In this you are not alone!

This chapter aims to do the following:

- to focus on studying with English if English is not your first language
- to help you to work out your strengths and weaknesses for studying with English
- to help you to understand the demands of a management course in which you will use English and which, for most of you, will require you to study alone and to study part time
- to help you to use your existing strengths to manage your studying.

ACTIVITY Take a few minutes to note down your objectives for this chapter. Remember to go back to these notes when you have finished working through the chapter.

If you 'keep something in mind', you remember it and continue to think about it.

Studying any management course in English will certainly improve your English. By the end of it, you will be more confident and competent in using the English language. However, you must keep in mind that you are not taking an English Language course.

Key points

On a management course, English is the means to an end. Don't make life impossibly difficult. Accept that your English will improve but keep this in perspective – any improvement will be a bonus.

To 'jot down' is to write some points or ideas in a fairly rough, instant sort of way.

You are probably a busy person coping with the demands of work, family and friends. Take a few minutes to jot down these demands. You will need to make extra time in your life for studying and for studying management through English. This chapter aims to give you a set of development strategies for using English for study.

It's not enough to say that if English isn't your first language, you'll be worried about using it for study. All of this book's readers will have different abilities and different anxieties. For this reason, it's important that you try to focus your own worries and to take from this chapter what you need. Don't just read through this chapter – use the Activities in order to make your own decisions and to become a manager of your own learning.

Here 'context' refers to the words before and after the word(s) you don't understand. It also refers to your overall understanding of what you read before and after the word(s) you don't understand.

In the margins of this chapter you will find explanations for some of the words and phrases that you may find difficult. Use these aids to understanding only if you need them and initially try to work out what is meant from the context of the sentence and paragraph. The margin notes give explanations of the words in the context in which they appear. If, after looking at the explanation provided, you're still not sure, then use a dictionary and make sure you read Section 5 on using dictionaries. Don't try to work through the whole chapter in one sitting. Spend an hour or so working and then do something else and let things sink in before returning to study.

To 'let things sink in' is to let ideas and information become settled and absorbed in your mind.

Where does English fit?

For some of you English will be your second language and you will use it every day. You may live in the UK and use English except when you're at home or with friends who share your first language. In a sense, English, for you, is a second language. For others of you, English may also be your second language although you may use it only very rarely. You may live in the country of your first language, but use English just occasionally for business purposes, perhaps, or to read a journal or magazine written in English. In a sense, English is, for you, a foreign language. Others of you will know and use two or three languages much better than you know English so for you English might be a third or fourth language. Think about your own use of English before you go any further in this chapter.

To avoid the complications of using terms such as 'English as a second language' or 'English as a foreign language', I will refer to English as 'ES' – English for Studying. I hope you will all feel that you can include yourselves in this category.

First of all, let us consider how it feels to be using ES. Perhaps you feel anxious about it, or confident about some things but worried about others. Your feelings are important, and if you feel anxious it is pointless for me just to say 'stop worrying'. I hope working through this chapter will help you feel more confident about dealing with your worries and about capitalising on your strengths.

ACTIVITY   You have already read quite a lot of text. The language is not designed specifically for you. I would write in the same way for students using English as their first language. Note your answers to the following questions:

- How do you feel about your understanding of this chapter?

- Have you used, or wanted to use, a dictionary?

- In general, how do you feel about studying with English?

- Have you answered these questions in English or in your first language?

- Whichever language you used, *why* did you use it?

This section tries to bring into the open the problems you may have and, at the same time, it reminds you that language is not the only worry learners have. A manager from the UK who has done no formal studying for years may be just as worried as you. The worries may simply be different ones.

Key points

Just because English is not your first language, this does not mean you will be less successful than other manager-learners. Like every student of management, you will have personal strengths and weaknesses. Hundreds of ES manager-learners are highly successful. Using ES is not an obstacle to success.

ACTIVITY   List your worries about using English.

Underline, or circle, any of the worries you've listed that a manager using English as a first language could have.

Add any worries that *any* manager, whatever their nationality, might have about studying.

Cross out or delete anything you've written in answer to the question above that you, personally, are not worried about.

I hope you've now started to focus on your worries and to be specific about your anxieties. Following the next section on feelings, I look at ways in which you can use your strengths and lessen your weaknesses. Knowing yourself is an important starting point. It is also very important to find out as much as possible about the course you are taking. Finding out what is expected of you and comparing this to previous experiences and to your expectations now is very important.

After this I explore your attitudes towards, and your approaches to, studying and I consider ways in which you can overcome language problems by adopting realistic study strategies. After this there are short sections on reading, writing, listening and speaking, and finally the chapter concludes with advice on making progress, controlling your own learning and using your strengths to advantage when you study.

By the end of this chapter:

- You should have started to make a study plan for studying with English. If you are reading this chapter before you start your course, this will mean you have time available before you start working on your course material.

- You will have a clearer idea about what worries you most about studying with English and you will have some strategies for coping.

To 'prioritise' means to order things according to their importance. So a 'top priority' is the most important thing to do.

- You will be ready to turn to other chapters in this book and, because you will have prioritised your strategies, you should have a good idea of a possible order in which you could work through the other chapters.

2 How it feels to be using English as a study language

The Activity below asks you to think about past experiences of using English. It then focuses on how you feel about specific uses of English for study.

ACTIVITY

1 Look back to your answers to the second Activity in this chapter. Expand on those answers now to complete Column 1 of the table in Figure 6.1 overleaf. I've already written 'Reading, Listening, Speaking, Writing'. You should add your other uses of ES but make them as specific as possible. What are you going to be reading? You might include textbooks, course books, magazines, newspapers, etc. Delete any categories I've written if they don't apply to you. You might like to add 'vocabulary' and 'grammar' but, again, be as specific as possible.

2 Complete Column 2, the 'Past experience' column. For example, if you've never used ES for reading course books, you would put a tick in the 'None' column.

3 Complete Column 3, the 'Feeling' column. If you feel confident about reading newspapers in English, you would put a tick in the 'Confident' column.

4 Now read through the table you have completed. For the final part of this Activity, you will need four different coloured pens or pencils.

It is much easier to highlight than to underline in this Activity. If you don't already have any, buy three or four highlighting pens now – they will be useful for your studying.

Start in the 'Feeling' column. Take a coloured pen and highlight, or underline, any 'Very worried' ticks, taking the line from right to left so that it goes through, or under, any types of ES that you feel very worried about. Take a different colour and do the same for the 'Worried' responses and then, in another colour, do the 'Confident' and 'OK' responses.

You should now have a four-coloured table that gives you an indication of how you're feeling about each type of ES you are required to use.

It's often very useful to do this type of activity when you're feeling worried about studying with English. Some ES learners have told me 'I'm worried about everything!' However, when we look carefully and start to break down the worries it usually becomes clear that some aspects of ES are causing more worry than others.

Key points

You need to know what you are most and least worried about and to be prepared for this to change as you start to study.

Column 1	Column 2			Column 3			
	Past experience			Feeling about ES skill			
Type of ES	A lot	Some	None	Confident	OK	Worried	Very worried
Reading:							
Listening:							
Speaking:							
Writing:							
Anything else?							

Figure 6.1

As far as your confidence is concerned you should now be able to prioritise your next step. You should concentrate on the things you are most worried about. However, as a busy manager time-management has to be considered.

Let us suppose that you are very worried about speaking English in a tutorial situation, writing English for assignments, writing English in examinations and reading English in textbooks. Now is the time to be realistic. How is your course of study organised? How much time are you required to take on each of those 'worry' tasks? Will you, for example, be assessed on written work, spoken presentations and/or case study interpretation, or by timed examinations?

Another 'being realistic' task concerns your ability and past experience. If you've put ticks in the 'A lot' column of the 'Past experience' section, but you're still worried about the skill, ask yourself if your worry is justified. Are you worried just because you would like to improve that skill for general English Language learning purposes, or is it a skill you really need to improve in order to succeed in your study programme? Remember what was said in the introduction – your study will almost certainly improve your English but that is not its primary aim.

What is required now is a study plan to help you feel more confident about ES tasks. If you're reading this book before starting your study programme, you can use this time to start improving these skills now. If you're already studying, you might be able to adjust your study plan to include more attention to skills you are particularly worried about if those skills are important on your course.

ACTIVITY

Step 1

Using the table you completed in the last Activity, prioritise your activities as the first stage of making an ES study plan. Ask yourself the following questions.

- Am I worrying unnecessarily? Am I being realistic in terms of my ability for study purposes? (You may want to come back to this question when you've seen the results of your first assignment; been to your first tutorial; read your first course unit, etc.)

- Am I worrying about the right things? Am I concerned about areas of study that are important to my success on the course or am I worrying about a general improvement in my language skills?

- Does my performance justify my priorities? You will need either to base this on past experience of using English as your study language or wait until the course starts before you can answer this. You might show the plan to other people and see if they agree. However, don't change things just because someone else says you should – this is *your* plan. Make a note on your study plan to return to this question.

Step 2

In order to organise your ES study plan you will need to understand the way in which your course works. Have you read the 'About this book' section, Chapter 1 'Getting started' and Chapter 2 'Learning opportunities'? When you receive them, read any introductory notes for your course in order to understand how your course is organised and what will be expected of you.

Step 3

Write a rough, or draft, ES study plan. Guidance on the steps involved is given below. Be realistic. How much time can you really devote to ES? Have you left room for work and family commitments? Remember, any study of management needs time management. Follow the six stages below to help:

Stage 1   Complete the thinking and review required in Steps 1 and 2 above.

Stage 2   Make a calendar for the time from now until you start your course of study. Divide days into blocks of time that are appropriate for you and show times clearly on your plan. (If you are already studying make sure you use an existing study plan – if you don't have one use this Activity to make one now.)

Stage 3   How much free time do you have? Make sure your calendar includes time for family and leisure as well as work commitments.

Stage 4   Calculate the number of hours you can devote to ES time.

For example, it is probably a good idea to work through this chapter and identify any worries you have. Then build in time to work on these topics.

Stage 5   Based on your priority list, calculate how long you can spend on the areas that you feel worried, or very worried, about. Take longer for the 'very worried' skills and make sure you've checked your original coloured table after considering the 'be realistic' advice. Include pre-course work if you have any, as well as working through other chapters in this book. It's all in English so it all contributes to ES pre-course planning and some of it is probably best done before your course starts, if that is possible.

Stage 6   You will almost certainly find that there aren't enough hours in the day. Can you reduce your list of things to do? At this stage you are only making a draft plan. Return to this when you've worked through this chapter. You may well find that you don't need to worry so much and that your skills will develop during the course. Above all, don't panic! Look at the two-week plan on the opposite page. It's an example of the sort of plan you might make.

However, this is a very detailed and apparently very 'tidy' plan. Life is rarely so tidy and you may find it easier to divide days into three or four blocks – such as before work, immediately after work, before bed. In this way you can still keep priorities to the fore, but use any extra time as a bonus. You must develop a plan that works for you.

The following abbreviations are used in the plan opposite:

MGSG	The Manager's Good Study Guide
hr	hour
min	minute

Days of the week are abbreviated – use your own abbreviations.

	Week 1	Week 2
Total time available	12 hours	10 hours
Priority 1	Reading and note-taking	Reading and note-taking
Priority 2	Improving reading time	Vocabulary
Priority 3	Writing summaries	Writing up notes
Priority 4	Grammar for writing	Assignment writing
Priority 5	Vocabulary	
Mon p.m.	30 mins – timed reading: text for MGSG Reading Chapter 2 hrs – MGSG: Reading chapter	1 hr – read & take notes from Course Reader 30 mins – update & revise vocabulary cards
Tues early a.m.	15 mins – timed reading: Financial Times 45 mins – read Course Reader following MGSG reading techniques 45 mins – note-taking from introductory course material	1 hr – read & take notes from Course Reader 15 mins – vocabulary update from reading
Wed p.m.	15 mins – timed reading: The Economist 1 hr – finish MGSG Reading Chapter	45 mins – timed reading & note-taking 1 hr – sort & summarise notes
Thurs a.m.	15 mins – timed reading: The Economist	15 mins – vocabulary from Course Reader
Fri p.m.	1 hr – make & revise vocabulary cards from timed reading/Reading Chapter 15 mins – timed reading: Course Reader	15 mins – vocabulary from Course Reader
Sat a.m.	1 hr – sort notes & summarise Reading Chapter 2 hrs – begin MGSG: Effective Writing Chapter	2 hrs – MGSG: Effective Writing Chapter 30 mins – grammar revision from week 1
p.m.	30 mins – timed reading: IPM Journal	
Sun a.m.	1 hr – check & update vocabulary cards	1 hr – plan draft assignment from MGSG
p.m.	30 mins – review week's work & revise next week's plan	1 hr – plan draft assignment from MGSG 30 mins – review week's work & make next week's plan

Figure 6.2

You should now have a *draft* plan that looks a little like mine. Some of you will have a much more fluid plan – that's fine. You may find planning in 15 to 30-minute blocks is hopeless – if so,

If something is 'set in concrete' then it is fixed for all time.

work on your own preferred planning system. At this stage, nothing is set in concrete. At the start of their courses, most people tend to overestimate the amount of time they have available for study. Use your plan for a week to see if it works and be prepared to revise it. You will almost certainly need major revisions. After a week you may have discovered other worries or realised that you're worrying unnecessarily. Perhaps you will find the reading easier than you thought but you will be increasingly worried about how to take good, brief notes.

Key points

Do keep revising your study plan. You need to make it work for you and it will almost certainly change over time.

3 Active learning

If you do not yet know this information, make a note to return to this section later.

In order to make your priority lists you will have found out about the type of course you are taking. You should now understand the course structure in terms of assessment, examinations and the approximate workload. You should know the order of the units and you may already have an idea of which units you might find particularly interesting or particularly difficult.

You should also be thinking about the conceptual demands of your course. What is successful management education all about? How can you make full use of management education? Are there any particular considerations for you as an ES user?

In any good management education programme you will be required to be active in your learning. This active learning requires you to play an important role in the learning process. Such a role may be unfamiliar to you – now is an opportunity to think about how you can make full use of the possibilities that your course will provide.

Think back to your last formal learning experience in school, college or university. How active were you? Were you one of a hundred or two hundred students in lectures, or were you involved in small group seminars and discussions? Did you study alongside your fellow students in study groups or did you always study alone?

Your past learning experiences will have an influence on your attitudes and approaches to learning now. However, don't just think about formal 'academic' study. Think back to your last learning experience in work. Perhaps you were on a course or maybe you had to learn something on your own. How did you learn? How can you use past experiences – good and bad – to help you now?

Because you are using ES, and because, for some of you, this will be your first experience of studying on a course written and produced by a UK university, you may need to prepare yourself for a new sort of learning experience. However, you should still be able to use previous learning experiences to help you now.

Active learners in management education:

Set out to *understand* what is to be learned by:

■ *relating* what is being learned to what is already known, and by

■ *relating* what is being learned to the workplace (now and for the future).

Set out to *take control* of learning by:

■ *questioning* everything

■ *personalising* everything, and

■ *managing* study time.

Set out to *achieve* by:

■ *understanding* the system of learning, and

■ *devising realistic strategies* for the learning system that allow them to

■ *remain confident* of eventual success.

If you have been taught in a system that tested your memory and not your understanding, those days are over!

Management education is about understanding concepts and theories taught on your course by relating them to management practice. Your work situation and your management experiences are as essential to you as your reading of course materials. You will be assessed on your ability to apply course concepts – not on your ability to regurgitate facts and figures. This has implications for both the learning and teaching process.

If you 'regurgitate' you take something in and then let it out again in the same form.

Your tutors will not provide quick answers to questions and there will be no miracle cures for study problems, just as there are rarely simple right or wrong answers to real-life management problems. You will all come from different backgrounds and you will all be working in different situations. It will be up to you to make sense of what you read and hear in the light of your *own* experience and situation. You may think, initially, that course writers are talking about management practices and contexts that apply only in the UK. Occasionally, this might be the case, and certainly some of the course writers will not have your first-hand experience of management in other countries.

In this sentence, context refers to situation.

Accept that many course writers are experts within a limited context – so, too, are you! Look for possible comparisons between countries and cultures. Use your knowledge and experience to draw out differences and similarities and question the relevance of what you are being taught for your own context. Frequently, you will be able to add information specific to your context that will increase knowledge and understanding for the rest of your tutorial group and for your tutor. Often course material will be universally relevant and your task will be to consider how your own work context fits into, or differs from, the scenarios and examples given. If you can see this as a positive opportunity to increase your understanding, you will be able to approach the course with an active, fully involved approach.

At this stage, you should be able to see ways in which you can become an active learner in management education. Consider the active learner characteristics outlined above and copied here with some additions as an Activity for you to try when you have started your course.

ACTIVITY

Do I set out to *understand* what is to be learned by:

■ *relating* what is being learned to what is already known?

■ *relating* what is being learned to the workplace?

ES learners in other countries need to pay particular attention to similarities and differences between UK scenarios and examples and their own contexts. Geographical, cultural, political and social similarities and differences should be noted and commented on if appropriate.

Do I set out to *take control* of learning by:

■ *questioning* everything in the light of experience and common sense?

■ *personalising* everything?

Just because English is not their first language, ES learners should not let this stop them from using their existing management experience, knowledge and practice to their advantage. By constantly trying to apply taught concepts and principles to the workplace they will be able to personalise learning in exactly the same way as a UK manager whose first language is English.

■ *managing* study time and getting to know my preferred way and time for studying?

Do I set out to *achieve* by:

■ *understanding* the system of learning?

■ *devising realistic strategies* for the learning system? If so I can:

■ *remain confident* of eventual success.

ES learners will need to develop the same active study approaches as students whose first language is English. However, certain strategies specific to ES learners should be developed.

It's probably a good idea to photocopy this Activity and return to it once your course has started. It can be especially useful if you are feeling anxious or unsure about your progress.

Thinking in English

Take a few minutes now to think about 'thinking in English'. Do you think in English already? We need to consider this point quite seriously. My advice is that you must try to think in English when you are writing. If you write assignment plans in English this will help. You could try to write notes or summaries of reading in English as this will help when you start to write. If you try to 'translate' sentences from your first language, you will quickly encounter problems. As you work through this chapter and then through other chapters in the book, evaluate your 'thinking' and start working out how and when you should 'think' in English and not in your first language. The more you practise thinking in English the easier and more automatic it will become.

   In the next section, we look first at vocabulary, dictionary use and grammar. This is followed by sections on reading, writing, listening and speaking. Work through the sections that are appropriate for you and then turn to the relevant chapters in the book for further advice and Activities.

4 Vocabulary

ES managers frequently say that vocabulary is one of their biggest worries. In this section I will look at vocabulary, and outline ways of coping with new words and learning important vocabulary.

If you work through all of this chapter, you'll read about 16,000 words. As I said earlier, I haven't consciously chosen words or structures that I felt would be easy for ES readers. Consequently, there may have been occasions when you needed to look at the explanations in the margin or use a dictionary to find fuller or additional explanations.

ACTIVITY   Ask yourself if you really needed the dictionary or margin help.

- Did you use it as a check on your understanding?

- Did you try to make an intelligent guess *before* using the explanation?

- Did you really need to check the word at all – could you have managed without a complete understanding of it?

- Were you looking up words that you thought would become important – because they occurred several times or because you'd seen them elsewhere and wondered what they meant?

- Having looked up words or phrases, what did you do then?

- Did you write down the words? If so, did you write an explanation in English or in your own language?

- Did you check whether the margin or dictionary explanation made sense in the sentence?

- Do you understand the word or phrase now?

Your responses to the questions above will help you to think carefully about understanding and learning vocabulary. Without going into too much theory, it's useful to start off with some understanding of vocabulary, how we use it, how we store it and how we retrieve it when we need it.

Active versus passive vocabulary

In your first language, you probably know and understand many more words than you use. Whilst understanding a word in context may not be a problem, you might feel less confident about using that word in a sentence of your own. Words available for you to use come from your *active* vocabulary. Words you understand but don't use easily or frequently are in your *passive* vocabulary.

In a foreign language, the distinction between your passive and active vocabularies will be more pronounced than in your first language. As a Spanish speaker, I can understand more or less any conversation provided that I can see the speakers and that I can listen to the conversation from its beginning. Using the context, speakers' gestures, guesses and my own passive vocabulary, I can usually manage. However, when it comes to producing words myself, then I have to rely on a much smaller, active vocabulary. (This difference also applies to grammatical structures. There are some structures I can readily understand but I have trouble using them correctly or appropriately myself.)

The question is how do we decide what to move from passive to active vocabulary and how do we set about doing this?

What is important vocabulary – what needs to be active?

To simplify, I'd say that the following criteria make some words and phrases more important than others.

- *Frequency* – is a word or phrase frequently encountered? If you see a word frequently, you probably need to learn it and to be able to use it.
- *Speciality* – is a word or phrase particular to, but frequently used and understood by, a particular community, for example, of accountants, lawyers, general managers? If you want to communicate in that community, you probably need to learn it and to be able to use it.
- *Utility* – is a word or phrase particularly useful? This probably relates to frequency and speciality above, but also includes certain words and phrases that you, as a non-native speaker of English, might need to become familiar with early on in your studying. Words and phrases such as 'however', 'nevertheless', 'in spite of', and 'as a consequence' might be examples.

Specialist vocabulary

Specialist vocabulary will not be a serious problem for you. Initially, you might need to learn the specialist words and terms for a particular management discipline. However, once you have learned these terms, you will be reading them and using them often enough for them to become familiar. A specialist management dictionary might help (see 'Recommended texts' at the end of this book).

ACTIVITY

1 If you are a manager in the UK and English is not your first language, list some specialist terms particular to your management context. Are you familiar with these terms in your first language? Are there any English terms that you are unsure of? Are there any first language terms that you don't know the English translation for?

or

If you are a manager in a non-English speaking country, list up to 10 specialist management words and expressions particular to your management context. You may have to think for a while – expressions familiar to you may, in fact, be incomprehensible to those not working in your specialism.

2 'Translate' the non-English word or expression into English or 'translate' the English word or expression into your first language. Use a dictionary to check your translation or to look it up if you have no idea of its English equivalent.

The problems of translation

Straight translations or direct equivalences are often impossible. In the Activity above you may have found that direct translations were impossible. Many words used in your first language will have no equivalence in English and vice versa. Accept this and be prepared to question equivalences, even when they appear to exist.

Is a dictionary definition good enough? If a word or phrase is used frequently, be prepared to test your understanding of it, with examples of its use, with your tutors and with any English-speaking colleagues or friends.

Be particularly careful to check words that 'sound' the same in English as in your own language. For example, 'sensible' in English is now used to mean 'having or showing good sense' (Concise Oxford Dictionary). Although it was once used to mean 'sensitive', this is rarely its use today. The Spanish *sensible* looks exactly the same but, in English, it means sensitive (*sensitivo*) whereas sensible in English can best be translated into Spanish as *razonable* or *sensato*. Similarly, in Italian *sensible* means sensitive and *ragionevole* translates to the English 'sensible'. In a question such as 'What measures might sensible managers take to ensure the commitment of their junior staff?' the difference in meaning is important.

Additionally, cultural differences frequently make direct translations difficult. A much quoted example of this is the Eskimo use of words for 'snow'. Eskimos have many different words for snow whilst in English one word usually suffices. Of course, if you are a skier, then 'powder snow', 'firm snow' and 'fine snow' might become necessary additions to the word in your vocabulary. Similarly, English has no equivalent for *bon appetit*. If you are a manager eating with English colleagues, you'll either have to use your own language's expression and explain what it means if necessary or, as in the UK, you'll say nothing as you start to eat.

Many languages use different structures to denote varying degrees of formality and respect. For example, in English the French 'tu/vous' and the Spanish 'tu/usted' distinctions cannot be translated by single words. Respect and status in English are conferred much more implicitly by the overall use of words and tone if you are speaking. Can you think of similar structures in your first language?

Translation machines

There are a number of hand-held translation machines or computers now available. If you have one of these, use it by all means but make sure you follow the advice given on checking the meaning of words in the context in which they appear.

ACTIVITY

Are there any words in your first language that look or sound the same as English but which in fact mean different things? List a few and, using a sentence or two in English, illustrate their meaning.

Are there any words or phrases in your own language that you already know to be 'untranslatable' into English? List up to five examples and try to follow these with a direct translation. Then write an English version that would be comprehensible to English speakers. An example is provided:

'Demasiado para el cuerpo' (Spanish) – 'too much for the body' – 'incredible (with a good or bad sense), amazing, wonderful, terrible'

You may want to add to this list as your course progresses.

Understanding vocabulary

I've already noted that the frequency of words and phrases provides a good indication of importance. When you read words you don't know, you have to decide whether or not you need to understand them in order to understand what you are reading. Sometimes this decision is easy, but frequently it is not. Consider the first two sentences of a text that I will ask you to read later.

The text used in this chapter is 'Germanity – reflections on a people' and can be found in Reading appendix 2 at the end of this book. You do not need to read it yet.

> Next stop Germany. You don't know the country well (maybe not at all or only through books) and the Germans you have met so far haven't been on their own home <u>turf</u>.

Horticulture is the cultivation or study of the cultivation of plants in gardens.

For many of you the word 'turf' may be new. Unless you are involved in horticulture or horse-racing you may not have met the word before. So what are you going to do? You have several choices. You could turn immediately to the dictionary. You could ignore the word because you think you understand enough of the sentence for it not to matter. You could guess the word in the context of the sentence. Or you could ask an English speaker for an explanation.

Let's forget the English speaker – many of you won't have one available. If we try to ignore the word, the sentence then reads:

> Next stop Germany. You don't know the country well (maybe not at all or only through books) and the Germans you have met so far haven't been on their own home ….

The grammar becomes slightly odd, but you can almost certainly paraphrase and make sense of it.

Let's try to guess the word in context. The best way to do this is to paraphrase and not try to translate the unknown word. So you might get something like:

> *... and the Germans you have met so far haven't been at home/in Germany/in their own country, etc.*

OK, that seems to work.

Let's try the dictionary. The Concise Oxford Dictionary gives the following initial definition:

> 'covering of grass etc. with earth and matted roots as surface layer of grassland; piece of this cut from ground ...'

Does this help? I think not. In this case, the dictionary was neither necessary nor particularly helpful. In modern usage, 'home turf' has taken on a particular meaning. Of course, another dictionary might have been more useful, but do you really need to use the dictionary in this example? Have you really got time? Do you really want to interrupt your reading?

Of course, sometimes you will have to go to the dictionary. As I have already said, the frequency of the word may suggest to you that it is important and that you will need to know precisely what it means and how you can use it. Additionally, it is sometimes *impossible* to guess the word from the context of the sentence or the text as a whole. You read on, you read back, and still you cannot make an intelligent guess. You think the word is important. At the moment you can't understand the sentence in which it occurs. Now you have little choice – you need the dictionary.

Consider the following sentence:

> Until you have got to know the people and figured out what makes them tick, your communication remains superficial and rudimentary.

'Superficial' and 'rudimentary' are essential in this sentence. If you don't know their meanings then you can't understand what has been written. Of course, you can still decide that you understand enough of the whole text to manage, but let's presume you don't feel so confident.

Some of you will have been able to use first language knowledge to help. Both 'superficial' and 'rudimentary' have close equivalences in some European languages. If this is the case for your first language, just check that your understanding fits the sentence and the text you have read so far. If it does, you need go no further. Be careful, though, that you don't just assume you can make a guess because the English word looks similar to a word in your language. Always check in context.

'Correspondence', here, means similarity. If something is 'called for' this means something is needed or required.

For some of you the words will have no correspondence and you will be unable to make an accurate guess. The dictionary is now called for.

Finally, in this section, consider the following sentence:

> Who are the Germans and what makes them t<u>ick</u>?

Possibly you don't know the word 'tick'. Perhaps you know that the English say clocks go 'tick tock'. That's a help, but you'll now need to make sense of that in the sentence. The Concise Oxford Dictionary suggests 'slight recurring click, esp. that of watch or clock' and then, under examples of use, it says: '*what makes* person (tick), his motivation'.

OK, we're getting there. By now you should have a pretty good idea of the 'what makes them tick' phrase. So you may now be able to paraphrase the sentence as 'Who are the Germans and what motivates them/keeps them going/interests them …? etc.

Learning vocabulary

As noted earlier, you will probably have a passive, or receptive, English vocabulary that is much larger than your active, or productive, vocabulary. The question is how to shift passive vocabulary to active and what vocabulary should be shifted anyway. As foreign or second language users, we have to accept that we can't learn every word or phrase we encounter – life is too short, the brain is limited, and the demands of a management course will give you enough to do.

If something is 'shifted' it is moved from one place or position to another place or position.

However, there may be certain items of vocabulary that you decide you need to learn for using when you speak or when you write; in other words, for production. One criterion to use when deciding what to shift to active vocabulary is 'semi-familiar' words and phrases. Learning requires effort and time. If you add half-known words and phrases to your dictionary of productive vocabulary this set will be easier, and probably quicker, to learn than a completely unknown set.

It is the case for all learning that different individuals learn best in different ways. However, the following tips for vocabulary learning might come in useful. Ignore them if you know you learn best using another method.

- Try to *write down* words and phrases. Repeating them in your head, or out loud, can help but the act of writing out the words will help them to stick in your memory.

- Always try to learn vocabulary *in context*. Write words and phrases into a sentence in order to learn the word itself and also the way in which it can be used.

If words 'collocate' it means they go together. For example, stop goes with bus, full, emergency, over, off and watch.

- Try to group items of vocabulary with other words. Writing sentences helps but think hard and note how certain words co-exist or collocate. An example of a word diagram for the word 'personnel' and its collocations is given opposite in Figure 6.3. Collocations – or words that frequently co-exist – with personnel are given above the word. A Concise Oxford Dictionary definition comes under the word and this is followed by examples of use.

- Efficient vocabulary learning cannot be done in one single session unless you have a photographic, or exceptional, memory. Return to vocabulary frequently in order to update your examples and to reinforce your learning. Because vocabulary is best learned in context, update your sentence examples as part of your reinforcement programme.

- Book regular, short periods of time in your ES study plan for vocabulary learning.

- Devise an efficient system for recording new vocabulary. Something like the 'personnel' diagram opposite could easily be fitted on to postcard-sized cards which could be filed in a box. Eventually you might sub-divide cards into sections, for example accountancy, law, human

personnel manager/director/officer

office/military/clerical personnel

personnel office/department/section

PERSONNEL

'body of persons employed in public undertaking, armed forces, factory, office, etc.'

Staff recruitment, training, conditions and counselling are frequently the responsibility of the personnel department.

All personnel should receive in-house training at least once a year. New personnel take part in a two-day induction course.

N.B. Personnel Dept. = Human Resource Dept.

Figure 6.3

resources, organisational behaviour, general English. Alternatively, keep notebook entries in alphabetical order and try to leave room between entries for updating and revision. Better still, use a ring-binder that you can add pages to as required.

- Use your own language to help in the construction of examples and explanations to yourself if you think this would help. On first encountering a word you might find this particularly useful, although eventually you will need to have English language examples in order to be able to use the word accurately and appropriately.

- Ensure that you regularly update your vocabulary learning system. You could highlight or underline selected vocabulary items when you are working with texts. Then, at the end of your study session, or twice a week, you could go through this material and add these highlighted words to your system.

- You might include passive vocabulary items in your system. This is fine but devise some sort of coding system so that, for example, when you sit down for your 10-minute vocabulary revision session, you concentrate on the active/productive cards and spend much less time on the passive/ receptive cards marked by another colour.

ACTIVITY Look back through this chapter. Have you underlined anything or put any notes in the margin? Are these underlinings or notes vocabulary related? If you've understood everything, that's great. However, some words, or phrases, might have been fine for reception – for listening and reading – but are you sure how to use them? Could you now include them in your active vocabulary? See if you can construct a sentence using them. Ask yourself if you could explain their meaning and their use to others if you were asked to do so a week from now. If you could, relax – you already have them in your active vocabulary. If not, add them to your vocabulary system and return to them to learn them.

Select two or three words or phrases that you would like to add to your active vocabulary. Try making a card similar to the one shown for 'personnel' in Figure 6.3 on page 155. Include a definition, examples of use in sentences and collocations – other words that co-exist – if appropriate. Remember to leave plenty of space on your card for additions. Make cards or use your own preferred system for the other examples you choose. Some phrases are provided below. These are suggestions – ignore them if you are happy to select your own items.

> update, commitment, regardless of, differs from, response, at the heart of, draft, counterparts, initially, nothing is set in concrete.

Key points

- Do not let vocabulary become a problem.

- If you are unable to understand a word or phrase used repeatedly by your tutor, ask for an explanation. Do not be afraid to ask.

- There will often be several of you in the group who don't understand – the others will be grateful that you have asked.

- Ensure that you understand frequently occurring words and phrases that you read. If, after using context and a dictionary, you are still unsure, then make a note and ask your tutor. Tutors will welcome your interest – they are there to help you.

Include vocabulary in your ES study plan. Familiarise yourself with key vocabulary when you are reading and develop a system, such as cards, for recording and revising vocabulary. Learn to be your own judge of what vocabulary you can and cannot do without. Remember the importance of being realistic. What vocabulary do you need for production? It is this productive, or active, vocabulary that requires the hardest work.

Learning vocabulary effectively requires effort and frequent attention. 'Little and often' is a good rule to follow. Could you take half an hour a week to add new vocabulary items to your system? Could you spend 10 minutes each day revising this vocabulary and checking that you still remember previously learned items?

5 Using dictionaries

I have already mentioned the use of dictionaries and I advised you to buy, or borrow, a specialised management dictionary for the initial stages of your studying. However, more importantly, you will need a good dictionary to help with your reading and writing. As you know, there are hundreds of dictionaries on the market. Before buying one you need to consider what you really need. (See 'Recommended texts' at the end of the book.) Answering the following questions should help:

- *Bilingual or English–English?* This decision will depend partly on your confidence. If you are confident, then it's probably better to buy an English–English dictionary. If, however, at this stage, you feel very worried about your vocabulary, then perhaps you should buy both an English–English dictionary and a bilingual dictionary. The English–English dictionary is important because it should give you examples of use. Bilingual dictionaries may provide the most efficient help for use when you are reading, as long as you check the dictionary definition in the context of the reading.

- *Big or small?* A pocket dictionary can be useful but you will probably need a bigger dictionary to use at home. Remember that pocket dictionaries can only provide very limited information. If I don't know a word, I want examples, details of use, and information on the word, such as pronunciation.

- *Old or new?* New – beware of old dictionaries because inevitably they will give old-fashioned examples. I frequently use a very large, but very old, Spanish dictionary but I now check words and phrases with a modern dictionary or with Spanish-speaking friends. I learned very quickly that my use of old-fashioned phrases amused my Spanish friends. Whilst this provided a smile, it didn't help me to learn the sort of Spanish I wanted to use.

A sight–sound language is one in which symbols or letters are always pronounced in the same way. Thus, when you see a word written down you know how to say it immediately. English is not like this!

- *What information to look for?* Because English is not a sight–sound language, you will probably want information on the pronunciation of words. You should also make sure a dictionary contains a good key, or explanation of, any symbols, including phonetics, that are used; examples of use; information on parts of speech, for example, noun, verb, adjective; and notes on usage, such as colloquial, literary, slang.

When you use a dictionary, make sure you read the word entries carefully. If you are using a bilingual dictionary, try to confirm your understanding of the word with an English–English dictionary. Because of problems with equivalence and translation, it's all too easy to use a word inappropriately and it's important to check.

6 Grammar

In Chapter 4 'Effective writing' you will find some brief notes on grammatical points that frequently confuse native English speakers and you might find these useful. However, even in that chapter, it is not possible to cover all the information you might need. You need to buy, or to borrow, a good reference grammar book, preferably one with exercises and answers, and to work through it. Like this book, it will contain sections that are unnecessary for you, but it should provide you with a learning tool and a reference source. Suggested grammar books are listed in the 'Recommended texts' section at the end of the book.

In the pre-course study period you should try to evaluate your strengths and weaknesses in grammar. Probably the best way to do this is to work through the exercises in each section of your grammar book. If you are getting the exercises right, then you can cross that section off your list. If you get exercises half right, then note that and allocate some time to checking and improving your understanding during this pre-course period. If you get more than half of an exercise wrong, then you will need to put that grammar topic high on your priority list.

However, as with all ES planning, you'll need to ask yourself if a particular grammatical topic is important for your study purposes. For example, you may find that you don't do well on an exercise requiring you to put direct speech into indirect speech and vice versa. The question is, do you really need this at the moment? Perhaps the use of hypotheticals, or conditionals, might be more important. Don't get carried away – remember you're going to study on a management course not an English Language course and prioritise!

Vice versa means the other way round.

7 Reading

Chapter 3 'Reading' contains more advice and activities related to reading and it would probably be a good idea to try those activities when you have completed this chapter.

Much of your study time will be taken up with reading. Although it is probably your writing that will be assessed on your course, this writing will depend on your understanding and on your application of the theories, ideas and concepts that you have read. In this section we look at some essential reading strategies that you can experiment with and adapt to fit your needs.

Reading for language acquisition versus reading for information

As a user of ES, you may view reading as an opportunity to learn, or to acquire, vocabulary and structures. There's nothing wrong with this, but everything has its time and its place. Effective reading for information will be a vital skill to develop for your studies. Effective reading for language acquisition is a separate activity and you should not confuse the two. Of course, when you are reading for information you may pick up new words and expressions. That's fine, but if you are reading for information, focus your concentration on that and that alone.

Key points

Reading can be a good way of learning vocabulary and structures, but don't try to learn language and to read to understand information at the same time.

Purposes and reading

You must be very clear about your purposes for reading. You might work through a text and consider every item of vocabulary that is problematic. This is a good exercise if your purpose for reading is to develop your vocabulary. It's a hopeless exercise if your purpose is to read for understanding and for information.

You always need to *set objectives* for reading – to say what your purpose is for reading a text. It is often helpful to divide objectives into a number of purposes. For example, your course notes, or your tutor, may tell you to read something and they might tell you to do so in order to 'get more information about topic X'. However, you should also try to personalise your objectives. You might know a great deal about topic X, in which case you could set 'check current understanding against text' as an objective. You might want to test the ideas in the text in your work environment, in which case you might say 'see how topic X works in practice'.

Frequently, you will have more than one objective for reading. Think about, or note, your objectives *before* you start. Then you can cover each one and see how you might need to read the same text several times in order to fulfil different objectives.

Key points

- You must always be clear about your purpose(s) for reading.

- Set yourself objectives.

- If you have more than one objective (for example, to learn vocabulary and to note information) make sure you allow yourself time for at least two different readings of the same text.

Preparing texts for reading

If you can do so, it's a good idea to photocopy texts you are required to read so that you can make notes and underlinings on the text itself. Of course, if the text is in your own book or course materials, you may not need to copy it again.

It's also useful to number paragraphs in texts you're reading as this helps with note-taking, especially when you need to refer from your notes back to the text.

If you photocopy the article you will find this easier than turning to the back of the book.

ACTIVITY Turn to Reading appendix 2 at the back of the book called 'Germany – reflections on a people'. Hereafter I will refer to this text as 'the Germany text'.

Look through the text to get an idea of its length and read the headings or sub-titles. Note what the text is about in very general terms.

I'm not sure about you, but I didn't find the headings very helpful at this stage. They're not headings that provide much help with what the text is about. However, sometimes, and especially in course books, you will find headings much more informative.

I've noted:

In general, the text is about the German people and what Susan Stern calls 'Germanity'.

The overviewing Activity you've just done enables you to skim over a text in order to see what it might be about, how long it is, and how it is organised. Skimming in this way can be a useful reading strategy when you are confronted with a lot of reading. You can skim three or four texts in order to see what they are about and to help you decide what to read and the order in which to read different things. In books you can get an overview by reading the contents pages and, if you want a more detailed overview, by reading the book's introduction or preface, if there is one.

Key points

Skimming can help you to see what texts might be about and can help you to make decisions about what to read.

Now you've skimmed the Germanity text, it is important to set your objectives for reading.

If you are not German, let's assume you are reading in order to find out what the Germans are like. If you are German, you could well be reading in order to find out if Stern has an accurate picture, according to your views, of Germans.

Whether you're German or not, let's say you're reading:

1 to find out what the Germans are like, according to Stern

2 to see if Stern's views fit with, or differ from, your own

3 to note what Stern chooses to write about in order to follow her structure and topics as a guide to writing a similar text about your first language user group. I haven't said writing about your country – you may be an Urdu speaker in Britain, or a Catalan in Spain

4 to consolidate vocabulary and to understand and record new, or extended, vocabulary.

If you put something 'on hold' you don't forget it or ignore it but you leave it for the moment whilst you are doing something else.

Initially I will ask you to put this fourth objective 'on hold'. ES readers frequently panic when they realise a text contains words or phrases that are unfamiliar to them. Let's start, instead, from what you do know rather than from what you don't.

Using knowledge about the subject of texts

ACTIVITY   What do you already know about the subject? If you're not German, list five or six things that you know, or think, characterise Germans.

If you are German, list five or six things that you know other nationalities often think characterise you as a nation.

You might include stereotypical things. If you were writing about the English you might say 'always talk about the weather, eat terrible food, are not very warm and affectionate, are punctual, are very organised'. These are stereotypes – I don't necessarily agree with them but I know they are what people often say.

If you're not sure of a word in English then, for the moment, use your first language. This is an exercise that focuses on what you already know – it's not a language production activity.

What is often said about the Germans?

1

2

3

4

5

6

Look back at your list. Does experience or knowledge tell you that anything on your list might be an outdated stereotype? Does first-hand or even second-hand knowledge tell you that anything on your list might be a prejudice you, or others, have?

Be aware of these things as you start to read. Will Stern confirm your thoughts or will she suggest that you should think again? Will you be persuaded by her point of view?

Critical reading

A good reader is a critical reader. You have to evaluate *any* text you are reading. Being critical of the text means you have to ask if the writer is prejudiced, biased or fair. Does the writer provide evidence for assertions? Is the writer's argument logical and based on fact?

You also have to be self critical. Being critical of yourself means that you have to ask whether you are prejudiced or biased before you start reading about a topic. Will you give the writer a chance or will you just dismiss what is said if you don't agree? Are you prepared to be persuaded and even to change your views *if* the writer provides a convincing, well informed alternative view?

Key points

Good readers are critical of the texts they are reading and of their own prejudices and biases.

ACTIVITY Return to the text and read the introduction. This should provide us with a clearer view of what the text is about, why the text was written and what the writer thinks about the subject. You will see that 'Introduction' is not a sub-heading. However, your scanning of the text for headings indicates that the first sub-heading comes after three paragraphs of text. These first three paragraphs can be safely assumed to be functioning as the introduction.

Read these three paragraphs without turning to a dictionary and, if you can, just keep reading. At this stage try not to stop on any unfamiliar or confusing words. Of course, words are important and I shall not ignore them but, for the moment, experiment with just trying to get a very general understanding of the introduction.

Let's now see if we can answer the three questions below. Don't bother to write complete sentences – notes are adequate.

1 What is the text about?

2 Why was the text written?

3 What does the writer think about the subject?

There are many possible answers. My suggestions are as follows:

(1) What the Germans are like – their 'rules' of behaviour, especially in a business context – how not to make mistakes when dealing with German managers.

(2) Because it's all too easy to make mistakes and to insult or irritate if you haven't got this sort of information.

(3) Some understanding of the Germans is necessary/helpful if you want to make the most of opportunities for business.

Being aware of personal reactions and expectations

In the Activity on page 161 you were asked to consider any existing ideas you might have had about German people. From reading this far, does the text confirm these ideas or does Stern suggest that there are more important things to consider? Are you learning anything new? Could it be that you're not yet reading 'new' information because Stern is, in the introduction, just setting the scene for what she's going to write about? Does the introduction suggest to you that the text is going to provide information about the sort of topics you thought it might? What are your reactions so far?

As well as reading the introduction to texts, you can sometimes gain an overview of the main points by reading the concluding paragraph(s). Don't feel you have to read texts from start to finish. Feel free to skip sections and/or to read out of order to suit your purposes.

Always try to add new information in texts to what you already know. This new information can extend existing knowledge or, sometimes, it can suggest that previous understanding and thinking requires modification.

Using existing knowledge

As well as always keeping their purposes for reading in mind, good readers work actively with texts and try to process text information in order to 'make it their own'. To do this you need to relate what you read to what you already know. You need to add what you read to what you know and, if necessary, to allow what you read to alter what you knew or thought before reading.

As you are reading, be aware of (and perhaps note) any information that either confirms or changes the views you had before reading the text. Additionally, note or highlight any new information that you find particularly interesting or helpful.

Reading the whole text

Now return to the text and, keeping in mind your purposes for reading it, go through the whole thing to establish a picture of what it's about. You may like to read it through from start to finish once without worrying too much about vocabulary and without worrying about highlighting or annotating important parts. You might, alternatively, prefer to highlight or underline the key points and difficult vocabulary as you go. If you do not already know how you prefer to read you should experiment now. Before reading the text, however, look at the Activity below so that you have an idea of what you'll be required to do next.

ACTIVITY Highlight or underline every key or important point that is relevant to your purpose for reading. Either immediately after this highlighting, or when you've highlighted all the important points, give each point a title or 'label'. For example, I might label the first paragraph coming under the Germanity heading 'Negative views about Gs'. Use any abbreviations that make sense to you and remember you are thinking of labels – you are not writing complete sentences.

I've used 'Gs' for 'Germans'. Use any abbreviations or symbols that make sense to you.

Check that you've provided a label for every relevant key point. In some cases, you might use one label for one paragraph – in other cases, you might have two or three labels in one paragraph. It's quite possible that you'll have *no* labels for some paragraphs. However, one of your purposes is to write your own account of your first language group using Stern's article to give you ideas of what you might write. For this reason, you might note her topics even if they're not of crucial importance to all of your purposes for reading.

My labels for the paragraphs numbered 4–10 are as follows. You'll need to check against the text if you want to go through them. Please don't think you have to have the same labels as I have used. Note that I've included the sub-headings, or labels, already used by Stern. My complete list of labels is given in the Appendix at the end of this chapter.

Paragraph   Label

Germanity

4   negative views about Gs

5   the uselessness of clichéd, stereotypical views of Gs

6   the need for an objective 'core' view of Gs

7   difficulties with an all-inclusive definition of Germanity

7   non-homogeneous population – introduction

8   non-homogeneous population – differences between states and regions

9   features/characteristics common to Gs

10   'cultural analysis' as a method of explaining common characteristics

Without returning to the text, your list of labels should give you a broad outline of the main topics. Additionally, the Activity should have helped you to extract the main points and enable you to go back to numbered sections of the text for further information. The actual process of labelling texts in this way provides a useful 'information processing' exercise. Further practice in this activity is given using another text in Chapter 3.

In 'Other ways of planning' later in this chapter, you will have an opportunity to experiment with other ways of processing information.

We shall use these labels in the next section on writing but, for the moment, take a few minutes to consider whether or not you found this Activity helpful. You may know other ways of processing information. Experiment with any method until you find the one that suits you best and be prepared to use different methods for different purposes.

Key points

When reading for information it is important to work at, or to process, the information in the text. Experiment with different ways of doing this until you find ways that work for you and for your reading purposes.

Break points in reading

Return to the list of reading purposes on page 160. In fairly general terms, I think you should have achieved purposes 1 to 3. Obviously, you might want to return to the text for a more detailed understanding and appreciation of Stern's points but, for the moment, let's consider the fourth of your purposes for reading.

Inevitably you will have encountered unknown, or only partially understood, vocabulary. I have, intentionally, left the language acquisition until now. If you have time or if you are struggling with understanding, then now is the time to work on the vocabulary in the text. If you struggle to understand every single word as you read you will inevitably lose the overall sense of the text. However, we need to be realistic. If a section of text contains five sentences and you are unable to understand significant parts of each of those sentences, then you will be unable to proceed with understanding. Sometimes you have to stop and work out the meaning of a word or phrase using a dictionary or, if you can, using the context of the difficult item. When this happens your reading flow is interrupted or broken. For this reason I call such interruptions 'break points'. What we need to do is to understand what happens during break points and to use this understanding to help us to regain the flow of reading with understanding.

Effective reading for understanding depends on an interaction between text and reader. When we're reading without break points, and hence without any difficulty or interruption, this interaction is virtually automatic. Think of reading a newspaper in your first language. Although you will occasionally have break points you will probably read fairly fluently and you will usually be unaware of the interaction going on between the text and your head.

When reading for study purposes, even in your first language, you may have more frequent break points. These might be caused by meeting previously unknown information, by a complex idea or concept, or even by vocabulary used in an unfamiliar context or introduced for the first time in a specialist or technical sense. When you are reading with English as your study language, then these break points will almost certainly increase. Although, in many ways, you cannot control this, you will need to take action in order to ultimately read texts interactively.

For study purposes you often need an understanding of what texts mean in their entirety. Understanding words and phrases is not enough. You need to go one step further. If you proceed word by word through a text you may eventually get to the meaning. More often, however, you'll just be left with an accumulation of word and phrase meanings that are unrelated to an overall picture of what you are reading. You must, therefore, try to fit parts of text into the whole.

■ Try to build a mental picture of what you are reading.

■ Put pieces of information together *as* you read and ask yourself how you are doing as you work through the text.

■ If you have a break point and need, for example, to turn to the dictionary, work out what the word or phrase means in the context of the sentence. *Then* fit the sentence into your developing overall picture of the text.

Remember that you will probably already know something about what you are reading. Good management education students fit knowledge and ideas from their reading into their existing knowledge and they try to relate their reading to what they already know. Don't let your break points stop you from doing this. Let's try with a few examples from the Germanity text.

Paragraph 6 contains only two sentences but the first sentence is long and may require unravelling. Read it again now.

> 'What we need is a succinct picture of a nation, one that captures its spirit, gives us an objective body of information which is concrete enough to be meaningful and yet broad enough to apply to one and all of its 80 million population, and which (above all) provides sufficient insight into the nature of the people to understand and predict their behaviour patterns. '

As a sentence this is demanding. It's long and contains quite a lot of information about the author's opinion. However, look at the sentence that follows it:

> 'In short – we are searching for the core of Germanity.'

The writer is reader sympathetic. She has summarised the rather complex sentence and clearly signalled, by the words 'In short…', that she has done so. This example makes the advice 'If in doubt read on' very easy to appreciate. It sometimes works and it's always worth trying.

So you've read the summarising sentence and, possibly, want to check your understanding of the word 'core'. The Oxford pocket dictionary defines it thus: '*Horny capsule containing seeds of apple, pear, etc; central or most important part …*'. Immediately you should realise that the first definition referring to an apple or pear is not exactly what you need. Reading on brings you to the 'central or most important part' and that, alone, is enough information.

However, your work on the sentence is certainly not over. First of all, re-read the sentence, fitting the dictionary definition into it. OK? 'In short – we are searching for the most important (or central) part of Germanity'. Now you have the meaning of the sentence *but* you might decide that the word 'core' is one that you'd like to add to your active vocabulary. As I noted in the Vocabulary section, this will require you to make some effort – what you must ask yourself is *when* you will make this effort.

My advice is to highlight or underline any new or confusing vocabulary as you read through a text. Of course, a break point will mean you have to stop and work out what a word or phrase means. However, having done this I would advise you to continue reading the text in order to understand it. Then, having completed your management education purpose for gaining information from the text, you should return to any vocabulary or structure you want to note or to work on for language acquisition purposes.

Key points

> If you try to do everything at once, at best you'll get a headache, and at worst, you'll be unable to build up the mental picture of the text that is so vital if you are trying to extract meaning from it.

Now you can return to the first sentence of the paragraph and start to extract meaning from that. You have an overall understanding of it, but I would divide it into information and structural parts. Immediately I can remove, and if necessary note, that Germany has a population of over 80 million. Returning to the start of the sentence, it's possible that you have a break point with the word 'succinct'. Relate it to the summary sentence and you're able to guess that it means something related to c*entral* or *most important*. As a word it's not essential for meaning. As an item for language acquisition, you might highlight it and return to it later.

What about 'portrait'? Maybe you have seen the word before: 'The National Portrait Gallery' or 'a portrait of the President' – you might know that it refers to a painting of a person. Take your existing knowledge of the word and apply it to the context of the sentence and text in which it appears. Replace it, if you like, with the word 'picture' and you'll have the meaning. Then we get a comma followed by 'one that..., ... which is... and... and which... and....' Using the 'in-between' words you can get a picture of the sentence and see how many 'bits' of information it contains. If necessary, take each one separately but after working out the meaning, re-read the whole sentence. If you leave each bit in your head, you might well have forgotten what each means when you eventually re-read the sentence. However, remember that for meaning purposes you don't really need to unravel the whole sentence – Stern has done that for you in the summary sentence. We are only doing it now because we are working on the language acquisition reading at this stage.

Key points

> When you have a break point caused by vocabulary difficulty, try first to see if you can understand the sentence by ignoring the difficult word(s). If not, work out the meaning of the word(s) using a dictionary if necessary. Then *always* relate your understanding of the word(s) to your overall understanding of the sentence and the whole text.

Remember – it's partly your *purpose for reading* that determines decisions about whether you need to stop and work out the meaning of words. Words and expressions *are important*. You can't always guess and, depending on your purpose for reading, you might actually need to understand every word. Some reading purposes and some texts themselves should suggest to us that we need only a very general understanding. However, consider the case when, in a foreign country, you need to change a plug or to operate a piece of potentially dangerous equipment. In a text containing instructions it will be vital to understand precisely what every word means. Of course, you will often have diagrams to help but you might still need to know, for example, the difference between a twisted mauve cord and a fine red wire. Nevertheless, in the Germanity text, there are probably many words that you can 'do without' and yet still understand the text.

Because I'm writing this chapter for a multi-lingual audience, it's impossible to predict which words and phrases you will, individually, have found difficult. Of course, you may not have found any items difficult. Some of you will find some vocabulary easy to guess from your first language. However, if, for example, you're a Punjabi or Chinese first language user then this guessing is not available to you and you may need to look in the dictionary more often than, say, a French or Spanish manager.

In this reading section we've stressed the importance of defining your purposes for reading. If a text has been recommended then you probably need to understand it fairly thoroughly. If you are using texts for writing – getting information from them and including this information in your assignments – then you need to extract the main points. Experiment with the labelling method suggested in the Activity on page 163 and then modify it to suit your purposes and preferences.

Key points

Try not to do too many things during one reading of a text. Inevitably, you will benefit from using texts as vocabulary sources, but try to keep your language acquisition purposes separate from your meaning seeking purposes.

Some ES readers complain that they read too slowly. Often this slowness is the result of struggling with every word when that struggle is not necessary. Be ruthless with yourself. Accept that your reading time will probably be greater than that for managers working in English as their first language, but don't forget that, like them, you have existing knowledge and the capacity to relate what you are reading to real-life, work-based situations.

Try to be aware of the strategies you use when you are reading. Always check that you are understanding and, if not, stop and start again. Always ask yourself what you want from a text and then, when you have finished reading, ask yourself if you've achieved your aims.

8 Writing

Most managers using ES say that writing is their biggest worry. Inevitably,
writing takes longer in another language than in your first language. This
has significant implications for your study plan. Until you have written
your first assignment you won't have a very accurate idea of how long you
will need. As the course goes on, and as you become more proficient, the
time needed for writing will decrease. However, if you are assessed by
examinations, then you need to remember that these require you to write
under timed conditions. For this reason you should add exam writing
under timed conditions to your study plan. Don't leave it until the week
before an exam to start writing to time.

You should certainly read and work through Chapters 4 and 5 on
effective writing and writing assignments, but here I will focus specifically
on writing in English as a study language. As with the advice on reading,
one of the most important things for you to realise is that you can't do too
many things at once. In common with English language-speaking
managers, you should sit down to write with every tool necessary at your
fingertips. These tools include all the information you need in order to
write. Ideally, the reading and notes for an assignment should be
completed before you start to write. If you are trying to compose an
assignment and, at the same time, you need to read more texts or to seek
information from your workplace, you will lose the flow of your writing.

All managers, using their first, second or third language, need to accept
that rarely, if ever, will their first attempt at writing an assignment be their
final version. You need to become self evaluators – to become aware of
mistakes you might make and to learn how to mark your own work.

Many ES managers worry about spelling. Use a dictionary and computer
spelling-checker if appropriate but, most importantly of all, be consistent in
your spelling. For example, you may use American spellings, such as 'color'.
Don't worry about this – just use the same form throughout your writing.

For all writers, but especially for ES writers, it becomes essential to write
complex ideas in simple, uncomplicated sentences. At first you might read
your writing and worry that it looks like the work of a child. Tutors and

examiners are not really interested in elegant prose. They need to see that you have understood course ideas and can apply them. What this requires you to do is to present your knowledge and understanding in the most coherent and efficient way possible. You need to do justice to yourself whilst accepting that your writing may never be as fluent nor as sophisticated in your study language as it is in your first language. However, on a more optimistic note, I have taught students who eventually write more effectively in English than they do in their own language.

Remember to use your tutor to help you with specific, individual questions and work through the writing chapters in this book. The most valuable thing you can do is to start writing as soon as possible. Don't wait until you write your first assignment. Try all three practice assignments in Chapter 5. That way you'll have practised writing assignment-length texts before you have to do so for assessment.

Key points

- Start writing as soon as possible and include assignment and exam writing in your study plan.

- In an assignment, or in an exam, you are writing in order to show your tutor or examiner that you have understood and can apply what you have been studying.

Copying and plagiarising

If you 'plagiarise' you take the writing of someone else and present it as your own. Such 'copying' is not as dishonest as it sounds and many of you, understandably, will be very tempted to do this. You may read something and think you could never explain it or write about it in such an effective way. You may be right! However, remember, again, why you are writing. Information from texts and tutors needs to become your own. Management education demands the application of theories and ideas in relation to your own individual work contexts. If an author can write something more effectively than you, that's fine! What you need to do is to show that you have grasped the author's ideas and can relate them to your own context. The best way in which you can do this is to process the information written by someone else so that it becomes your own.

When you are taking notes, make sure you make it clear if you copy the words of the original text. If, for example, I read 'Cultural differences have been exaggerated and, indeed, misunderstood' in my notes, then I know this is taken directly from a text. I use the '...' to tell me this. You must devise a similar method for your own note-taking.

Other ways of planning

This book stresses the need and desirability of devising and developing your own preferred ways of studying. The labelling technique I used for the Germanity text will not work for all of you. It is a linear step-by-step way of working and some of you will prefer to use a non-linear method.

The diagram in Figure 6.4 below exemplifies another non-linear method. Play around with these methods until you know which suits you best and then you will be able to use a variety of approaches to manage a variety of study tasks.

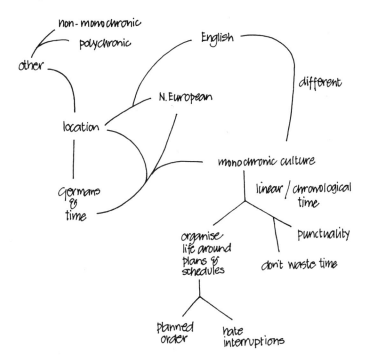

Figure 6.4 *A non-linear plan*

Key points

Experiment with a variety of planning methods until you know which work best for you for different study tasks.

ACTIVITY Take a section from the Germanity text and using either linear (labelling) or non-linear notes, prepare to write a summary of the text.

The words and structures you choose

The golden rule of sentence construction is to keep it simple. Just as the structure of your sentences is best kept simple so, too, should your word selection be simple. If you are absolutely sure about a word's use and meaning, then use it. If, however, you are doubtful, then don't use it! An exception, and the only exception, to this rule concerns the use of words in the title of the assignment or words that come up frequently as part of the subject you are writing about. For example, if the title or question reads 'Under what circumstances can IT be detrimental to companies?' then it is imperative that you fully understand and use the words 'IT' and 'detrimental'. The language of your subject should be a high priority on your list of words to work on and to add to your active vocabulary. What you should never do is to use a long, clever sounding word if you are at all unsure about it. In the end you will not sound clever if you misuse words.

Key points

Remember – your tutors want to evaluate your understanding of management, not your ability to write wonderful prose in the English language.

9 Listening and speaking

Many of you will be students on distance-taught courses. Speaking and listening will form only a small part of your study time. However, tutorials, discussion with colleagues and tutors, and perhaps telephone conversations, can be very important.

Listening presents you with its own particular problems. Hopefully your tutors and colleagues will speak clearly and reasonably slowly. More importantly, they will speak sympathetically – clarity is a part of this and so, too, is clear structuring of what they are saying. As ES managers you have a certain responsibility before listening. Preparation is essential – try to familiarise yourself with the key concepts of a tutorial or residential seminar before you have to listen. Ask your tutor for help if pre-tutorial material is insufficient.

Key points

Listen out for the key points. Be aware of the speaker's signals. Comments such as 'To sum up…', 'What's important is…', 'Don't worry too much about …' and 'This is a really important point …' are essential clues.

Additional things you can do are to expose yourself to spoken English on the radio or television. However, remember that, for example, radio news in English may be much more difficult to understand than your tutor. You will have a much better idea of what your tutorials will be about – you can prepare for them. Remember, too, your responsibilities as a learner and as someone with a right to understand. Supposing another manager in your tutor group speaks too quickly for you to understand – say so! Ask for clarification or repetition. Don't sit there becoming more and more lost.

Similarly, if you are talking you need to be sympathetic to your tutor and to your colleagues. Perhaps because you are anxious about your English you speak quietly. Don't – it will make you more difficult to understand. If you are worried about your English accent, try to slow down. Don't worry if you hesitate and have to think of the words you want – this is normal. Listen to English speakers and you will hear them doing the same thing.

You may be studying in a group where a number of you are using English as a study language. You need to be particularly sympathetic in your listening and speaking if this is the case. You may all speak with accents that make you difficult to understand at first. Ask for clarification but try to do so in a sensitive way. Instead of saying 'I can't understand you', try saying 'This is interesting but could you just explain it again – a bit more slowly.' I have seen people go into shops when they're abroad on holiday and ask for something in English. If the shop staff don't speak English then, I'm ashamed to say, I've heard the tourists repeat their requests three or four times, getting louder and louder as they do so. Inevitably, this is a hopeless, and an insulting, communication strategy. If you, or anyone else, uses a word that is not understood, then the trick is to think of another word to say the same thing.

Always remember that your right to speak is as important as anyone else's – so, too, is your right to understand. If you find your tutor difficult to understand, try to work out why this is – does she or he speak too fast? Does she or he have an accent that's difficult or unfamiliar to you, or wander from the point and leave you unsure of what the point is?

Key points

Your tutors will want to help you – help them to help you by talking to them if you have problems and by explaining to them as precisely as possible what the problem is.

At the end of a tutorial, go back to your preparatory notes or reading. Re-evaluate your understanding of the topic and make notes if necessary. Include notes to yourself such as 'Not sure about this' or 'Very important'. Don't leave too much to memory – keep on top of things as you go.

You may find it helpful to tape-record seminars and lectures and to listen to them later. This provides you with an opportunity to check on anything you missed or didn't understand at the time. If you want to do this, you should ask your tutor for permission to record. Similarly, if you are recording a seminar with fellow students, then you should ask the group for permission to record. If you explain your purposes for recording them, almost certainly you will find that people are happy for you to do this. Do remember, though, that it takes time to listen to recordings. If you don't have enough time to do this listening properly, then it is best to concentrate during the seminar and select key points for attention.

An OBS tutor suggests 'replaying' spoken messages twice. He frequently has meetings with associates in Eastern Europe and the discussion is always in English. Both the English and Eastern Europeans try to express their points in two ways as a check on understanding and as a way of communicating as effectively as possible.

Talking and listening on the telephone is a difficult medium for many of us in a foreign language. Make sure you 'replay' the message to the speaker. So, if your tutor has been answering a question, try saying something like 'So you mean...' or 'So if I include... then that will be enough.' 'Replaying' the message gives you a useful chance to test your understanding.

10 Summary

You should now have a clearer idea about ways in which you can work at improving your English in order to help you in your course. The most important thing to keep in mind is that you are studying on a management course and not an English course. Your English will improve and if you follow the advice in this chapter, and work through the other chapters, you will be better equipped to enjoy your course and to be successful.

This chapter should have helped you to realise the importance of gaining control over your studies. Awareness of any language difficulties and worries you have is the first step to putting things right. Often you will find that your worries are not as serious as you previously thought, or you will be able to see a clear way to improvement. Be positive – English is not your first language, but you will nevertheless be able to draw upon experiences and to relate your course to your work and indeed to your cultural and linguistic background. You have as much to offer and as much, if not more, to gain as any other manager–learner. Remember this when you are studying.

Appendix 6.1 Paragraph labels for Reading appendix 2

Linear time

11 Time as part of cultural programming

11 Punctuality

12 G as a monochronic culture

13 Polychronic cultures

14 Contrasting notions of time

15 Problems of differing notions of time

16 Contrasting notions of time within the same time culture groups

Encapsulated space

17 Space as part of cultural programming

18 Close correlations between time and space attitudes

18 G need for 'encapsulation'

19 Effects of time–space correlations re: G orderliness and efficiency

Refined information

20 G as 'low-context' culture as a result of time/space attitudes

21 High-context culture views of Gs – Gs as pedantic/ irritatingly thorough

22 Need to understand and predict Germany

23 Advantages of cultural analysis for greater understanding of G

Chapter 7 Working with numbers and diagrams

1 Introduction

This chapter is divided into two parts. The first part will help you if you are the sort of person who shies away from information which contains numbers. In reading management literature you frequently come across displays of information in numerical form. If you tend to skip over tables and graphs there is something for you in the first part of this chapter. It's deliberately written at a basic level and does not set out to teach you material you would expect to learn as part of your course. Indeed, much of the content revisits topics you should have covered at school but which you might have since forgotten. So you will read about percentages, decimals, graphs, tables and averages. If this sort of material is too basic for your needs, then skip this part of the chapter and carry on to the next part.

In the 'Recommended texts' section at the end of the book I have listed some additional reading for those of you who want to develop your numeracy a little further.

If you really need very basic help with numeracy then that is more than this chapter can provide. There are courses available to which you would be able to turn and there are numerous books which might set you on the right road.

ACTIVITY Skim through Sections 1 to 6 of this chapter. In the space provided list your objectives for working through this material and remember to check these at the end of your work on it. Use this Activity to decide whether or not this part of the chapter is at the right level for you.

The second part of this chapter deals with the representation of ideas in diagrammatic form – and particularly how you might develop and use diagrams for your own purposes, whether in personal notes or in written assignments or reports. It's a skill that you will find valuable, not only as a student, but also as a practising manager.

2 Getting to know numbers

We work in an environment where a great deal of information is communicated in the form of numbers. Sometimes these numbers come singly, as when a delivery driver tells us the number of boxes to be unloaded. Sometimes they come as sets of numbers that are presented together, such as the ordering of stationery, giving quantities, catalogue numbers and prices. Sometimes a lot of numbers are put together in the form of a chart or graph, such as the diagrams used to show sales figures, or those that show how one currency has been rising or falling against another.

Many of these sorts of numbers are so familiar that you have learned to take in their meaning without stopping to think about it. When planning an outdoor promotional event, you might consult a weather forecast. If it says that the temperature is to be 30°C, you immediately know it is going to be hot; and you have a much better idea of how hot than if the forecaster simply said, 'It will be hot.' Yet, in making instant sense of these small clusters of numbers, letters and symbols, you bring into play a lot of knowledge and experience. To interpret the information, you have to know:

- that the symbol '°' stands for 'degrees'
- that degrees are units of temperature
- that 'C' stands for 'Celsius'
- what it feels like when the temperature is in the 30s C.

After years of exposure to weather forecasts, all this knowledge is something you take for granted. You are probably not aware of being an expert at reading this particular form of numerical representation.

At work, numbers are perhaps even more prevalent. Everything seems to revolve around them. Think of invoices, forecasts, sales figures, purchase orders, contracts, expenses, salaries, production data, wastage, marketing spend, market share, and so on. Much of this is related to information

Numbers can be difficult because numerical information comes in a very condensed and highly abstract form. A number on its own means very little. You have to learn how the number is used (i.e. what the conventions are) and what the number stands for. Thirty years ago, 5/- (five shillings) was a very meaningful sign in the UK. Now the convention for representing that quantity is 25p or £0.25. It is hard to imagine 5/- being the natural way of writing it – we have learned the new conventions so thoroughly.

Do you need refreshing on percentages? If you started with sales of £300,000 and there was a 10% increase, you would then have £330,000. 10% means 10 for every 100 (centum is Latin for a hundred). To work out what 10% of something is, you multiply it by 10, then divide by 100. (Similarly, to calculate 6% you multiply by 6, then divide by 100.) If you multiply 300,000 by 10 you get 3,000,000 – then dividing by 100 you get 30,000. So, if your increase is 10%, you have 30,000 more to add to your original 300,000 making 330,000.

Numeracy is not a single ability which you either have or don't have. It is the skill, experience and knowledge you need to 'read' the specific kinds of numbers and tables used within a particular field of discussion. You can be numerate in one field, such as when looking at market research data, but innumerate in another, such as accounting. As we have already seen, we all display a wide-ranging numeracy in our daily lives without even noticing it. We tend to be much more aware of the numbers we don't understand.

about money; for example, how much money is spent, how much money is earned, how much profit is made or how profits are made up. Numbers might be thought of as the key language of business.

When you become a manager for the first time, you may be moving into unfamiliar territory and you will have to make a time investment in order to acquire the relevant numerical 'vocabulary' and the conventions of presentation. At first new uses of numbers may be difficult to make sense of, but as you get practice, reading numerical information eventually becomes second nature.

The point I am making here is that it is quite normal, nowadays, to be expected to take in numerical information at work. In most organisations it is assumed that you know that 10% stands for 10 per cent and that you know what it means if sales rise by 10%. You are probably expected to become familiar with quite complicated tables, such as marketing research data or departmental expenses, which lay out information precisely, and where the position in which each figure is placed is very important in interpreting its meaning. For example, you see that the figure 525 appears along the line labelled 'Stationery' and under the heading 'Feb.' on your departmental expenses sheet, and so you know how much your department spent on stationery in February. So long as you understand the conventions and have plenty of experience of reading such information, it is something you can do very easily and quickly.

In your studies you will encounter numbers very often. They might crop up in case studies – in this chapter I shall use an example from a case study – or in written text and other situations. To be an effective management student, and indeed an effective manager, you must become comfortable with numbers. I hope that this chapter will give you the confidence to handle numerical information whatever form you encounter it in – whether in the form of tables, graphs or diagrams.

Each time you come across a new kind of numerical information, the question arises as to whether it is worth making a fresh investment in learning how to make the numbers meaningful to you. Since there is so much numerical information around these days, the answer will often be 'No'. You are unlikely to have the time to discover the significance of all the numbers you come across. On the other hand, within any given area of knowledge there is quite often a general level of numerical 'literacy' which is taken for granted. So, if you intend to become a regular participant in discussions within that field, then you have to take the time and trouble to develop the relevant numeracy. If you want to understand how your organisation is funded, for example, you will need to know how to read balance sheets.

Key points

In order to be able to use numerical information you have to invest some time in learning:

- *how* the numbers are being used, and
- *what* they are being used to represent.

Are numbers precise?

The way we present, and are presented with, numbers varies according to the circumstances. Sometimes great accuracy is needed whilst at other times a more general 'feel' is required. Indeed, in some situations, lots of decimal places can lead to 'false accuracy'. This commonly occurs when estimates or rounded numbers are used in calculations. In many circumstances, it is better to be 'approximately right' rather than 'precisely wrong'. For example, take the number 68.5189276. Depending on the circumstances, the appropriate way to present this figure could be:

(a) 68.5189276 in, say, a scientific report, where the seventh place of decimals might be significant

(b) 68.5 as in, say, a cost schedule, where the '0.5' was relevant

(c) 70 in a list of approximate percentages to give a broad percentage with other data in a schedule

(d) 2/3 where it was sufficient to know that the number represented this proportion of the total.

3 Working with tables

Let's look at a concrete application of numbers in a business setting. Imagine that you want to introduce a range of products for cleaning kitchen appliances into Europe. Before embarking on such a venture, you need information about the size of the appropriate markets. If I summarised my research with a statement like 'as most people in Europe have kitchen appliances, there is a potential market for our new cleaning products' you might respond by saying, 'What do you mean by "most"? Exactly how big is the potential market? And how does the market differ across Europe?' To support my original statement, I need to quote some detailed figures – which you will find in Figure 7.1.

You will come across tables like this one in many situations at work. In the world of academic study, you will come across such tables in an equally wide variety of situations. This one has come from a case study. If you read across the top row of figures, the figures for Austria, the table shows the percentage of homes that contain washing machines, tumble dryers, dishwashers, refrigerators, electric freezers and microwave ovens. The rest of the table gives you the same information for the other countries. The second to last row tells you the total percentage of homes in Europe, covered by the survey, that contain each type of appliance. The last line shows ownership in the USA.

It is important that you know how to extract information from tables such as this one. The following Activity will show you how, with a little bit of effort, information is readily available from them.

Country	Washing machines	Tumble dryers	Dishwashers	Refrigerators	Electric freezers	Microwave ovens
Austria	89	5	28	94	57	8
Belgium	83	28	21	98	58	6
Denmark	88	32	24	100	71	5
Finland	86	2	23	85	58	13
France	86	5	26	98	44	9
Germany	91	17	32	96	56	11
Greece	69	n/a	3	73	24	n/a
Italy	96	n/a	22	99	22	3
Netherlands	95	15	9	98	42	3
Norway	92	n/a	25	96	n/a	n/a
Portugal	43	n/a	9	83	12	n/a
Spain	92	4	10	98	5	2
Sweden	93	28	38	96	73	12
Switzerland	96	19	36	99	63	10
United Kingdom	87	31	10	97	45	33
Europe	85	15	22	95	41	18
United States	70	42	48	100	41	66

n/a = figures not available

Source: Adapted from Dess, G. G. and Miller, A. (1993) *Strategic Management*, McGraw-Hill, New York, p. 761.

Figure 7.1 *A table showing the percentage of households containing kitchen appliances in Europe and the United States in 1987*

ACTIVITY Work out the answers to the following questions by studying Figure 7.1. Write your answers down, so that you can check them against mine when you have finished.

1 (a) What is the lowest figure for refrigerator ownership in Europe?

  (b) What is the highest figure for refrigerator ownership in Europe?

  (c) Would it be reasonable to say almost every household in Europe has a refrigerator?

  (d) Does owning a refrigerator depend on which country you live in?

2 (a) What percentage of homes in Spain have electric freezers?

  (b) Can you express this as a fraction or a ratio (roughly)?

  (c) What fraction or ratio (roughly) of homes in Greece don't have electric freezers?

  (d) Do most households in Europe have electric freezers?

3 (a) In which country or countries do less than half of the homes have washing machines?

(b) Does a higher percentage of homes in Europe or in the United States contain a washing machine?

(c) What is the percentage difference?

4 (a) On which type of appliance is there the biggest percentage difference between Europe and the United States?

(b) Which appliance shows the biggest difference in ownership between Germany and Portugal?

(c) Would it be reasonable to assume that very few Portuguese homes contain a tumble dryer?

(d) Would it be reasonable to assume that about half of Norwegian homes contain a microwave oven?

5 (a) Which appliance has the greatest variation in uptake in Europe?

(b) Which nation, or nations, have the least number of appliances?

(c) In which country, or countries, do two-thirds or more of homes contain electric freezers?

(d) Would it be reasonable to say that only washing machines have achieved a place in most homes in Europe?

6 The number of homes containing large kitchen appliances in Europe is broadly similar to those in the Unites States. True or false? Explain why.

7 Are all European nations represented here?

8 What other problems might there be in using these figures for current decision-making?

Answers to Activity

Here are my answers. Give yourself plenty of time to check back to the table if you disagree. The 'Summary of tips for table readers' on page 183 may help you.

1 (a) 73% – for Greece.

(b) 100% – in Denmark. This figure shows that all or nearly all homes in Denmark contain a refrigerator. If you have not chosen the same answer as I have, hunt back through the table to see where my figure comes from. Then try to work out how I arrived at that figure.

(c) Yes, it would – 95% of, or 19 out of 20, homes in Europe contain one.

(d) No, refrigerator ownership is not dependent on country, as most homes in most countries contain a refrigerator. Even in the country with the fewest refrigerators, Greece, 3 out of 4 homes contain one.

2 (a) 5%

(b) $1/20$ or one-twentieth. 5% is one-twentieth. As a ratio, we would say that 1 home in 20, or 1:20, has an electric freezer in Spain.

(c) Approximately $3/4$, three-quarters, or 3 out of 4, of the homes in Greece don't contain an electric freezer. (Note that these are rounded figures. The exact figure would be $76/100$ of Greek homes don't contain a freezer.)

It is useful to be able to switch back and forth between fractions and percentages because, although percentages are often more accurate, you can begin to lose touch with what the figures mean. If you remind yourself from time to time that 50% is the same as a half, that 75% is three-quarters, that 20% is a fifth, and so on, it helps to fix in your mind the kinds of quantities you are dealing with.

(d) This is a difficult question. Over the whole of Europe 41% of homes contain an electric freezer. This cannot be considered 'most homes'. However, in a number of countries the majority of homes do contain an electric freezer: Austria, Belgium, Denmark, Finland, Germany, Sweden and Switzerland. It is debatable what the term 'most' actually means. It could mean: more than half, substantially more than half, or almost all. In Denmark and Sweden more than 7 out of 10 homes contain an electric freezer. I would say that only in these countries could one argue that most homes contain a freezer. These figures may be distorted because we are not given any information on fridge/freezers. Are these counted in the refrigerator column or the electric freezer column, or both?

3 (a) Only in Portugal.

(b) More homes have a washing machine in Europe – 85% of homes compared to 70% in the United States.

(c) 15%. You need to be careful of percentages when used in this way. The difference between Europe and the United States is 85% minus 70% which equals 15%. However, you must remember that these are percentage points. The populations of Europe and the United States are different, so 15% of the European population is different from 15% of the United States' population.

4 (a) The biggest difference between Europe and the United States is on microwave ovens. In Europe 18% of homes contain one, whereas 66% of American homes contain one.

(b) Washing machines – where the difference is 48%. However, there are no figures available for Portuguese ownership of microwave ovens or tumble dryers. Sixty percent or more of Portuguese homes would need to contain a microwave oven or 66% or more would need to contain a tumble dryer for one of these products to be the greatest difference between Germany and Portugal. This seems unlikely, as Portugal generally has one of the lowest saturation rates of large kitchen appliances in Europe.

(c) Given what we know of large appliance ownership in Portugal generally, this seems a safe assumption. However, it is an assumption and one which we need to qualify.

(d) From the figures it is impossible to say. Norwegian kitchens do contain a large number of appliances. But to say this is indicative of the uptake of microwave ovens would be purely speculative.

5 (a) Electric freezers. At the lowest end of the range, only 5% of Spanish kitchens contain one, whereas 73% of Swedish homes contain one. This assumes that all the figures that are not available lie somewhere near the bands of quoted figures.

(b) You cannot calculate this without more information. To do so, you would need the total number of domestic kitchens for each country and then multiply out the figures. For example, assume that Denmark has 5 million kitchens and Greece has 10 million. Denmark would contain about 5 million refrigerators, whilst Greece would contain about 7.3 million refrigerators.

(c) Only in Denmark and Sweden.

(d) No. Refrigerators have penetrated the market even more than washing machines.

6 You could answer either true or false to this question. Some appliances, particularly refrigerators and electric freezers, do exhibit similar uptakes in Europe as a whole, and washing machines are not that dissimilar to the United States. However, there is a marked difference between the other appliances and if one looks at each country in Europe you can find both greater or lesser uptake of appliances than in America.

7 No. Eire is not, and some of the smaller European countries such as Lichtenstein, Luxembourg and Andorra are also missing. In addition, there are no figures for any country in Eastern Europe.

8 First, they are out of date. One suspects that there is a life cycle to the adoption of some of these products, such as microwave ovens, and that therefore a greater number of kitchens now contain one. Second, there is the problem of how combined appliances are included in the figures, for example the washer/dryer or the fridge/freezer. Third, if we were going to make any decisions based on these figures, we would probably want to know how many kitchens there are in each country and how the figures have changed over time, at the very least. We will look at some of this information a little later.

Sampling errors

In the example we have been using, it seems very unlikely that the researchers conducted a census of the kitchen appliances in each European country and the United States. Instead, they probably selected a sample of 'typical' homes and asked the householders what appliances they had in their kitchens. The researchers would then have assumed this represented the normal pattern of kitchen appliance ownership and used information about population or number of homes to find out what their sample meant for the whole country. The assumptions necessary to obtain this information may cast doubt on the accuracy of the figures.

The total number of people in any particular group is known in statistics as a 'population'. This population may be very big, for example everyone in a country, or very small, the people who shop at the corner store.

If you follow the political opinion polls you will know that every now and then a freak result comes up. The 1992 UK General Election is a good example, as all opinion pollsters predicted a Labour Party victory. Most surveys rely on studying a *sample* from a given *population*, or group of people. This means that the researchers could be unlucky and by chance pick a lot of people of one kind and fail to pick many of another kind. This will bias the results.

There are several ways of trying to avoid being misled in this way. One is to make the sample very big, since the effects of chance ought to even out when you select lots of people to be in the sample. But large samples are very expensive, so another safeguard is to do small surveys on several occasions to check whether you get the same results. The variations in results that you get from different samples are called *sampling errors*.

Out-of-date data

Many figures are almost always 'out of date', simply because of the time it takes to collect, process and publish them. This is something you have to look out for when you examine tables.

On the other hand, just because a table is not completely up to date doesn't mean it isn't worth looking at. You can never get *exactly* the figures you want. And *some* data is a lot better than none. The table we have been looking at has enabled us to answer a lot of useful questions, even if we have had to put a note against our findings to the effect that there are likely to have been important changes since the data were collected.

It is usually the case that you have to work with data gathered by someone else, for some other purpose, some time ago. You haven't the time, or the resources, to gather for yourself all the figures you might like to have. Primary research can be very expensive. The trick is to learn how to make intelligent use of the data that other people collect.

> Primary research is research you have conducted yourself.

Summary of tips for table readers

Take your time and be cautious

As I have said, numbers are a very abstract and condensed form of information. They can tell you a great deal in a very compact and efficient way. But, as with any table you want to read intelligently, you have to allow time to understand – to work your way through the figures and the words, so as to be sure that you know exactly what kind of information you are looking at. It is easy to be misled by numbers. You need to approach them in a careful and questioning frame of mind just as you would any other information. There is a lot to learn from most tables if you take the trouble to become familiar with them.

Finding your way in

It's often difficult to get a grip on a new table. When you look at the headings and labels they may be a bit too cryptic to take in on their own. Often the best way in is to pick on one or two of the numbers and see if you can work out what they stand for by checking across to the left-hand edge and top edge of the table. Try to cross-check against what you know of the 'real world' to see if the figures as you understand them seem likely. (For example, in the table we have been looking at, does it seem likely that 10% of kitchens in Spain in 1987 contained a dishwasher? Yes, it does.) If you seem to be making a plausible reading of the figures, then try some other checks. It would be reasonable to assume that a greater proportion of people in the richer countries of Europe bought more large kitchen appliances than those in the poorer parts of Europe. If you scan the dishwasher column, does this assumption hold true? There would seem to be 'blips', but broadly speaking, it does seem to hold true.

If the figures seem to make sense, then scan across some of the rows and up and down some of the columns to see whether you can see any patterns in the way that the figures rise and fall – in other words, look for any trends

> A 'blip' is a number in a table that appears to go against the trend, or a point on a graph or chart that seems unusual. Picking out the blips is one of the 'tricks of the trade' of table reading. You scan down columns and across rows, looking for patterns of steady rising or falling. Wherever you find a blip it is worth stopping to take a closer look and to think what might have caused it.

in the figures. If you can spot patterns, think whether they seem to make any sense.

Reading the words

When you have had a good look at the numbers, go back to the words to check them more thoroughly. Once you have something of a feel for the figures, the significance of the main title of the table will be clearer to you. You also need to check the headings of the columns carefully. Make sure you know what the units of measurement are. Are you dealing with numbers of people, or numbers of millions of people, or percentages of people; with pounds, or millions of pounds? Then look at any other notes that go with the table. Who collected and published the data and when? You may find that you need to change your understanding of the numbers in the table once you have read the small print that goes with the table.

Extracting information

When you have satisfied yourself that you really have grasped what the figures in the table mean, then you are ready to start pulling out the information that you want to know.

- Look for the highest figure and lowest figure in each row to see what the range of variation is. Then do the same for each column. Are any of the highs and lows surprising?

- See if you can find an interesting trend. If so, how could you summarise it in a few words?

- Are there any 'blips' in the trends? If so, can you think of any reasons for them?

- Try quickly to summarise for yourself in words the main patterns which emerge from each of the rows and columns of the table.

What I have been outlining here is the 'super de luxe' treatment. You won't have time to look at every table you come across in such detail. However, you should make a point of building up your experience in reading tables, by picking on one from time to time and really giving it the full treatment. Once you are used to reading tables, you will become quite comfortable with them.

Producing tables

Once you are comfortable reading information from tables, you will probably want to use tables to support your own arguments. As I said, they are a very compact and efficient way in which to supply information. Tables are as simple to build as they are to read, but there are several points you should bear in mind.

Layout

Before building your table you need to identify clearly what information you wish to communicate. Tables quickly become confusing and daunting if you include additional, but unhelpful, information.

You must then decide which way round to orientate the table. There are no set rules, but tables tend to have the main category at the left-hand side and the sub-categories across the top forming the column titles. In our example, the main category is the nations of Europe and the sub-categories are the kitchen appliances. So we place the main object of enquiry at the left-hand side so that we can easily read across. Accounting and financial data commonly come in this format as the sub-categories are often the months of the year or whole years.

Checking the numbers

If you spot a mistake when using a table, you instantly become suspicious of all the data contained in the table. How can you be sure that other numbers, which look right, are not also incorrect? It is vital, when preparing tables, that you thoroughly check all your calculations. There is a simple little trick that can be used on many tables which have total columns or rows. Add up each row so that you have a list of totals for each row. Then add these totals up to come to a total for all the table. Then add up the numbers in each column so that you have a total for each column. Add these column totals together so that you again get a total for the whole table. This number must match the first total you calculated. Then compare your sub-totals with those in the table – they should match. This is an excellent way to reveal mistakes made sub-totalling a table.

Tables (such as the one we have been using) containing sub-totals or percentages that are not the sum of the row or column need an extra check. The best way to check these tables is to ask someone else to check that you have made the correct calculations and put the right numbers in the right places. A fresh eye usually spots mistakes well. It can sometimes be quite difficult to spot your own mistakes.

The dangers of calculators and computers

We depend on calculators and computers to do our calculating for us these days. There are dangers in this. Some people have said that we are losing our numerical ability and that our over-dependence on machines causes us to make foolish mistakes, that we tend to just copy output without giving thought to it, or we may not check the answer from the machine for reasonableness.

Computer engineers have a saying: 'garbage in, garbage out'. This means that machines are only as good as the data you put into them. It is very easy to make a mistake when putting numbers into a calculator – adding a zero or transposing two numbers – and, if using a spreadsheet, to alter a formula without realising it. In order to combat these problems, always find ways to check your answers. Check your figures for reasonableness, that is, ask yourself, 'Are these the sorts of numbers I would expect to get?'

Key points

When reading tables:

- Take your time and be cautious.

- Read accompanying headings and notes carefully.

- Try to cross-check figures against what you know of the 'real world'.

- Look for patterns, trends and 'blips'.

When producing tables:

- Pay careful attention to layout.

- Check the numbers carefully and apply a 'reasonableness' test.

4 Working with diagrams and graphs

Tables are just one way of communicating numerical information. However, it is a method that requires the reader to do a lot of work to uncover the message. A much more immediate and powerful way to do this is to use diagrams and graphs. When you use tables the reader has to visualise the meaning of the numbers. Diagrams and graphs help the reader do this. To show how powerful these can be, let's look at a bar chart created from the table we have been using.

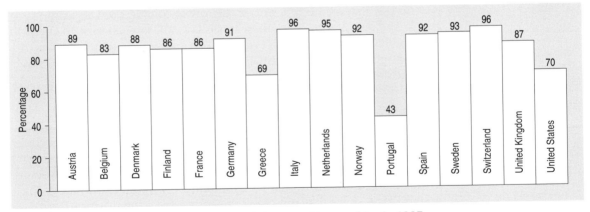

Figure 7.2 *The percentage of households containing a washing machine in 1987*

From this bar chart we can immediately see that Greece and Portugal have a much smaller percentage of homes with washing machines. We can also see straight away that all the other countries have similar percentages of homes containing washing machines, about 90% or 9 out of 10. A series of bar charts for each appliance would show us the trends almost instantly.

ACTIVITY   To check that the bar chart is nothing more than the data from the table presented in a different way, try comparing the numbers in them.

I hope that you can see the trends I've already mentioned. The bar chart brings the message of the figures out much more clearly and forcefully. This is the basic purpose of presenting data in diagrams rather than in tables. If you choose the right kind of diagram it makes the patterns in the data very much clearer and more obvious than tables.

Bar charts are just one type of graph. You can immediately see that most homes in most European countries contain washing machines and that Portugal, and to a lesser extent Greece, go against the trend, and by how much. Other charts are used as the situation suits. Imagine, for example, that we have data for the sales of large kitchen appliances for a number of years. We would use a different type of graph to show the trends – a line graph, as in Figure 7.3.

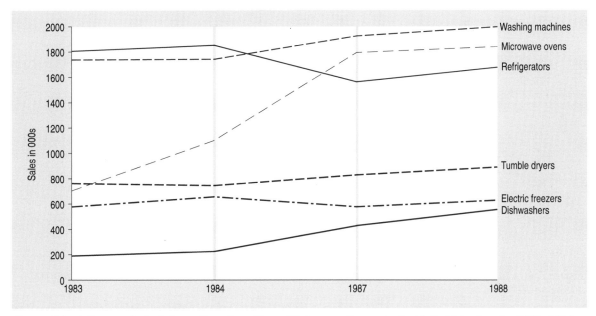

Figure 7.3   *A line graph that shows the sales of large kitchen appliances in the United Kingdom in 1983, 1984, 1987 and 1988*

You can see, for example, the rise in sales of dishwashers and microwave ovens as you move from 1983 on the left to 1988 on the right. In fact, it appears that sales of microwave ovens rose dramatically between 1984 and 1987, whilst sales of dishwashers only increased steadily. The graph is so clear and direct that you might ask why anyone would bother with the bar chart. With the line graph the figures are condensed to just a set of points, so that you have to work just a little harder to remind yourself what the picture is telling you.

Another thing the line graph does is to make it easy to predict what the levels of appliance sales might have been in the years left out of the original graph. For example, if you look along the line for tumble dryer sales to the point one-third of the way between 1984 and 1987, it suggests that about 800,000 tumble dryers were sold in 1985. In other words, we can read off predictions from a line plotted on a graph. The bar chart is one snapshot, whereas the line graph is a series of snapshots.

One more thing we might want to do, while we are looking at the trends on the line graph, is to ask: 'What about the unevenness of the lines? Perhaps the shape of the line graph would be different if we showed all the intervening years so that each year is the "proper" distance apart.' Figure 7.3 is actually incorrect and it misrepresents the figures. The amended and corrected graph can be seen in Figure 7.4.

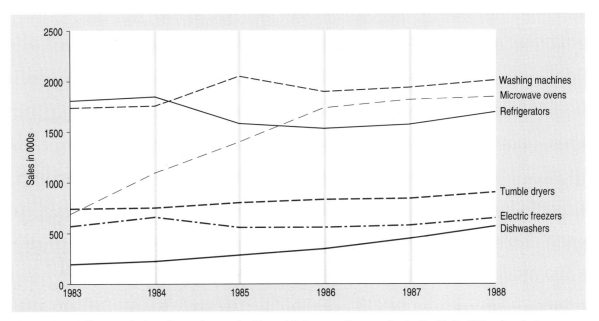

Figure 7.4 *A line graph that shows the trend of large kitchen appliance sales in the United Kingdom between 1983 and 1988*

Figure 7.4 is the same as Figure 7.3, except that the years 1985 and 1986 are included. This line graph shows the whole picture. As a consequence we can spot the trend in microwave oven sales more accurately: a rapid rise in sales from 1984 through to 1986, followed by a slowing down in the rate of growth in 1987 and 1988. In addition, the trends on all the other appliances are all easier to detect. Yearly sales of tumble dryers and electric freezers seem fairly static; sales of dishwashers are growing at a steady rate, as are those of washing machines, if one ignores the blip in 1985. I hope you can see that the trends are more gradual than suggested by the previous line graph.

Other forms of diagrams and graphs

In this chapter we have looked at bar charts and line graphs. These are probably the most commonly used graphs. However, there are a myriad of other diagrams and graphs that you might come across. Each type illustrates a different aspect of numerical data. For example, if you wanted to show how a total is split you might opt to use a pie chart, as in the figures below.

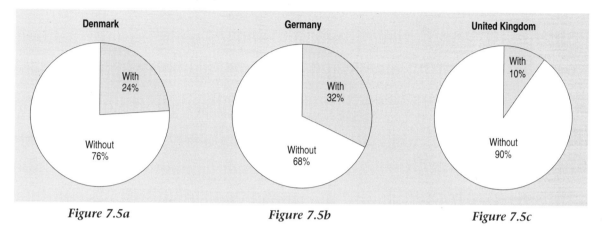

| Figure 7.5a | Figure 7.5b | Figure 7.5c |

Pie charts which show the proportion of homes containing dishwashers in three European countries

Keeping the pies the same size has made it easy to compare the proportions of the slices from one country to another. However, we have no information comparing the overall size of the three markets. We could have made the pies different sizes to represent the size of the markets, but then the size of the Danish pie would have been minuscule compared with Germany and the United Kingdom, as its population is roughly a tenth of the other two. Every way of presenting data has its advantages and disadvantages. You have to decide what information you want to bring out most clearly and then choose the most appropriate form of presentation.

Many managers have access to personal computers and regularly use spreadsheets and these are often used to produce tables, graphs and charts. The latest versions offer a wide range for you to use. Spreadsheets are an excellent way to try out different diagrams and graphs on the same data without the need for lengthy recalculations. By trying many different kinds you will see the data represented in many different ways and this helps you to choose the most appropriate way of displaying it.

The problems and dangers of graphs and charts

Graphs seem to appear everywhere. Perhaps this is because they are such a good way of presenting information and supporting arguments. However, because they are used to support arguments there is a temptation for the producer to make graphs and charts show the information in a way that best suits him or her. Graphs and charts are easily 'designed' to emphasise certain trends. The three graphs overleaf, Figures 7.6a, 7.6b and 7.6c, all show exactly the same information, but the reader of the graph might interpret each graph differently.

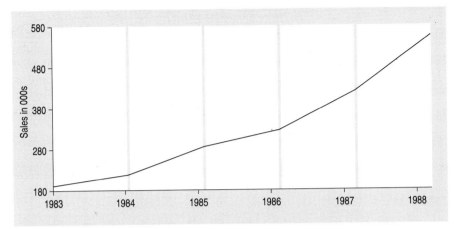

Figure 7.6a *Sales of dishwashers in the United Kingdom, 1983–88*

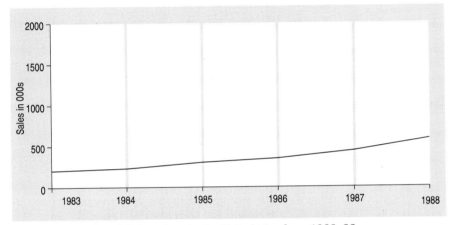

Figure 7.6b *Sales of dishwashers in the United Kingdom, 1983–88*

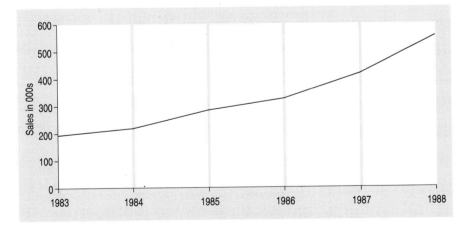

Figure 7.6c *Sales of dishwashers in the United Kingdom, 1983–88*

ACTIVITY Look at the three graphs above. Think about how you might have interpreted these graphs had you not read this chapter.

These graphs look, at first glance, to be completely different. However, if you examine them carefully, you will see that the numbers are exactly the same, only the vertical scale is different. In the first one the impression given is that sales of dishwashers has rapidly increased from a very low base; the second line graph suggests a static amount of sales; whilst the third line graph is, perhaps, a truer representation of the trend in dishwasher sales. The lesson from these line graphs is that you need to examine the graph carefully before jumping to conclusions.

You might have noticed that all the graphs I have used in this section have been rather simple and designed to show just one feature or trend. This was deliberate. Graphs and diagrams quickly lose their impact when they contain too much information. As an example of this, look at Figure 7.7 overleaf. This shows, in graphical form, all the information in our original table of data.

Having said that graphs can show trends and that you should keep graphs simple, there is one warning I should give. Do not take information from graphs without thinking about what the information means.

ACTIVITY   Refer back to Figure 7.6c. How would you describe the trend on the graph? What conclusions would you draw about future sales of dishwashers in the UK?

This graph looks like very good news for manufacturers of dishwashers. The trend is upwards and in 1988 over half a million dishwashers were sold in the UK. But this sales growth corresponds to the 'consumer boom' of the mid-eighties. One would expect most products to be selling well in this period of relative prosperity. Indeed, a product with 'flat' sales during this period might well be thought of, in real terms, as underperforming. Predicting the future from the trend in the graph is likely to be ill-advised without the use of other supporting information, particularly information relating to the economy. In the following years, of course, the UK economy started to slide into recession.

So, be careful when extracting information from a graph. Try to find ways to check the information and also try to get a broader picture.

Key points

- If you choose the most appropriate kind of diagram or graph it makes the *patterns* in the data much clearer and more obvious than tables do.

- There is no one perfect way to represent data graphically – it depends on your purpose.

- The golden rule with graphs and diagrams is to keep them simple.

- You need to examine carefully how information is presented in graphs and charts before accepting conclusions.

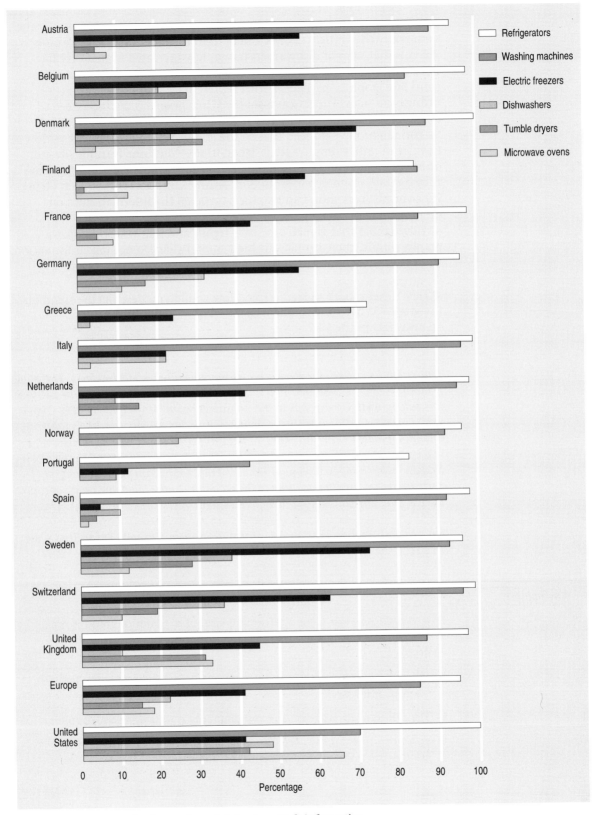

Figure 7.7 *An example of a graph containing too much information*

Summary of tips for reading graphs and charts

My advice for graphs and diagrams is similar to that for tables of numbers.

Take your time and be cautious

Graphs and charts ought to be easy to read, since the whole point of turning figures into diagrammatic form is to bring out their meaning more clearly. However, like numbers, graphs and charts are highly abstract representations, which attempt to summarise certain aspects of the world in a very condensed form. Consequently, they require a degree of mental effort on your part to bridge the gap between the formal pictures on the page and the aspects of 'reality' they represent. As with tables, it is important to approach graphs and diagrams *carefully*, allowing yourself time to get the feel of what you are looking at. Don't assume you know what information a graph contains. Take a thorough look.

Finding your way in

The sheer visual impact of a diagram can make it difficult to look past the attractive layout and shading to the underlying message. As with tables, it is a good idea to look quickly at the main headings and then focus on a point to check what you are being told. Pick on one of the bars and tell yourself what it stands for; for example, 'this bar tells me the percentage of Belgian homes containing a dishwasher', or 'this line shows the number of sales of microwave ovens in the UK for each year from 1983 to 1988.' Scan your way around the diagram – up and down and from side to side. Check that it makes sense in terms of what you already know of the world.

Reading the words

When you feel reasonably comfortable with what the diagram concerns, examine in more detail the words written around it: the main headings, the key, and the axes. The axes are the bottom edge (the horizontal or X axis) and the left-hand edge (the vertical or Y axis) of the diagram. The axes should always be labelled to tell you what units you are counting in. Read any small print by the diagram to be sure you don't draw the wrong conclusions from it. And do you remember the three graphs in Figure 7.6? Check the scale of the axes and where they start.

Extracting information

When you are sure you know what the chart or graph is all about, then start to check for any main trends. Jot down for yourself a few conclusions that you think can be drawn. It often takes a little time before you can interpret the diagram properly. However, it is worth the effort, because information held in the form of a graph is highly patterned; and since our memories work by finding patterns in information and storing them, graphs are all set up ready to be stored. As a result, it can be a lot easier to remember information you have taken in from a diagram than information from a table or from a text.

When you are reading diagrams or graphs you should:

- Take time to get a 'feel' for what the diagram is telling you.

- Pick on one or two points and make sure they make sense.

- Read the words around the edges very carefully.

- Look for patterns, peaks and troughs, and blips.

5 Working with averages

How often do you hear people refer to 'the average'? But what do they mean? There are several ways of calculating an average.

The mean (or arithmetic mean)

When people refer to an average we normally assume that they are referring to the mean. This is the most widely used average. To calculate the mean of a group of numbers you add together all of the figures and then divide by the number of figures you added together. For example, the mean of the following nine numbers 3, 3, 3, 5, 6, 6, 7, 14, 16 is:

$$\frac{(3 + 3 + 3 + 5 + 6 + 6 + 7 + 14 + 16)}{9} = \frac{63}{9} = 7$$

The brackets are used to tell you which calculations to do first. If you come across multiple brackets within a calculation, start from the inside and work out.

Simple arithmetic means like this are easy to calculate. But how would you calculate a mean from the first column of data in Figure 7.1, i.e. the European average percentage saturation rate for washing machines?

This is more difficult because we are dealing with percentages. To produce an average from this data we must calculate a *weighted mean* that takes into account the fact that some of the numbers are more important, i.e. have more weight, than others. The percentages would have to be weighted by the number of households in each country. This means that you need extra data over and above that in Figure 7.1. As I do not have the number of households in each of these countries to hand, I need to find a substitute. It seems a reasonable assumption to me that the comparative pattern of total populations across Europe is similar to the comparative pattern of households across Europe. The total population figure will obviously be much higher but the pattern (i.e. the weighting) should be broadly similar to the pattern of households. This is not a perfect substitute because some European countries have larger families than others, but it seems a reasonable one. The calculation of the weighted mean is shown in Figure 7.8 on the opposite page.

	Percentage of homes with a washing machine 1987	Total population (in millions)	
Calculation	a	b	a x b
Austria	89	8	7.12
Belgium	83	10	8.3
Denmark	88	5	4.4
Finland	86	5	4.3
France	86	56	48.16
Germany	91	62	56.42
Greece	69	10	6.9
Italy	96	57	54.72
Netherlands	95	15	14.25
Norway	92	4	3.68
Portugal	43	10	4.3
Spain	92	38	34.96
Sweden	93	8	7.44
Switzerland	96	6	5.76
United Kingdom	87	57	49.59
Europe		351	310.3

Figure 7.8 A table showing how to calculate a weighted mean for the average number of homes with a washing machine in Europe, 1987; the data in column a are 'weighted' by the data in column b

The final calculation is: (310.3/351) x 100 = 88.4%, which suggests that about 88% of kitchens in Europe contain a washing machine.

The original Figure 7.1 provides a figure of 85% as the total for Europe – presumably this was calculated from the original data. We have found a way to check this figure and our decision to weight the percentages by the total population figure seems to have been a reasonable one. A bonus is that in making this calculation we have gained a feel for the size of each market.

Whenever calculating a mean, make sure that you are dealing with 'real' numbers – not ratios, or mixed formats (e.g. some numbers in millions, others in thousands, or some rounded and others not rounded). If you are at all unsure, return to the original data and calculate a simple mean.

The convention in the UK is to use a comma to separate each group of three whole numbers when writing down large numbers. For example, 12,500,000 is twelve and a half million. In some countries on the mainland of Europe, however, the convention is to use spaces instead of commas and to use a comma where the UK convention is to use a decimal point. For example, 12 500 000,25 is 12½ million and a quarter in some countries. If you have to use numbers from another country, you should check to ensure that you understand the conventions of that country.

The median

The median is another type of average. The median is the middle ranking figure. So in a group of nine numbers, the median would be the fifth ranking number. Using the nine numbers we used earlier – 3, 3, 3, 5, 6, 6, 7, 14, 16 – the median would be **6**. No tricks, it is that simple. When there are an even number of data points the median is the arithmetic mean of the two 'middle' numbers.

The median tends to be used when the numbers represent individual items such as the performances of particular people on some activity. In this case, the median might accurately represent the average performance without the distorting effect of especially good or bad performers. Imagine sales of washing machines through 100 retail outlets in the United Kingdom. There might be some outlets that have particularly good catchment areas or additional sales. Conversely, there might be outlets in particularly poor areas. These extremes might distort the mean to produce an unrepresentative average. A median (in this case a mean of the 50th and 51st figures) would be more appropriate to show 'typical sales'.

The mode

The mode is, perhaps, even simpler than the median. The mode is simply the figure which occurs the most times. Using our nine number example again – 3, 3, 3, 5, 6, 6, 7, 14, 16 – the mode would be **3**, as this occurs three times, which is more frequently than any other number.

The mode is used when you want an insight into frequency. So, if you were a distribution manager, you might want to know which products were moving most frequently through your warehouse. The mode would give you this information, the mean and median would not.

6 Summary

Some people use numbers to hide their inadequacy with words. Perhaps this is part of the reason for the large number of appendices at the end of some reports – lots and lots of numbers because the writer cannot make sense of them or find trends in them. In this situation appendices become like a lamp-post to a drunk – more support than illumination. Your reading of this chapter should help you to see through such subterfuges.

We have focused on numbers in this part of Chapter 7 because making use of them requires specific skills, which you may not have had a chance to pick up before. It is important that you become increasingly competent at examining tables and that you are able to summarise data using averages.

If you are new to tables and diagrams, you will have done some hard work so far in this chapter. Perhaps some of what you have attempted will have baffled you. If so, don't worry about it. Any course you attempt that requires you to work with numbers is likely to give you further assistance. Indeed, there are many other interesting and valuable things to learn about statistics, tables and diagrams, but you will have these explained to you as you need them. All I have been aiming for here is to begin the process of building up your skill, experience and confidence. I hope you will also feel encouraged to develop the habit of stopping to look carefully at tables and diagrams and to work out what they mean, rather than skipping over them. As you have seen, tables and diagrams offer you a lot of information in a very compact form. If you follow the basic steps outlined here, you will soon be able to make yourself familiar with the common ways of presenting numerical data. Then you will be in a position to start finding things out for yourself instead of waiting to be told.

Key points

- Making sense of numbers is a normal part of modern life.
- The ability to work with numbers is more a matter of building up experience with specific ways of using them rather than a special gift.
- You have to be prepared to invest time in learning how to read unfamiliar kinds of numbers, tables and diagrams.
- If you invest this learning time, numbers can give you a lot of information very quickly and effectively.
- Numbers help you to give weight and form to your arguments.
- You need to be careful when you read tables – approach them in a spirit of exploration and questioning.
- When you approach a new table you need to:
  - focus on a few specific numbers and work out what they stand for
  - check all that is written above and below the table and along the edges
  - scan for patterns, trends and blips
  - be aware that the figures may be no more than approximations to the truth, so draw conclusions cautiously.
- When you approach graphs, charts and diagrams you do much the same as for tables.
- Graphs, charts and diagrams help you to see the patterns in sets of numbers.
- Because of this they help you to remember information.
- You need to check how any averages that you encounter are calculated.

Additional reading

You may wish to develop your numeracy a little further. If you do, you may find it useful to have a look at the 'Recommended texts' section at the end of the book.

7 Communicating through diagrams

The purpose of the rest of this chapter is to help you make the best use of diagrams as you work at your studies.

ACTIVITY Skim through the section headings of the remainder of the chapter. List your objectives for working through the material and check these after you have completed the work.

Many people find diagrams useful. I hesitate to use the old saying about 'one picture saves a thousand words', but if I didn't mention it you would be thinking it. This word-saving quality is valuable in writing course assignments. Diagrams are useful in general communication, too. Often, when two or three people are sitting discussing some complex issue, you will see a pad of paper in front of them with rough circles, lines and arrows on it; not drawn to any particular 'system' and incomprehensible to the passer-by, yet a valuable visual framework for the people concerned.

I realise there are people who feel very strongly that diagrams are not for them. If this is how you feel, do please still consider what follows, as you may find some of it useful. However, if after working through these sections diagramming is clearly still 'not for you', then it would be wrong to force yourself into an approach that doesn't suit you.

The rest of this chapter is divided into four parts covering:

- how diagrams help
- using diagrams from course material
- using diagrams of your own choice and design
- an Appendix listing widely used diagrams.

8 How diagrams can help you in your studies

Diagrams are useful as a means of expressing yourself when preparing and presenting written work and as an aid to learning itself. These purposes overlap and both can be operating at one and the same time. Expressed as a diagram these ideas might look like Figure 7.9.

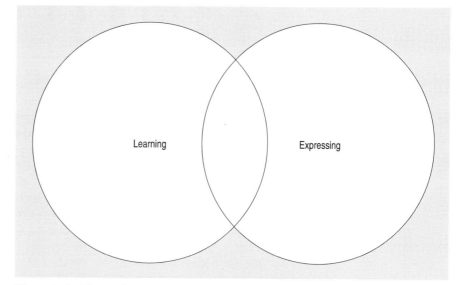

Figure 7.9 *The overlapping uses of diagrams for study purposes*

It is worth taking an example to show more clearly how this works. Suppose you were writing an assignment about the changes in the structure of an organisation in the years around 1993/4. Such an account would probably reflect the characteristic changes of the period, where organisations have changed from tall hierarchies towards flatter, more flexible organisations. It would be quite natural in the course of that assignment to draw the following two diagrams, Figures 7.10 and 7.11.

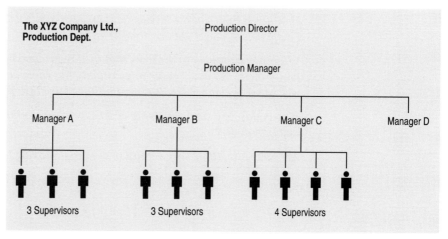

Figure 7.10 *Structure before reorganisation, 1992*

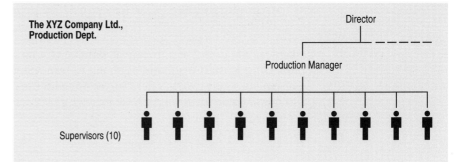

Figure 7.11 *Structure after reorganisation, as at October 1993*

As shown here, the diagrams meet the purpose of expressing our thoughts. Indeed, they do this quite well: set out in this way the diagrams make the structural changes easy to appreciate. But while the main purpose might be to express our thoughts in a clear and economical way, maybe there can be some of that overlapping purpose of learning here, too.

ACTIVITY Spend a few minutes studying the two diagrams (think of a real organisation where this sort of thing has happened, if you like) and see what queries and questions arise about the two structures and the changes.

I'm not sure what questions came to your mind – but here are mine. If you've got a different list, don't worry – it is quite likely that we will have seen this from different perspectives.

In the old structure

What communication links were there between the areas of Managers A, B, C, D?

What is Manager D doing? Whoever has that job seems a bit alone and separate.

How do the supervisors relate to each other? I suspect there may be a great deal of informal contact that does not show on the diagram.

In the new structure

How much time can the Production Manager give to each supervisor? Has the Production Manager got any time at all for staff?

What has happened to the work that used to be done by the managers who are no longer there? No doubt some responsibility has come down to supervisors. How well are they coping? Do they need training? Are they feeling stressed?

How is this new single grouping of 10 supervisors communicating, both formally and informally?

Are functions still clearly defined or are people having to be flexible across areas?

I expect your list is different from mine. The point is that whilst the diagram has a use for expressing our thoughts, at the same time it can also stimulate further learning. The reverse is also true: diagrams we use for exploring ideas and situations may also be valuable in expressing those ideas.

As we move on to consider the use of various sorts of diagrams, these two purposes for using them – helping us express ourselves and helping us learn – will be there under the surface. As we saw in Figure 7.9 earlier, these purposes overlap.

9 Using diagrams from the course materials

Using diagrams from the course materials in assignments is a good idea. Properly used, they will help you express yourself concisely, gaining the maximum advantage from any word limit to the assignment. They offer an opportunity to deepen your learning about the theory and the practical circumstances you are exploring. In the text which follows you will find practical guidance on how to get the most out of using diagrams in this way. In order to make the ideas come alive, the content will be based around a diagram used on basic management courses in The Open University's Open Business School. First of all, I shall explain the diagram and the theory involved, then we shall consider how it might be used most effectively. The diagram we shall use is on the subject of what motivates people to perform well and is usually referred to as 'Expectancy Theory'. (An easier diagram could have been selected – but part of the learning here is about how effective diagrams are in expressing complex subject matter.)

Expectancy theory – motivation

It would seem common sense to say that performance in a job is related to the effort put in. So we could draw:

Figure 7.12 *The link between effort and performance*

However, someone may be putting every effort into the job, but other things intervene. Unless there are clear goals, they may not give a good performance. Likewise, sufficient time, resources, ability and skill, as well as things we term 'job design', such as feedback on performance, feeling the job is important, etc., all affect performance. So it is not quite as simple as our first picture indicated. We might change it to look like Figure 7.13.

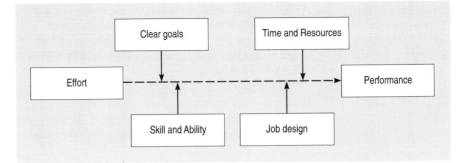

Figure 7.13 *Factors affecting performance*

We can now see the relationship between Effort and Performance more clearly. But the theory we are considering suggests there are *outcomes* from performance:

■ *intrinsic outcomes* which no one else has to give you – they come from the relationship between you and the job, for example the feeling of doing a good job

■ *extrinsic outcomes* which are external to you, for example payment, praise, etc.

These outcomes, intrinsic and extrinsic, may be perceived as fair, to a greater or lesser degree.

Arising from these outcomes and the perception of fairness, the theory then suggests 'job satisfaction' arises to the extent caused by the outcomes and the perceived fairness. Finally, this job satisfaction leads to the person being prepared to put more effort into their work. This might be represented as in Figure 7.14.

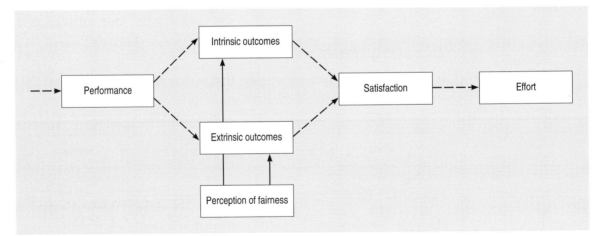

Figure 7.14 *The link between performance, job satisfaction and effort*

If we now join these two parts together, we have a complete model which can analyse people's motivation (or demotivation) (see Figure 7.15).

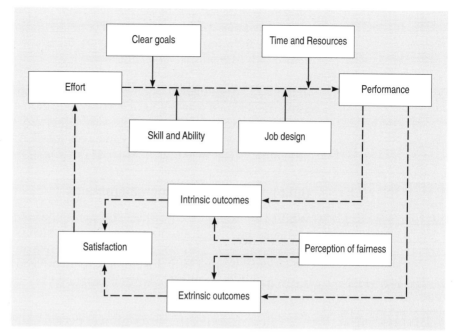

Figure 7.15 *The Expectancy Theory model*

The theory has not been explained to the depth in which it would be given in a management course, but we have sufficient for our purposes here. Please re-read and check that you have a reasonable grasp of these ideas before we move on.

Let us now imagine that you have been asked to write an assignment that analyses why a person in your workplace is not performing particularly well and to make recommendations. (If you are not yet a manager, imagine that you have that position, for our purposes here.) After due reflection you feel that Expectancy Theory is an appropriate concept to apply to this case. In the text that follows we shall consider a number of options about using the diagram and the implications in each case, both for learning and for expressing our thoughts. While the application will be to a specific diagram, the points arising should have general application to using any course diagrams. Let us consider the options available.

Option 1: Don't use the diagram at all

ACTIVITY   It is quite feasible to write a good answer analysing a person's motivation, applying Expectancy Theory without using the diagram. What do you think are the advantages and disadvantages of not using the diagram?

I'm not sure what you thought, but if you are someone who is not a 'diagrams person' as we discussed earlier, then not using the diagram would save you struggling with something you really were uncomfortable with using.

For those who do feel able to use diagrams, then this particular one is quite complex to draw – certainly time would be needed if you chose to use desk top publishing software to draw it. (Most tutors, though, would quite happily accept tidily drawn manually produced diagrams.)

In terms of advantages, it is generally felt that diagrams save words, so using the diagram leaves you free words to gain marks elsewhere. I would also argue that diagrams can express thoughts very powerfully and clearly, but you may want to wait until you have looked at the options below a little more before deciding whether or not you agree with me.

Option 2: copying out course diagrams

See Chapter 5 'Writing assignments' for more about communicating your understanding in assignments.

Whilst I am trying to encourage you to use the course diagrams, there is a particular pitfall you shoould try to avoid, which is the option we are considering here. This option is one that management students do use, so it's worth exploring why it is not a particularly good one. The following is a slight parody of the sort of written assignment I have in mind. The text reads something like this:

'In considering the motivation of person "X" I would apply Expectancy Theory, see Figure 1.'

There then follows 'Figure 1' which is a direct copy of the diagram from the course book, after which there is no further explanation or application. The answer simply continues on to another aspect of the question.

Let's consider this in terms of diagrams being useful for learning and expressing our thoughts. In terms of learning, to simply copy out the diagram from the course book doesn't achieve very much; there is no indication of understanding the diagram, or of its use to help understand the situation being considered. In terms of expressing our thoughts, simply copying the diagram is not a great deal of use either, because it is not expressing *the student's* thoughts. So, this option in using diagrams is to be avoided – it doesn't take us very far at all.

Option 3: linking the diagrams to the case

This is the option which could be useful for you. Let's imagine the case of 'Jo', working on a particular project. Jo is working long hours and is really interested in the project. Now, we could continue discussing Jo's motivation using text, but that would take quite a lot of writing. On the other hand, in the diagram shown in Figure 7.16 we can get a great deal of information across very concisely.

If you draw a lot of diagrams by hand you may find special templates helpful. These can be purchased from good stationery retailers.

The diagram outline has been drawn with the help of a computer software package but it could equally well have been done by hand. If you feel uneasy about putting the detail on to the diagram tidily, an alternative approach is to put as much as you can on the diagram and then use reference numbers or letters to link into the text that follows. To cross-reference in this way is perfectly acceptable.

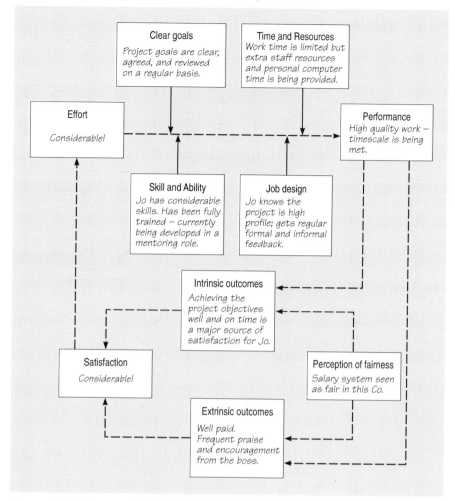

Figure 7.16 *Factors affecting Jo's motivation*

ACTIVITY If you were asked to analyse your motivation in studying this book, the answer, in text form, might take a little while to write. However, in the same way that I have analysed Jo's motivation, try working through the diagram shown in Figure 7.17 overleaf in respect of your motivation in studying this section, making notes at each stage, or using reference numbers to link the stages in your diagram to your notes.

Our answers will vary (see Figure 7.18 on page 207). I've had to guess at what your circumstances might be. What is important is that you have marked the diagram with relevant aspects of your situation, thus applying the theory from Figure 7.15.

Reflection and discussion

I hope that using the diagram is helpful in showing how powerful diagrams are in expressing our thoughts. What is perhaps relevant here is to pause for a moment to reflect on the potential of diagrams in helping our

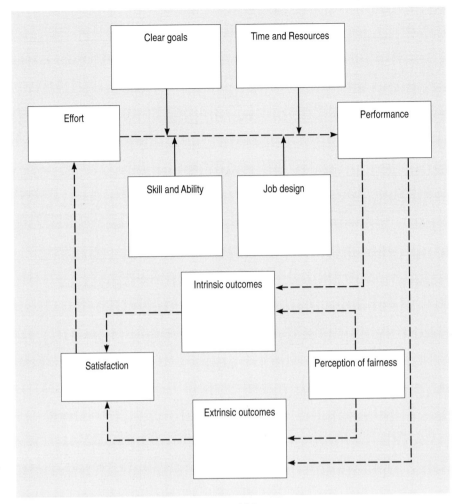

Figure 7.17 *Diagram for Activity on page 205*

learning. For example, in the work we've done together now on this diagram, do you feel you have some sort of grasp of what is known as 'Expectancy Theory'? Of course, it's the task of the course you are doing to teach such theories – yet by simply applying our minds to the diagram, and in particular doing the Activity, we have probably gained quite a good understanding of the main points of the theory.

We can now go one stage further. One of your ambitions may be not just to pass, but to get the highest marks you can and learn as much as possible. Diagrams, used as we are using them here, can help in this respect too.

Let me explain. Suppose now, instead of considering 'Jo', we were considering why someone else – person 'X' – was demotivated and not performing well in their work and that we were that person's line manager. We might have failed to consider our responsibility for their demotivation, our own part in this person's condition. It would be very easy to write an assignment that focused on them alone, rather than on all the factors leading to their state. The diagram won't let us get away with that too easily! If we refer back to Figure 7.14 or 7.15 we will find that it poses uncomfortable questions. We can't simply accept that 'X' is not performing

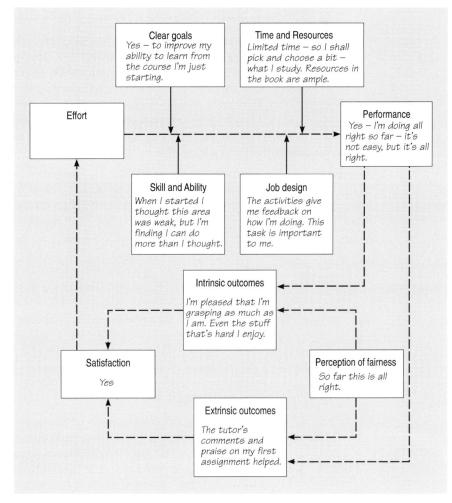

Figure 7.18 *Answer to Activity above*

because they are not putting the effort in, maybe because they are unhappy at home. The diagram challenges us: 'Have they got clear goals and objectives?', 'Have they got the skills and abilities?', etc. All of a sudden it's not so much a question about 'X's' motivation, as about our performance as managers! If the goals and objectives are not clear, what are we going to do about it? Or maybe we say 'Of course they are clear', but how do we know? Have we checked recently? What feedback are we giving this person? Then we might focus on the 'ability and skills' as being lacking. That may be right, but if that's the case what have we done about training and staff development, and by the way, what about our processes for induction and staff selection?

It is easy to see how using the diagram exposes the whole of the model and offers us the opportunity to use it rigorously and to ask the questions that subconsciously we might try to avoid. The sort of answer which deals with the issues in the paragraph above will not only gain better marks, it will also be of practical benefit to us as managers. The study skills here link straight back to the workplace.

Let's now return to our options and consider one final one.

Option 4: challenging and adapting course diagrams

In this option we take a diagram from the course material and either adapt it or challenge it. This is fine and indicates a thinking approach to the course. There is one golden rule: 'State clearly that this is what you are doing.' It is important to do this. Staying with our example of Expectancy Theory, here are a couple of examples. In each case assume the approach in Option 3 has been followed, though for the sake of clarity I haven't filled in all the detail and I've only shown the relevant part of the diagram, rather than the whole of it.

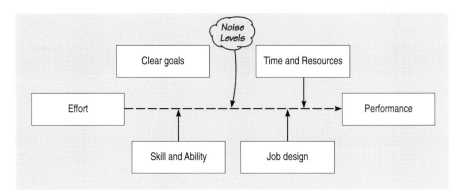

Figure 7.19 *Example 1 of changing course diagrams*

The student's text might read:

> 'Whilst the diagram covers many of the factors affecting the performance of person "Y", in our particular office the noise level from the factory is so high that however good the other aspects are, she simply cannot perform to the best of her ability in that noisy environment. The question of the noisy environment also relates to Herzberg's theory of ...'

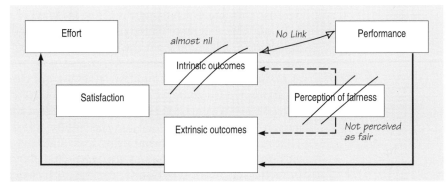

Figure 7.20 *Example 2 of adapting course diagrams*

The student's text might read:

> 'I have adapted the thinking of the diagram above because in our context the model does not apply in full. All the points about the link between effort and performance do apply and people do get extrinsic

rewards. However, there are few, if any, intrinsic rewards. In effect, the link is direct from extrinsic outcomes (pay) to effort; satisfaction doesn't come into it. We do realise how unsatisfactory this is, and in Section ... below I make recommendations for improvements.'

In both cases, the writer has taken a thoughtful approach to the diagram and made changes and justified the approach. By doing so, they have made good points which are relevant to the situation.

Review

In this part of the chapter we have considered the use of diagrams from the course material to help us learn and to help us express ourselves in assignments. As we saw earlier, these two uses of diagrams overlap.

Key points

Provided you feel able to use diagrams, then:

- Use them if they are relevant – they save words and make an impact.

- Remember that simple line drawings can be very effective.

- Don't simply copy the diagram from the book, but rather link it to the real situation – either by showing details on the diagram at the appropriate points or by reference numbers to following text.

- Use the diagram to challenge your thinking – follow it right through, as it may prompt you to consider important issues you might otherwise not address. Use it to make your analysis more rigorous.

- If you choose to adapt or challenge the diagram, that's fine, but do justify your approach and state that your alteration is intentional.

10 Using diagrams of your own choice or design

In this part of the chapter the content will be split into two parts:

- use of diagrams for general study skills
- use of diagrams in assignments.

As you might expect from the two sections these uses may overlap. The 'private' diagram that helps you understand a complex issue as you make notes on a subject could end up in an assignment.

The appendix to this chapter is an index of the sorts of diagrams that are widely used by managers. You may find it useful to read quickly through that material now before continuing with this section.

We shall now consider some specific types of diagrams that people find useful when studying, and conclude with some general points about using diagrams of your own choice and design.

Mind maps

When we are at the start of a course assignment it is similar in some ways to starting a new project or task at work. The mind can go as blank as the sheet of paper in front of us. Somehow, if we try to list our ideas, we keep on coming to a halt.

Mind maps are very useful in getting past this 'blank piece of paper' stage and are a little bit like brainstorming on our own. They allow us to get the ideas we have (and we have more than we credit ourselves with) out on to paper in a relatively unstructured way. Many of us, through the education and training we have received, tend to want ideas set out in a structured way, which is what hinders us when trying to list our ideas. Mind maps help get us past the problems we have when trying to list things; they help us get ideas out in a less structured way.

To produce a mind map:

- Use a large sheet of paper.

- Start in the centre of the page with a box or circle labelled with the title of the map. The main ideas or thoughts radiate outward from this, and the subsidiary ideas radiate from them, and so on, fanning outward from the centre. If you run out of space on the paper, add more sheets beside it and ensure you have plenty of space to work in.

- Label each idea with just one or two words.

- Feel free to start subsidiary mind maps if a new topic seems to be emerging, rather than trying to cram in extra main branches that don't really fit.

An initial mind map may take only three or four minutes to produce. Once drawn, it is then possible to mark related concepts or clusters of ideas by using different coloured pens, by underlining, and so on.

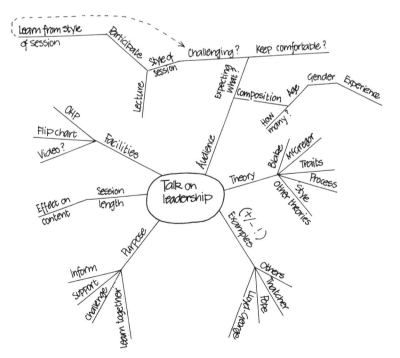

Figure 7.21 *Mind map for a talk on leadership*

While my thoughts so far have been about using mind maps as a fast tool to get ideas on paper, they can also be useful to help ideas grow over time. You could leave a mind map on the office or study wall to 'grow' over days or weeks, using it as a display and filing system of information or options.

As an example, I drew the mind map shown in Figure 7.21 in three minutes as a response to a hypothetical requirement: 'A colleague who was going to do a talk on management and leadership at the Chamber of Commerce tomorrow has gone sick. Will you fill in, please?'

This is my personal response and includes both practical issues about equipment as well as content issues about leadership style and theories. The map may not be complete, but the process seems to me to be an effective use of time.

ACTIVITY Imagine that you are required at short notice to give a talk about stress, either in your work, or in your particular situation if you are not employed. Follow the process outlined above. Start with the words 'stress and work' or 'stress and unemployment', 'stress and caring for children' or a situation relevant to you, in the centre of the page. Don't judge the ideas you have – just let them out on to paper, with the main ideas starting at the centre and working outwards, then starting again at the centre with each new theme. Spend no more than 5 minutes. Use a separate piece of paper – minimum size A4, larger if possible.

Figure 7.22 shows what my version looked like.

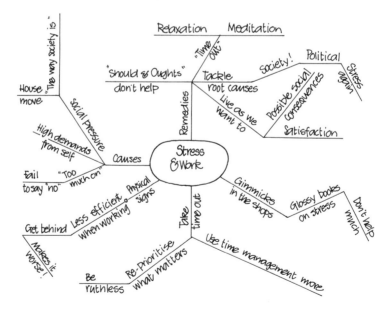

Figure 7.22 *Mind map about stress*

What is interesting for me is that I can now group ideas, using a different coloured pen, in ways that might form sections in a talk or piece of written work. Can you do the same with your map?

At this stage with our map we have various options. If we are thinking in the longer term, we can put the document on the wall and let it grow over time. Alternatively, we can use it immediately, extract the ideas that we captured in this very fast way, and use them as the basis for some more structured thinking. Perhaps the process of re-ordering the ideas for a more structured approach will itself stimulate further ideas.

The practical applications are many and the technique is especially useful when you start a new task or project. For study skills purposes, it would seem valuable as an initial process at the start of a written assignment, or if you are required to give a presentation.

Spray diagrams

These may look similar to mind maps, but the source of the ideas is different. In mind maps we are being creative, getting out from our minds, in a very effective way, the ideas and thoughts that we have.

Spray diagrams are, in a sense, the reverse, as we use them more to capture or encapsulate the ideas of others or to lay out our thinking on a subject. However, if you find yourself using these sorts of diagrams and it's not quite clear whether it's a spray diagram or mind map – don't worry; what matters is that the diagramming technique is being useful to you in learning or expressing your thoughts.

For example, if you had attended a lecture where the subject was about taking notes, your notes in spray diagram form might look like Figure 7.23.

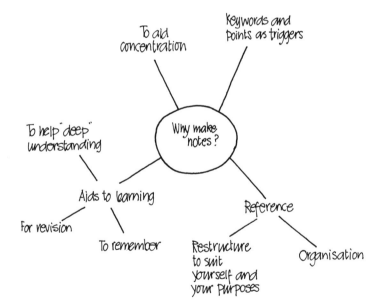

Figure 7.23 Spray diagram from a lecture on taking notes

There is one particular use of spray diagrams which, if the technique suits you, can be very useful. When you have finished studying a book or a section of a book, it is useful to make notes of the key concepts and issues whilst all the ideas are fresh in your mind. You may find it easy to do this in a simple list, but some people certainly find the spray diagram a useful alternative. These notes are valuable as memory aids if you need to come back to the material and, in particular, for exam revision.

ACTIVITY Draw a spray diagram for this part of Chapter 7 on diagramming. I am assuming you have glanced through the Appendix to this chapter, as suggested earlier, so all that will be missing will be the rest of this section.

The diagram you will have produced omits part of the chapter because of the point at which you did it. If you want to turn your diagram into a useful revision aid, though, simply add in the notes for the parts that are missing – I have done this on the shaded part of the diagram. If you have found this Activity easy to do, then when it comes to the management course itself, draw your own spray diagrams for each book or section. That way you will have a valuable revision aid that links in well with your own pattern of thinking.

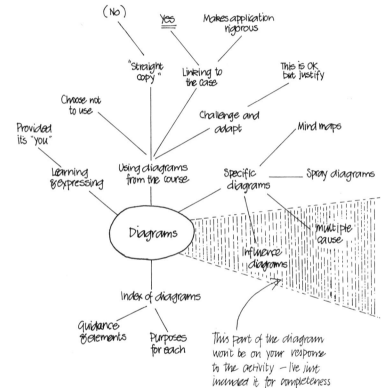

Figure 7.24 *Answer to Activity above*

This technique and the one before, mind mapping, are both primarily for learning rather than expressing ideas in assignments. While not impossible, it is unlikely that you would include this sort of diagram in an assignment.

Our next two types of diagram also help your thinking, but could be used in assignments as means of expressing complex relationships.

Multiple cause diagrams

You don't need to be a manager for very long to realise that problems and difficulties seldom have single causes. Multiple cause diagrams help us represent these relationships in a way that is easy to understand. The text in the box overleaf relates to some of the pressures on management in

213

voluntary organisations. Read through it (some of it may seem a little strange) and then compare it with the diagram in Figure 7.25 below.

Recently, the nature and quality of management in voluntary and non-profit organisations has taken on a new significance. Government policies mean that voluntary and non-profit organisations are becoming increasingly, and more closely, involved with organisations in both the public and the private sectors. Sponsorship, corporate community affairs programmes (which include secondments, employee volunteering schemes and donations in kind), partnerships and 'service agreements' or contracting-out are all the order of the day. Along with the opportunities they present, these developments are making new demands on the managers of voluntary and non-profit organisations. Moreover, those they deal with in the public and private sectors have an understandable tendency to view things in terms of their own organisational practices and experiences. As a result, voluntary organisations are increasingly being expected to imitate business or public authorities – or both.

(Source: Open Business School course B789 *Managing Voluntary and Non-profit Enterprises*)

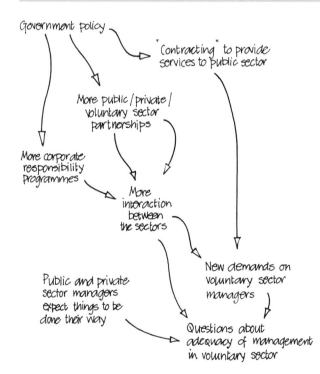

Figure 7.25 *Pressure on management in voluntary organisations*

The text and the diagram present basically the same message, but in different ways. I hope you will have found the diagram easy to interpret. I suspect, too, that even if some of the terms are not quite clear, it is easier to feel you understand the overall picture through the chart than simply from the text.

In the chart, the arrows mean 'leads to' or 'contributes to'. The other components are the phrases referring to events, developments or other factors. This sort of diagram is used to explain why or how something happened, or to represent a person's thinking about what may happen.

The diagram may be entirely sequential, or it may have loops, for example 'vicious circles'. In constructing a multiple cause diagram you normally begin at the factor or event to be explained and work backwards. Because the arrows may represent different kinds of contributions or causes, it may be helpful to label them. It helps in checking a draft diagram to ensure that each individual relationship is clear. If not, insert any necessary intermediate factors. Multiple cause diagrams do not distinguish between different types of causes. If the distinction of types is important for your purposes, you will need to annotate your diagram to this effect.

Influence diagrams

This is a useful technique for expressing relationships and influences between people and groups within an organisation and between it and the external environment. In our early consideration of organisation charts and the reference to them in the Appendix, we recognised that they don't show what is really going on. Influence diagrams help us represent the more complex relationships that exist. In these diagrams, roughly drawn circles or 'blobs' represent activities, people or groups. Assorted arrows or lines indicate relationships. Words are used to label the 'blobs' and sometimes the arrows. The outlines of 'blobs' represent boundaries so that you can show what is a part of what. Figure 7.26 shows an influence diagram loosely based on a Village Playing Fields Committee.

One Open Business School course refers to the *written* and the *actual* structures that occur in organisations.

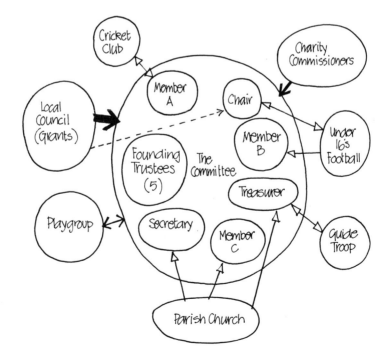

Figure 7.26 *The Village Playing Fields Committee*

The big circle or 'blob' represents the committee itself, the small blobs inside portray the various members of the committee and the larger blob represents the founding trustees. The blobs outside indicate other village organisations and various other bodies which influence the committee. I have used arrows to represent the direction of influence; a double-headed arrow denotes a two-way influence. Arrows are not always used; sometimes ordinary lines are quite sufficient. Arrows and lines denote a capacity to influence, not a sequence in time. Different thicknesses of lines can indicate different strengths of influence. Resist the temptation to overload the diagram with information. It may be helpful to write down all the influences that you can think of at first, but for use in an assignment, select the significant ones.

The Appendix to this chapter is an index of some of the charts and diagrams used by managers. Before moving on to the Appendix, a final word about diagrams of your own design. If you can use or adapt one of the more standard forms of diagram described in this section, then it is probably wise to do so. But if you are going to devise your own, some of the advice that would apply elsewhere in this chapter is also applicable.

- Give the diagram a title.

- Don't try to squeeze too much information into it.

- Make sure the logic is consistent. If there is a circular logic, i.e. one arrow leads from A to B and there is another leading back from B to A, then be sure this is what you intend. In some contexts (e.g. influence diagrams) it may be correct; in other contexts (e.g. a precedence diagram) it would be an error.

- Check the diagram out with someone not involved in the situation. If they understand it, then it probably is useful.

- If your diagram is similar to, or an adaptation of, a standard form of diagramming, acknowledge this. If symbols are used differently from accepted methods, then acknowledge this too.

- Keep the diagrams as simple as possible.

Appendix 7.1 Index of management charts and diagrams

The material in this Appendix is adapted from the Open Business School course B789 *Managing Voluntary and Non-profit Enterprises* Resource File.

Charts and diagrams are widely used in management because of their value in analysing, planning and communicating. This alphabetical listing of some of the main types of charts and diagrams suggests in general terms when they will be helpful and the conventions for drawing them. You will come across further charts and diagrams as you progress in your studies. While the guidance for use is general (these are practical tools used by managers), I want to stress that this section is a rich resource to help with your studies. Almost all of the diagrams and charts can be used in written assignments. I list below just a few of their uses which are specifically about helping you in your studies.

1 Bar charts (Figure 7.29) or key events plans (Figure 7.34) – useful for planning to get assignments in on time.

2 Cause and consequence maps (Figure 7.30) – use in tutorials or self-help groups when a group of people are exploring a real management problem or case study.

3 Precedence diagrams (Figure 7.37) – use as a tool to work out the *order* of events if an assignment requires you to produce an action plan.

4 You can use diagrams and charts in assignments. For example, a bar chart together with an assignment chart (Figure 7.28) can be used to show a plan of action; an influence diagram (Figure 7.26) can express complex relationships; an evaluation matrix (Figure 7.33) or a decision tree (Figure 7.32) can help justify the course of action in your 'Recommendations' section.

Algorithms

Purposes

Algorithms provide instructions for a complicated task. They explain a process as a series of activities and decisions. For example, this sort of diagram would be well suited for displaying a sequence of tests in applying rules for eligibility.

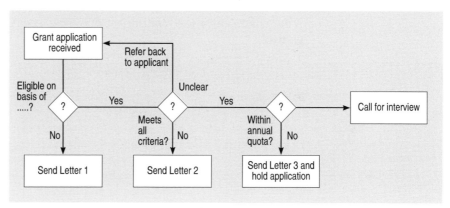

Figure 7.27

Elements

The test questions or decision points are usually in diamonds. Activities are usually in boxes. Lines or arrows with 'yes' and 'no' labels connect test questions and activities.

Guidelines

Algorithms require careful preparation. It is preferable to maintain consistency in the arrangement of 'yes' and 'no' outcomes – for example, 'yes' arrows are all horizontal and 'no' arrows are all vertical. The logical nature of the approach for analysing decisions is valuable. In the management context other variable factors (e.g. exceptions, special cases) may need noting on the diagram.

Assignment charts

Purposes

An assignment chart displays responsibilities, i.e. 'who does what'.

Task	Person(s)	Deadline	Notes

Figure 7.28

Guidelines

This is basically a table with suitable headings.

Bar charts

Purposes

A bar chart can be used for project planning, project monitoring and control.

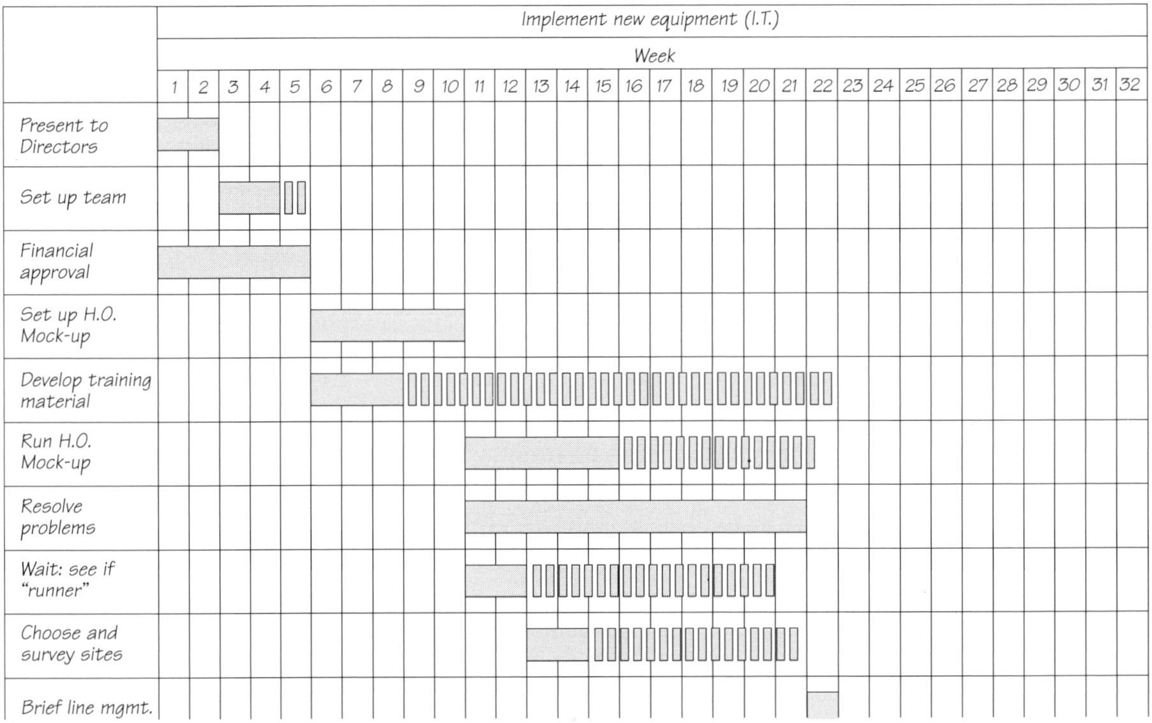

Figure 7.29

Elements

Activities are listed down the left-hand side of the chart. Time-scale is shown across the top. 'Bars' represent the duration of activities. A variation of this is known as the 'Gantt chart', where the planned activities are shown on every other line; the lines between are used for drawing bars, often in a different colour, to show progress to date. (If the blank lines between activities on Figure 7.29 were to be used in this way the chart would, in effect, be a Gantt chart.)

Guidelines

This chart is simple, versatile and widely used. Various embellishments are possible (e.g. showing resources). It is helpful if the activities listed on the left side of the chart are broadly similar in scale and size. It is common practice to list activities in start date order (giving the pattern shown in the example), but other sequences can be used.

Cause and consequence maps

Purposes

A cause and consequence map can be useful in exploring and understanding the complexities and relationships in problem situations and for capturing these issues on paper.

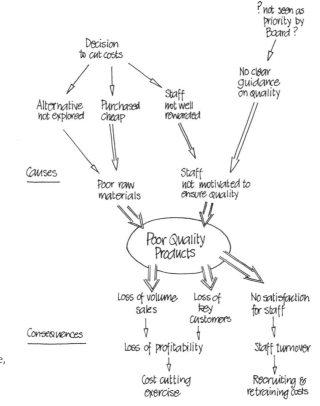

Note: As in this example, there may be links between some of the causes and some of the consequences.

Figure 7.30

219

Elements

The problem statement is shown in a circle in the centre of a large sheet of paper. Immediately above this are concise expressions of what seem to be the main causes. The causes are joined to the main problem by an arrow or line going towards the centre. Contributory causes join on to these like branches of a tree, fanning out. Similarly, going downwards, like roots, are the main consequences of the problem. Secondary consequences fan out from the main ones. Each cause and consequence is concisely labelled.

Guidelines

A cause and consequence map is easy to use. It is sometimes helpful to work on this chart on flip-chart paper and with a group of people. It is sometimes necessary to draw in 'dotted line' links where causes and consequences are linked or reinforce each other.

Commitment charts

Purposes

Commitment charts can be used for planning and managing change, and for identifying where effort in persuasion or education, for example, might be best placed.

KEY PLAYERS	NOT COMMITTED (OPPOSE)	LET	HELP	MAKE
Community UGM		O ——→ X		
GP Senior Partner		X ←———		O
Junior GP 1	O ———			→ X
Junior GP 2	O ———		→ X	
Community Physician		O ———		→ X
Social Worker	O ———		→ X	
Chairman of Community Health Council		OX		
Assistant General Manager of Family Practitioner Cttee	O ———		→ X	
Health Visitor		O ——→ X		
District Nurse			OX	
Nurse Manager				OX

Figure 7.31

Elements

Key people (or groups of people) in the situation are listed on the left-hand side of the chart (in our example, they are Health Service people). Your best judgement of their current disposition is then shown by a circle in the relevant column: oppose, let (i.e. they will let it happen but won't actively help), help, or make (i.e. they give strong active support). Crosses are then used to represent the necessary or desired dispositions for your purposes. Arrows indicate any necessary movement.

Guidelines

Basically, this is a table which makes you think through what stance people are likely to, or will need to, adopt for change to happen.

Decision trees

Purposes

A decision tree can clarify possible options for decision, and help identify key choices when many options exist.

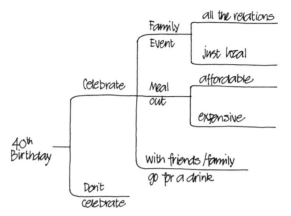

Figure 7.32

Elements

These consist of branching lines with phrases for options.

Guidelines

Each branch should be a clear choice ('either … or … or'). These diagrams can be used as a first step in comparing options (see evaluation matrix). The more complex uses of this type of diagram, which assign values and probabilities to each option, should probably not be attempted without special study of the subject.

Evaluation matrix

Purposes

This sort of chart is helpful in comparing alternative options against a specified 'ideal' outcome or end result, for example in recruitment, equipment purchase or project appraisal.

Elements

The desired outcome is broken down into a set of criteria which are ranked in some way. Some techniques separate them into 'musts' and 'wants', others use a rank order system. The criteria are listed down the left side of the chart. The alternatives are listed across the top of the chart and scored on how they perform against each of the criteria.

Figure 7.33

Guidelines

To avoid bias as far as is possible, the options are assessed against each of the criteria one by one. The process is still one of judgement rather than scientific accuracy, but the chart does lay the information out clearly. This chart may also reveal the necessity for further information.

Gantt charts

See under Bar charts (page 218).

Influence diagrams (sometimes known as organisation maps)

See the full description in the previous section (page 215).

Key events plans

Purposes

This chart can be used for expressing the key points of a plan simply. It is useful for reports and presentations to senior managers or others (for instance, clients) who may not wish to see the more detailed planning documents.

THE KEY EVENTS LIST [EVENT Something that happens / is achieved at a set time]

KEY EVENT PLAN FOR :– Offsite Stockroom PREPARED BY: – IKW

DATE	KEY EVENT	OTHER EVENTS
12th May	SHELL COMPLETE	FITTINGS ON SITE
3rd June	ALL FITTINGS & WORKS COMPLETE	
10 July	RACKING COMPLETE	DELIVERIES ON ORDER
11 July	STOCK DELIVERIES	
20 July	STARTS SERVICING STORE	

Figure 7.34

Guidelines

This chart is not a planning tool itself. Its value lies where people have already used detailed planning techniques. The main thing here is to select a limited number of key events in the life of the plan or project that can act as intermediate deadlines. These are listed as indicated above. It is wise not to prepare a key events plan without having done more detailed planning first, for example using a bar chart. If you go directly to a key events plan it is likely that you will miss time-consuming intermediate events and commit yourself to a timescale you cannot meet.

Multiple cause diagrams

See the full description in the previous section (page 213).

Objectives trees

Purposes

The diagram helps in the shaping of a coherent set of goals and objectives. It is valuable for explaining goals and objectives and analysing the relationship between them.

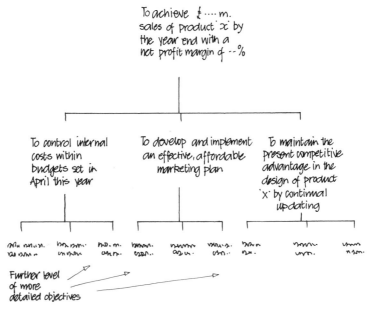

Figure 7.35

Elements

The diagram consists of statements of goals and objectives with branching lines to indicate which lower-level purposes contribute to the attainment of the higher-level purposes.

Guidelines

The diagram requires clear thinking and expression of goals and objectives – it is not an easy diagram to use. It may be a useful one to use to help clarify your own thinking about objectives.

Organisation charts

Purposes

This chart shows formal organisational structure – roles, departments, supervisory relationships, and so on.

Elements

Roles or people are represented on the chart. Branching lines are then arranged vertically to show authority relationships. The horizontal lines are used to separate roles and people. Dotted lines are used for additional reporting relationships.

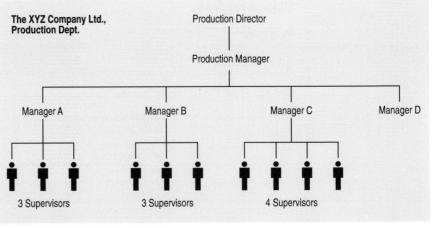

Figure 7.36

Guidelines

Plenty of space is needed. Even if the hierarchy in the organisation has been 'flattened', lateral space will be needed at the bottom of the chart. If vertical positioning is used to indicate status, the lengths of vertical lines must be varied so that people or roles at a particular level in the diagram are of commensurate status, though this may make the chart more difficult to draw. If dotted line relationships are shown, it may help if a footnote is used to explain the exact significance of the dotted line in the particular case. It is worth remembering that this chart only depicts the official structure and not invisible or unofficial relationships that may well exist.

Precedence diagrams (sometimes known as flow charts)

Purposes

A precedence diagram can be used in the planning or analysis of a sequence of tasks, or of a decision-making process. It is useful for the display and communication of the information.

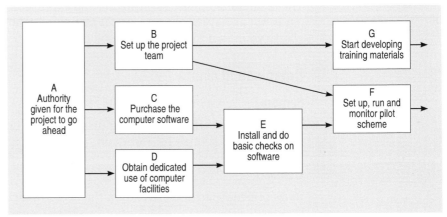

Figure 7.37

Elements

The diagram consists of boxes with phrases briefly stating the activity or decision. Arrows link the boxes, working in a logical sequence across the page from left to right.

Guidelines

Arrows going to a box indicate that the event or activity from which the arrow has come is a precondition to that box. In the example, which represents the early stages of a pilot project to use new computer software, B, C and D are dependent on A being complete before they can happen. C and D are preconditions for E; F can only start once E and B are complete. This type of diagram can be elaborated with 'test questions' to become an algorithm, or with other adaptations it can be used for project planning.

Spray diagrams

See the full description in the previous section (page 212).

Key points

- Diagrams help us express ourselves and help us learn.

- Using diagrams from the course can save words in an assignment.

- If you use course diagrams – apply them, don't just copy them out.

- Keep diagrams in assignments as simple as possible.

- Use spray diagrams, mind maps and other charts to help you in your thinking and planning.

- BUT, if after studying this book diagrams are still not for you, don't force yourself to use techniques that aren't helpful.

Chapter 8 Preparing for examinations

1 Why exams?

This chapter is about a particular style of written examination familiar to most UK students at least – the unseen, three-hour paper and its variants. It will not address multiple-choice, oral or practical exams. While I concentrate on preparing more for the extended written exam where a report or similar answer is required, much of the general advice is equally relevant to exams which are more numerically based, when coupled with the advice given in Chapter 7. I shall, however, add some extra advice on questions involving numbers. Even if you have never taken the sort of exam I describe, or last did so years ago, this chapter should help you to cope effectively and efficiently – to *plan, prepare, practise* and, most importantly, *perform* in the exam. If you are at all worried about revising for and taking an exam, do glance through this chapter before you start your course and then return to it later. This is because you'll benefit from reflecting on your experience of studying and because some of the activities will make more sense in the light of your experience.

By multiple choice exams I mean those that offer a series of possible answers to each question. You have to choose the correct answer.

The chapter is organised so that you can easily sort out your own appropriate route through it. If you already understand and are happy with the learning purposes of exams and, on the basis of experience, are not overly concerned about taking them, you may wish to move rapidly to Section 3.

ACTIVITY Jot down on a separate piece of paper a list of any worries you have about exams. Use your list to draw up your objectives for reading this chapter. Remember to check back to them when you have worked through the chapter. Raise with your tutor any points which still cause you concern.

Management education stresses relevance, with improved management performance as the key objective. It would be understandable to question the role of a traditional examination in such circumstances. It seems to be something remote from the real managerial world. However, it's not as artificial a task as it might at first sight seem.

ACTIVITY Can you think of any parallels between the skills and techniques needed for a successful exam performance and those required in some management situations?

In real life, managers do not always have the luxury of plenty of time; we often need to work fast but be clear and succinct in getting across essential points. To be asked to 'let me have one page on that before I go to see X at 12.00' is not an uncommon experience in the managerial world.

An examination sets up a framework within which you expend exceptional amounts of effort on developing skills and knowledge which you might otherwise never take the trouble to master. It presents a challenge which puts you under pressure, and which can thereby produce very positive learning effects. Properly approached, exams will help you greatly in achieving an overall grasp of what you have been studying.

Exams create pressure through bringing a performance element into the task. In a written assignment you can write when you choose and for as long as you choose, until you are ready to submit your work to your tutor. In an exam you have to perform at a specified time and place, to the satisfaction of an audience you don't know. You have to 'think on your feet', so to speak, and you have to get it right first time. This brings considerably more pressure to bear on you, but the pressure is potentially a very creative force. In effect, the exam creates the conditions to enable you to draw a peak performance out of yourself.

Key points

The pressure created by exams is a positive force which you can harness to help you consolidate your grasp of the course. Your aim is to find ways to 'manage' the pressure to ensure a good performance on the day.

2 Some myths about exams

Many unhelpful myths have grown up around exams. It will be useful briefly to dispose of some of these myths before beginning the essential task of exploring revision and exam techniques.

ACTIVITY Before reading on, check back to the first Activity. What beliefs about exams does your list of worries highlight?

What if I fail?

In the previous Activity, you may have put the possibility of failure high on your list of worries. Experience shows that, for those who have worked at their course, the overwhelming reasons for exam failure are:

- not answering the question set
- writing without reference to the course material
- not allocating time in the exam efficiently.

If, by some mischance, things do not go right on the day, there's usually a possibility of resitting an exam.

These elementary failures of exam technique are nothing to do with basic intelligence or memory. Remember that, in a pass/fail exam, you only have to gain a pass mark to succeed. If this is, say, 40%, it puts the matter in perspective. Most people, if they have prepared properly and are clear about appropriate techniques for tackling an exam paper, will pass the exam they are sitting. This chapter aims to help you with these techniques. So I suggest the question at the head of this section should be rephrased as 'What do I have to do to pass?' We can tackle this question positively together, with the aim of your not only passing, but passing *well*.

Finally, don't be misled into thinking that exams are a battle of wits with examiners who are looking for an excuse to fail you. Exams are not at all like that. The examiners are pleased to have students pass and they usually go out of their way to seek out what is good in the answers they read. If you have made a genuine effort to understand the course, and if you have made progress with your written assignments during the course, then you stand every chance of success.

Key points

Everyone *wants* you to pass, including the examiner.

Let's now look at some of the myths in detail.

Myth 1: You should have studied everything in the course before attempting the exam

Most students, and especially part-time ones, have to cover some material in any course more lightly than other material. Within reason, it is not usually much use, at the revision stage, worrying about what you have had to leave out, providing that it is not obviously essential. It is usually far better to consolidate what you *have* done rather than to attempt to read fresh material. An exam is an occasion when you draw on the products of your months of study and use them to achieve a peak performance. For most people, it is too late for studying from first principles. The advice in this paragraph needs to be read in conjunction with the section 'Getting hold of old exam papers' (page 241).

To put things in perspective, just think about the practical constraints that apply to exams. How much can you write in a three-hour exam? If you have to answer, say, four questions, all of which carry equal marks, you need to know enough to write, say, three or four pages on each question you tackle – although it is difficult to be precise as a shorter, more concise answer may still cover the content. Equally significantly, the person who marks your script, rather than checking over it in fine detail, will be more concerned to see whether the general approach of your answer seems right, whether a reasonable number of the key points are there, and whether it is reasonably well structured. That is what exams are like. Your written assignments during a course are your chance to put together detailed and carefully thought out arguments for close reading by a tutor. The exam is of necessity a less precise exercise, both in the writing and in the marking. So you have to worry less about having left things out, so long as you can pull together enough from what you *have* studied to write relevantly for 30 to 40 minutes on a topic.

An idea of what marking notes for an exam question might look like appears in the Activity on page 237.

Key points

Work out how to make the best use of what you have done, rather than worry too much about what you haven't done during the course.

Myth 2: If you have not understood what you have read it isn't worth taking the exam

It is quite normal to feel uncertain about your grasp of some areas of course content as you reach the later stages of a course. You can be sure that many other students will be harbouring the same doubts. Naturally, in any course, there will be certain central ideas you will be expected to have made progress with. If you have *tried* to make sense as you studied, you will probably have developed more of an understanding than you realise. But if the course is at all challenging you could hardly expect to arrive at a resolution of every issue it raises by the time of the exam. In fact, as I have suggested, the exam may be just what you need to spur you on to sort out some of these central issues. The point is to use your preparation for the exam to pull things together, to make the best sense that you can of what you have studied.

A good course will have set all kinds of ideas whirling around in your mind, some of which you will still be sorting out a year or two later. Indeed, it is hard to imagine what a final and complete understanding of a topic of any significance would be like.

Key points

No one understands everything. There are bound to be some areas where you feel under-prepared and uncertain.

Myth 3: Exam papers are unreadable

Your first look at a past exam paper for the course you are studying may give you cause for concern. Exam questions may look very broad and demanding at first sight. They may also be rather abstract in form and may seem somewhat oblique in their wording. This is usually because the examiners want to point you towards a specific topic in the course without answering the questions *for* you. In other words, they are trying to be helpful without giving the game away. You need to remember at all times that the exam is a test of your understanding of the course you have been studying, not of your general knowledge. So somewhere within what you have been studying lies the answer to each question on the paper. Don't panic at the sight of the paper. Instead, carefully match what you know of the course against what the questions seem to be asking, until you find the specific part of the course each is pointing you to. There is no mystery. The examiners want you to display an understanding of some specific parts of the course. It's just a matter of working out *which* bits.

Key points

Don't panic when you read exam questions. Every exam question is linked quite directly with something you have covered on the course. You just have to work out the link.

Myth 4: Exams are for people with a good memory

Mnemonics such as STEP to help you remember Sociological, Technological, Economic and Political factors in the external environment will, after all, only make sense and be worth remembering if you understand the concept of the external environment in the first place.

Everybody has a good memory. It is a matter of how you use it. However, that is not the key point. Most of the exams adults take are *not* intended as pure memory tests. You are not being asked to take part in a management quiz. The purpose of the course you study is to develop your ideas. And the purpose of the exam is to provide you with the chance to show how well you have grasped the ideas in the course. You will be asked to *use* the ideas in arguing a case or in applying them to a management situation. If you revise constructively before the exams the role of pure memory will be relatively small, albeit that memory will be needed to trigger chains of ideas.

If you have an organised understanding of what is in the course, and if you can see the relationship between the course material and the question, you will have the core of an answer. On this basis you will find it fairly easy to remember sufficient details of examples, names and so on from the course. So don't worry about your memory. Concentrate on organising your notes during your revision. Let your memory take care of itself. It's ideas which are vital; you will lose comparatively few marks if you can't quote a name.

Mind maps are referred to in Chapter 7. If you have not found diagramming a technique which suits your way of working, then try to brainstorm a list instead (i.e. write the items down in the order in which they come into your mind under the stimulus of the topic you have chosen).

ACTIVITY You already know more about the key course content than you think. Take a blank sheet of paper. Put a key topic from the course in a box or circle in the centre as a stimulus and try to develop a mind map to show the main themes, concepts, ideas and authorities related to the topic. Do this from memory. Now check back to your notes or to the course material.

Don't worry if you haven't done too well at this stage as you still have your revision ahead of you. However, I suspect you will have been pleasantly surprised at how much you already know. Incidentally, such techniques will be useful ways of testing yourself during your revision.

Key points

Exams tend to be about what you understand rather than tests of pure memory. Getting your course notes organised is the crucial step to sorting your memory out.

Myth 5: The exam will show up all the gaps in your education and experience

An exam is not a test of your general knowledge, nor of your unique management experience. (It would be impossible to mark in a standardised way if it were.) It is a test of your grasp of the course and your ability to apply the ideas. In fact, it is a grave mistake to read a question on an exam paper and then try to answer 'off the top of your head', using just your general knowledge and personal management experience. The person marking your paper is unlikely to be impressed. The examiners' marking guide will indicate specific points from the course for which marks can be given. An answer which does not use course ideas is thus almost bound to fail. Where your personal management experience *is* likely to add real value to your answer is in illustrating course ideas in order to provide a more rounded answer. You should be used to this in writing course assignments and in testing the course material against your experience as part of your learning strategy.

Key points

Don't worry about what you didn't learn *before* the course. Consolidate on what you have learned *during* the course.

Myth 6: Exams are just a speed test

Can you think quickly enough and write quickly enough to pass an exam? Probably. As far as the *thinking* is concerned, you need to make sure you have done most of that in advance of the exam itself, as we shall see in Section 4. So the extent to which sheer speed of thinking matters is very limited. What *will* matter is how well you have organised your ideas and how well you have planned your exam strategy. If you are working to a good plan, you can be extremely efficient in your use of time in the exam.

If you have doubts, and particularly if you usually use a word processor or if English is not your first language, then it is essential that you give yourself some practice in handwriting at speed. If you have a physical disability which makes you a slow writer, then you should get advice on whether you can be given special support for the exam.

As far as your speed of handwriting is concerned, this may have an effect if it seriously restricts the amount you can get down. If you can get down, say, 500 to 700 words of appropriate content in 40 minutes, that should be sufficient to get a good mark, although it is impossible to give hard and fast rules on this. Some students write short pithy answers which are very effective, while others write pages without saying much.

The fact that you are geared up to peak performance in an exam will help you to write much more quickly than usual. In general, however, it is far more important to focus on the quality of what you write than the speed at which you can produce it. In any case, your speed of progress is as likely to be affected by the rate at which you can work out the next point in the argument as by the purely technical process of putting the words on the page. As we shall see, this has a great deal to do with how you prepare yourself in advance of the exam.

Key points

Speed in an exam is to do with having a very clear plan of how you intend to use your time.

Myth 7: You have to revise until you drop before an exam

The folklore of exams is full of stories of amazing last-minute efforts involving working late into the night. There may be some truth in them, in that we *are* capable of extraordinary feats when the pressure is on. But the telling of the stories is as much to do with the feelings that preparations for exams produce as it is to do with accurately describing reality. It is *not* the case that all preparations can be done effectively at the very last moment, particularly as you get older. This is especially so if you are studying part-time and have other commitments.

Remember the 4Ps: plan, prepare and practise in order to *perform*.

Our minds function somewhat differently from normal under pressure, and you need to understand the differences if you are to manage yourself well in building up to peak exam performance. In the days immediately before the exam, you will probably find that the tension builds up and you have plenty of nervous energy. You can get lots done, but it is perhaps harder to keep yourself under control, in order to channel the energy in the best directions. Being highly charged can make you very good at focusing attention on specific matters in hand, but conversely it can make you less good at sorting out broad, abstract issues. The obvious answer is to do your broad planning well in advance so that, by the final stages of revision (and in the exam itself), you have clear-cut strategies already worked out – strategies for tackling the revision, for allocating time in the exam, for taking the exam questions apart, for structuring your answers, and so on. If you have a well developed sense of purpose and a framework within which to work, you may find you can think surprisingly clearly once the exam has started. But none of this is likely to happen if you leave all thoughts of exam preparations to the last couple of days and nights before the exam.

Key points

> You probably *will* do a lot of work just before the exam. But you need to do it in a planned way, using your time efficiently and conserving your energies. You don't want to turn your life upside down just because of an exam.

These, then, are some of the myths about exams. But, as we have seen, the reality is much more mundane. Exams are just another part of the education process – admittedly a part which presents a different challenge and perhaps puts you under greater pressure. The essential secret of achieving the results that you deserve in exams is to take a practical approach to them; to be realistic about yourself and about what is required of you by the exam, so that you can prepare yourself carefully and sensibly to give a peak performance.

3 What examiners do not like

Having disposed of some of the myths, let us look in more detail at the reality. One way of getting a sharp focus on what *is* wanted in exams is to consider what boards of examiners are likely to say in their reports after marking exams. Often these reports stress how well many students answer questions. However, here I think it is useful for us to highlight some of the faults examiners frequently find.

ACTIVITY You will have seen what your tutor does not like in written assignments. Now imagine you are an examiner. What things do you think *you* would not like to see in exam answers? Make a list before reading on.

Failing to answer the question

In answering exam questions, it isn't just *what* you know that counts but *how* you say it. A great deal of emphasis is placed on being able to use what you know to argue a case that relates directly to the specific question. If you don't do this, your script marker regretfully writes 'Doesn't answer the question' below your answer. According to examiners' reports, there are several ways in which you can miss the mark:

- *Failing to recognise what one of the key terms in the question means* (answering a question, say, on the *external* environment as though it meant the same as the *physical* environment). You have to think carefully about what each of the words in the question means. If there is a key term in the question you don't know, avoid the question. You will get very few marks if you guess and get it wrong.

- *Failing to realise which issues from the course are being raised.* These may come from one part of the course or straddle more than one area. Every question is intended to direct you towards particular issues that have been discussed in the course. You have to spot which ones.

  Suppose a question asks you about, say, appraisal and feedback on performance. You recognise rightly that this is focused on the 'people' area of the course you are studying. That, however, is not sufficient. You are not invited to write about, say, recruitment and selection, induction and initial job training as the core of your answer just because these might figure in that section of the course. If the question asks you to write about appraisal and feedback on performance, then this must form the core of your answer if you are to gain pass marks. Depending on the exact wording of the question, a reference linking recruitment and selection, induction and initial job training to appraisal and feedback as part of a process could, however, gain bonus marks. Similarly, a question on 'managing change' cannot be answered by using course concepts about 'conflict'. None the less, an answer that uses managing change concepts could perhaps be enhanced by reference to the issue of conflict as a part of the answer.

- *Failing to offer analysis and argument relating to the question.* However the question is posed, it is generally expected that you will be presenting analysis and arguments in your answer. This requirement is indicated by 'process' words in the question, such as 'address', 'comment on', 'describe', 'highlight', 'outline', 'identify', 'draw on', 'recommend', 'consider', 'explain', 'discuss', 'suggest', 'show' and so on. No exam question ever asks you merely to 'write all you know about …'.

- *Failing to take an objective enough stance in relation to the question.* You cannot get away with haranguing your reader with your opinions dressed up in lots of committed rhetoric. If a question asks, say, about disciplinary procedures, then you should not use your answer to vent your feelings about a recent disciplinary case in your organisation about which you feel strongly. You need to preserve a cool detachment. Throughout the exam you have to remember that your real audience is the examiner.

- *Failing to end the answer with any conclusions.* You greatly increase the impression of purposefulness and relevance in your answer if you make a point of coming back quite specifically to the question at the end of your answer and *briefly* showing how what you have said helps to answer it.

- *Failing to answer in the appropriate format.* If the question asks for a report, then an essay-style approach will lose all the marks allocated for format; in which case you will have thrown away easily gained marks.

These are all familiar points. We came across them in connection with assignment writing in Chapter 5. So there is nothing particularly new to think about here; you should simply note that exam answers, though much shorter and inevitably less polished, are judged along roughly the same lines as written assignments in terms of content and approach (but to lower levels of expectation, in recognition of the constraints).

If a question is genuinely susceptible to more than one interpretation and you cannot avoid answering it, then you should state clearly how you define it and thus how you intend to answer it. This should not be seen as an invitation to bend questions to your own wishes. That would be to fall into the trap outlined in this paragraph.

You'll find the meaning of such words considered in Chapter 5.

You have to observe the same principles of objectivity as in your written assignments (see Chapter 5).

Chapter 5 gives further advice on the difference between essay-style answers and reports.

Failing to draw on material from the course

Use your management experience to illustrate a point in relation to a course theory or idea, or indeed to indicate a reservation about its applicability in certain situations. But do recognise the possible limitations of your experience as evidence. So don't rely solely on anecdotes or on-the-spot analysis, even when you are desperate. Use material from the course.

Examiners complain that it is sometimes hard to tell whether some students have actually studied the course. In other words, these students completely forget one of the basic principles of an end-of-course exam; namely that it is set up as an opportunity to demonstrate that you have worked on and thought about the content of the course. It is essential that you treat each question as an opportunity to bring in relevant terms and ideas presented in the course. When you are arguing a point, you must back up your case by citing evidence and examples from the course.

More important than using names of authorities is to use theoretical frameworks from the course and to make them stand out. For example, 'I would analyse the job using Hackman and Oldham's model' tells the examiner little. However, an analysis of the job with the content laid out under each of the appropriate headings of 'skill variety', 'task identity', 'task significance', 'autonomy' and 'feedback' tells the examiner clearly that you know the theory, understand it and above all can *use* it.

You cannot expect to impress the examiner without showing that you know what others have said on the subject. Equally, you cannot base your answers entirely on your own experiences or those of people you happen to know. You have to be able to bring in some more generally recognised evidence, as appropriate.

Stuffing your answers full of names and facts

Use names or references only where *relevant*. Putting in a few important ones shows that you have studied the course.

You should use the course material in a discriminating manner. The exam marker is not interested in whether you can memorise a diagram or a section of a book and repeat it. He or she wants to know whether you can select useful material from all that you have come across in the course and use it to answer a specific question. To give a simple illustration, in Chapter 1 I used a force field diagram on page 5 to show the forces acting for and against Michael's success in his studies. I labelled the diagram specifically for that purpose. If you cram your answer full of facts, names and diagrams without selecting them for their relevance or explanatory power, or without placing them in the context of an argument, the marker will suspect that you don't understand the subject and are hoping that sheer memory for items of information will do as a substitute. It won't.

Using your time badly

Suppose your exam asks you to answer four questions from a three-hour paper, each of which is worth 25% of the total marks. A very common failing is to produce a very long first answer, followed by a somewhat shorter second one, a very short third, and finally a fourth which is just a paragraph and some rudimentary notes, or is even missed out entirely.

Good work on one question cannot be carried over in any general way to your overall score. It is very difficult to get more than 90% of the marks allocated to a question for your best answer. If you did manage 90% for your first answer, but followed it with 45%, 30% and 15% of the available marks because you had spent too long on your first question, your overall exam score would be 45%, no matter how brilliant your best answer – a case of the best being the enemy of the good, and a wrong strategy in the circumstances. On the other hand, if you allocated your time better and got, say, 75% of the marks for the first question, and then set about the considerably easier task of pulling the other question scores up the lower mark range, you might end up with, say, 60%, 55% and 50% on the remaining three. This would give you an overall exam score of 60% which, as you can see, is a much better result.

It is much easier to gain a solid base of marks in the lower range of the mark scale than to gain marks in the upper range, so it always makes sense to spend roughly the same amount of time on each question, *provided* they carry an equal number of marks, however weak you feel on some of them. Of course, you'll always aim to build extra marks on that solid base in the time available – but not at the expense of the easy marks to be gained on other questions. Where, however, a question on the paper carries higher marks than others, you need to allocate it an appropriate proportion of your time but no more. For instance, if the paper contains a case study or a compulsory question which is worth, say, 50% of the marks, then it's worth 50% of your time. More than this will be at the expense of the easy first marks you can accumulate on the remaining questions.

> This advice also applies to multi-part questions. You must allocate your time appropriately to each part, paying particular attention to information guiding you on the relative worth of individual sections.

Poor presentation

Finally, examiners also complain about answers which are:

- unstructured (i.e. lacking a beginning, a middle and an end) or not in the format required by a particular question
- lacking any division into paragraphs or sections
- written in note form rather than sentences where the questions did not ask for notes, and vice versa
- in illegible handwriting.

> You cannot help the generally poorer presentation of your exam answers as compared with your course assignments, but neither can the exam marker help being influenced to some extent by the relative difficulty of working out what you are trying to say, although he or she will try hard not to be.

Again, these requirements are familiar enough from your assignment writing. Obviously, it is harder for you to pay attention to presentation under exam pressures. But, equally, the exam marker's job is harder than your tutor's, as he or she has to work through a large number of scripts. No matter how well disposed the examiner may be, it is hard to do justice to an argument which is very difficult to read. It is very difficult for an examiner to keep in contact with the train of thought you might be developing if he or she has to stop continually to interpret your writing. Unlike your tutor, the script marker doesn't know you and can't draw on previous knowledge of your approach to guess what you might be intending to say, so it is all the more important to provide coherent and legible answers.

These, then, are the things examiners are likely to complain about in their reports (alongside the very pleasant and encouraging things they also say).

ACTIVITY   Now here's a chance to put yourself in the examiner's shoes for a fictional basic management course exam.

Thanks are due to Gilly Salmon for permission to adapt this material.

Read the following question and examiner's marking notes, then read the examinee's answer to the question. They have been made up specially for this Activity.

In what ways do you broadly think this student could have improved her answer, bearing in mind the marking notes and the advice given so far? You obviously do not know the detail of the student's course, and that's not the point of the Activity, but there are some general areas that you might home in on in the answer. You may wish to discuss your answer with a fellow student or make this a group activity.

The question and marking notes

'Write a report on the leadership style in your organisation. Make recommendations for improvement.'

Up to 15 marks are awarded for the analysis, 8 for recommendations and 2 for structure and presentation.

I thought I'd try to give you a broad idea of what examiner's marking notes might look like.

A very good answer (i.e. 20–25 marks) will clearly but briefly describe the leadership scenario in the organisation and analyse it using several appropriate concepts from the course (I have not listed these). Recommendations will arise directly from the analysis and be presented in the form of an action plan. For more than 20 marks, the answer will need to be concise, clear and well presented with a structured report format, references and diagrams.

A good answer (15–19 marks) will include most of the above.

A pass grade (10–14 marks) will need to show evidence of study, understanding and application of course concepts as well as the ability to make recommendations emerging from this analysis.

Fail grades (under 10 marks) will repeat material from the course without attempts to use it for analysing the real scenario, or will be mainly descriptive or anecdotal.

The student's answer

The characters and organisation in this report are fictitious.

Report to: Jonathan Greenford, Chairman
From: Gilda Santos, Manager
Date: 1.9.9X
Subject: Leadership Style

1. Introduction

Here I describe my organisation, The East London Counselling Centre (ELCC), a large voluntary organisation, for which I am a paid full-time manager. I analyse the leadership style of my Chairman and Area Manager and make recommendations for changes.

2. The Scenario

I manage one branch of the London Counselling Association, based in East London. The organisation provides a relationship and bereavement counselling service for an urban population of three-quarters of a million people. Most of our clients are self-referred or from local hospitals, doctors and social workers.

I am responsible for fund-raising and budgeting, the management of paid and voluntary staff, publicity and the office building and counselling outposts. I report on a day-to-day basis to a voluntary management committee chaired by a local businessman. My area manager is also my boss within the organisation.

We are funded by direct client donations, local council grants and a small amount of voluntary donations. We pay a tax to the national counselling service and they provide training for counsellors, library and administrative services and national media links.

3. The Chairman

JG is a local magistrate and managing director of a successful local printers. He used to be a counsellor with ELCC but became frustrated with the lack of money and poor management so took over management of the committee when no one else wanted to do it. However, he likes to keep his caring attitude and be seen as a 'player-manager'. I would consider his style to be on the left of the System 2 manager on the Likert scale, i.e. benevolent, but this sometimes means he doesn't give me help on more material matters! Although JG wants to improve management, he wants to do it by concern for people.

JG allows me a great deal of freedom and asks for support from the management committee, but this sometimes means that no decisions are taken. If he used more authority, then sometimes it would be easier for me to use resources and get things done.

4. The Area Manager

IY has been with the organisation for six years. At first he was manager of the West London Region but was soon promoted to South Area Manager with a reorganisation. He was trained in leadership as a Major in the British Army. I asked him what concepts he uses for leadership and what he described was similar to the John Adair model.

Generally, his manner is not liked by the part-time staff and counsellors at ELCC. They see him as focused too much on money, and 'cold'. He has spoken at some of our meetings and is seen as boring. However, I find he is clear in setting objectives for me and will support me if I need help. He tries to value my contributions and has secured training for me.

5. JG and IY compared

I place below both the Tannenbaum and Schmidt model and the Blake and Mouton model and indicate where I think my two leaders could be placed.

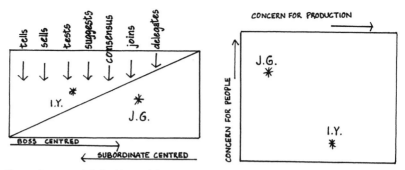

Tannenbaum and Schmidt model   Blake and Mouton model

6. Recommendations

I think JG and IY should get together and work out what contribution each has to make in managing me and ELCC. If IY were able to set objectives for the management committee then it would be easier and clearer to get things done. The different management styles could have advantages if they were properly organised.

What did you make of Gilda's answer? You were asked to consider broad issues and not worry about the detail. For me a fundamental weakness was that Gilda spent something like half the answer in describing the organisation rather than analysing the leadership style. Her answer lacked balance. She could have been more concise and ruthless in cutting unnecessary detail and anecdote. An organisation chart would have helped to clarify reporting lines to this end. She did introduce course concepts, including the diagrams she adapted. However, she did not take an opportunity to define 'leadership style' in her introduction, and she tended to 'name drop' rather than demonstrate understanding. She produced her answer in a report format as the question asked, but her recommendations were weak and diffuse, thus compounding an overall sense of vagueness in her answer. Gilda didn't do herself justice. She needs some help from this chapter!

How can you make sure that the examiners make positive comments about *your* answers? There are three areas in which you can improve your performance, by careful planning and sensible application. These are the revision process, preparing during the last day or two and sitting the exam itself. These areas are the subject of the next three sections of this chapter.

Key points

- Do answer the question set. Ensure you understand it fully before beginning to write.

- Do apply and use *relevant* course concepts in your answer.

- Do plan your time.

- Do pay attention to presentation as far as is possible under exam conditions.

4 Revising for exams

What is the point of revision?

The most important purpose of revision, as I have already said, is to pull together all the work you have done in studying the course. It serves the function of rounding off the course. While you are studying you are constantly challenging your existing ideas and throwing them into disarray. Revision is the process of tidying up the result and getting your ideas back into a usable shape. Without this period of revision, the course would just drift away from you.

The consequence of this is that revision has to be made into an active managerial process – not just a mechanical 'scanning through pages hoping something will stick'. It won't – or at least not in any meaningful way that will help you to write good exam answers. It needs to be planned in a purposeful way and to be designed around activities that are meaningful, engaging and thought-provoking, not repetitive, tedious and boring.

What kinds of things, then, are worth doing, given the strictly limited time you have available and the importance of making all your efforts count? We shall now consider some of the key strategic questions.

ACTIVITY Before reading on, try to list the key strategic issues for revising. Write them down and check them when you've read this section to see if your questions have been answered satisfactorily. If not, ask your tutor.

When should you start your revision for the exam?

There is no correct answer to this question. Basically it is something you have to work out for yourself. Some students leave it to the last fortnight, while others make a start two months before the exam; some make a point of briefly reminding themselves at intervals of key points from earlier parts of the course as a general way of consolidating their learning and making connections. This is made easier if you have taken the opportunity during your studies to use a highlighting pen on your course material, to make marginal notes and to make brief notes of key concepts at the end of major parts of the course. I personally find it helps me to round off such activities by trying to pull together my understanding in a diagram. Such materials are then readily available for building on for exam revision when the time comes. But the right time for you depends on:

- your personal commitments in addition to studying, and the time you can spare for the revision process
- your personal approach to studying – whether you are more capable of short intensive bursts of effort, or longer sustained periods
- what you are trying to get out of the course.

I'm not suggesting that you spoil the later parts of the course by being obsessed with revision. On the other hand, it is a mistake to avoid thinking about the exam until the last moment and then just hope for the best. You will get far less out of the course and you will suffer in the exam itself if you leave yourself no time for revision. It is a good idea to begin to have some thoughts about revising a couple of months before the exam, even if you don't actually start the revision itself until later. If you were just to jot down a first attempt at a plan of the last weeks of the course, sketching out how you might try to fit in some blocks of revision time alongside the normal course work, it would be a useful start. It doesn't matter if you have to revise the plan. The effort of making a tentative start on a revision plan on the back of an envelope will set in process the necessary shift in orientation as you move towards the final stages of the course.

Getting hold of old exam papers

Open Business School courses always supply students with a specimen exam paper and it is usually possible to obtain other past papers. If you are not an OBS student, can you get hold of past exam papers? Make a point of finding out how to get hold of old papers. Ask your tutor, or experienced fellow students, or, for professional and other such exams, write to the examining body.

It is an excellent idea to get hold of some old exam papers in good time in order to get a feel for the style of questions, the sort of content they cover and to use as a guide to your revision strategy. Don't worry if you feel you can't answer the questions at this stage – you haven't begun your real revision yet. But you certainly don't want to have the experience of seeing the style of the paper for the first time in the exam itself.

It is sensible to be suspicious of exams, particularly if you haven't done one for a long time. You need to find out as much as you can in advance about the nature of the exam and what is expected of you. Have you, for instance, a free choice of questions, or are you constrained by having to answer questions on specific parts of the course? Your tutor, or more experienced fellow students, will be able to give you a lot of tips and clues about how the exam process works in practice. But in order to focus your mind on the task in hand, most people find that there is no substitute for looking at past exam papers. From them you will be able to see exactly how the questions are set out on the page; how many there are; whether there are separate sections from which you have to choose questions; how much choice you have; whether any questions are compulsory; what kinds of questions are set; whether there is an obvious relationship between the structure of the exam paper and the structure of the course; whether there is a question set on each major section of the course; whether questions straddle major sections; what sort of language they employ; and so on. This information is crucial in guiding your revision strategy. Your revision time will be limited and you need to be sure you are using it wisely.

> **Note**
> Exams vary in length and in the number of questions you have to
> answer. To avoid unnecessary complications, I am going to write
> generally in terms of a three-hour exam, in which you answer four
> questions, each of which requires a report-type answer, and each of
> which carries 25% of the marks. I shall also include a case study
> variant. When you have found out the details of *your* exam, you will
> have to make the necessary adjustments to any figures I give for time
> per question, length of answers, etc.

By the time you take the real exam, you need to be very familiar with what
the paper is going to look like and to have a pretty good idea as to what
questions you are looking for on it. You cannot guarantee getting the
specific questions you want, but you should be able to form a reasonable
idea of the general areas the questions are likely to cover. You cannot afford
to waste time in an exam hesitating or changing your mind half way
through a question. One of the most important projects before an exam is
to form a clear plan of attack on the paper. Both for your general revision
strategy and for detailed planning for the exam itself, you need to make
yourself very familiar with the way the exam paper is likely to look.

Should you re-study the whole course?

Prioritise. Remember,
'must do', 'should do',
'could do' ... and by
implication, 'don't do'.

This is far too idealistic. It would take much too long, and it would be very
tedious. More importantly, it would waste all your previous work on the
course. You need to take a much more focused and more active approach as
you return to your earlier weeks of study. You need to make a careful
judgement, based on your study of past papers, your study of the course so
far and any advice you can get from your tutor about the key ideas,
concepts and areas of the course to concentrate on. Then decide exactly
where to focus your efforts.

Drawing up a detailed timetable for your revision

As I have said, exam folklore is full of legends of people leaving things to
the last few days and then studying 'around the clock'. However, as a part-
time student, possibly with further exams ahead of you in future years, a
more temperate approach is likely to serve you far better. You have to
retain a balance between the exam and your other commitments. You need
to make out a timetable of the last weeks of the course and see how many
hours, in total, you can reasonably hope to set aside. Allow a proportion of
your time for studying the last part of the course. Set aside some time for
practising exam questions, and for the final stages of drawing things
together. Then divide the remaining time into equal parts for each of the
areas of the course you are going to revise.

It is tempting to allow more time for sections of the course where you
feel particularly strong and to try to squeeze the weak areas in at the end.

However, it is best to allow equal time for each area if we assume each question carries the same number of marks. It is easy to end up with too little time for the topics which most need sorting out, or to leave no time for revising the very topics you had hoped to do best in. Fill in your timetable with a rough schedule showing how you hope to spend the time. Although you won't be able to stick to it, having some kind of plan will help you to focus on the nature and the size of the task. You can then keep adjusting your plans in the light of your monitoring of your progress.

Sorting out your course material

One of the central features of revising is getting yourself organised. Unless you have a superbly efficient filing system, you will have accumulated assorted bits of paper, notes, written assignments, handouts, photocopies of articles, and so on. Setting aside an evening to do nothing other than sort everything out is more than just 'housekeeping'. The act of putting all the material into a new, tidier form reminds you of what material you have and pushes you into thinking about the overall shape of the course and how things can be grouped together. When you can look around you and see what you have got and where, you will be in a much better position to get a clear run at a spell of revision.

Identifying the central questions at the heart of each section of the course

This is a very powerful strategy. Try to identify one or two central questions in each section of the course that you are revising, and try to write notes that answer those questions. In other words, what is this part of the course all about? What is the point of it? Sometimes an author will have identified the key questions for you. Look, for instance, at section and sub-section headings. At other times, you will have to tease them out and pose them for yourself. Similarly, the author will sometimes have made a point of drawing conclusions on the main issues for you, while at other times you will have to summarise and draw conclusions for yourself.

Don't neglect to look back over your course assignments in this process. They usually pull together some of the key areas and themes.

The process of seeking out key questions and answers to the questions will get your mind working in the way in which it needs to be working during the exam. It will alert you to the kinds of questions that *could* be asked on the course content you have been studying. It will also help you to think in terms of the broad sweeps that are needed for putting together answers that are based on the course material.

Is it worth writing new notes at this late stage in the course?

Yes, it is an excellent idea to work with a pen in your hand, creating something as you work. This gives a much more constructive feel to the task of revision and will engage your mind more effectively for long spells of work. One such way of working is as follows:

Remember, too, that you can do some of this as the course progresses.

1 Make very condensed notes from various materials that you have gathered together for revision on a particular topic.

2 Then extract the main points from these condensed notes in order to produce a single summary sheet of headings with key points, names, etc. for that topic.

3 Finally, having done this for the topics within a given section of the course, take the main headings from all the topic summary sheets and produce a single master summary sheet which outlines the main subject matter for that whole section of the course.

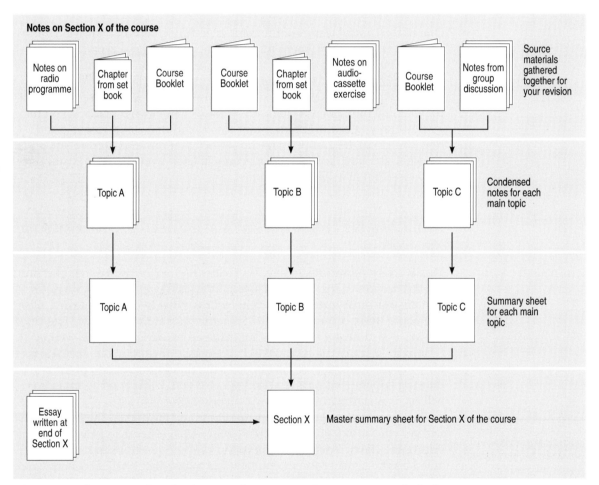

Figure 8.1 *The process of condensing notes from a range of sources on to a single sheet*

Figure 8.1 shows this method of working in the form of a diagram. However, there's no one right way. An example of one person's approach to summarising a topic from their course is shown in Figure 8.2.

The effort to condense the course down in this way, so as to extract its essentials, is particularly valuable because it converts the broad themes and the detailed discussions of the course into a form which is much more manageable for the purposes of answering questions in exams. As you know, you do not have time to write at great length in exams, so you don't

Using different coloured pens can also be a great help in organising information and making it stand out. Don't forget that section and sub-section headings in course books can be a useful organising framework.

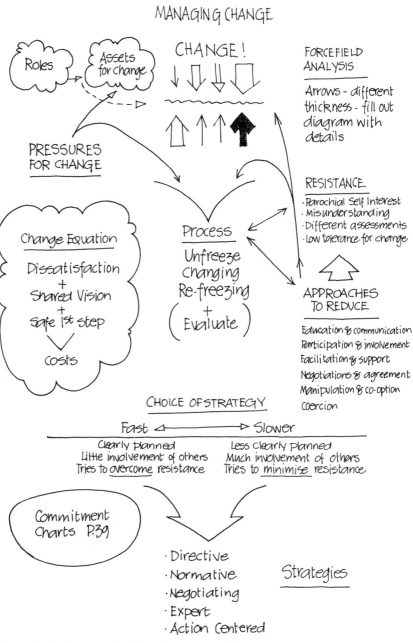

MANAGING CHANGE

CHANGE!

Roles — Assets for change

PRESSURES FOR CHANGE

FORCEFIELD ANALYSIS

Arrows - different thickness - fill out diagram with details

RESISTANCE
· Parochial self interest
· Misunderstanding
· Different assessments
· Low tolerance for change

Change Equation

Dissatisfaction
+
Shared Vision
+
Safe 1st step

Costs

Process
Unfreeze
Changing
Re-freezing
(+
Evaluate)

APPROACHES TO REDUCE

Education & communication
Participation & involvement
Facilitation & support
Negotiations & agreement
Manipulation & co-option
Coercion

CHOICE OF STRATEGY

Fast ⟵⟶ Slower

Clearly planned   Less clearly planned
Little involvement of others   Much involvement of others
Tries to overcome resistance   Tries to minimise resistance

Commitment Charts P.39

· Directive
· Normative
· Negotiating
· Expert
· Action Centered

Strategies

Thanks are due to Ian Williams for permission to use this diagram.

Figure 8.2 *An example of a topic summary sheet*

want to wade through mounds of detail in your mind trying to sift out an answer. This condensed version of the main points of the course is much closer to what you will have time to think through and write about.

What is more, when you come to answering a question on a particular section of the course in the exam, you can remind yourself of the master summary sheet or diagram, to identify what main topics are relevant to the question and remind yourself of the topic summary sheets or diagrams concerned. You scan mentally through the main items on any given topic summary sheet and select whichever are relevant. This then leads you back

The practice is rarely quite as neat as this, but at least this 'note-condensing' approach provides you with the basis for a systematic overviewing and retrieval system.

towards the condensed notes that lie behind those items on the topic summary sheet. In other words, having in your revision constructed pathways down from the basic source materials through condensed notes and topic summary sheets to a master summary sheet, such as the one illustrated in Figure 8.2, you can then, in the exam, quickly trace your way back up those pathways to locate exactly the material that is relevant to the question.

A strategy such as this gives you a well focused and absorbing task to be getting on with, rather than the aimless scanning back over old material – which will only lead to boredom. And what is more, condensed notes will supply you with just the kind of condensed version of the course that will be invaluable in the future when you want to remind yourself of what the course was about.

Finally, use the techniques you used for the Activity in the section 'Myth 4: Exams are for people with a good memory' on page 230. Test yourself before you start revising a topic to see how much you already know and to get your mind working. At the end, go back and see what progress you've been able to achieve in the session, by adding in missing data. Use these techniques for spot checks on your revision progress. You can do this mentally when waiting on the platform for a train, while doing the household chores and so on, literally thinking on your feet, and this is good practice for the exam.

Should you try answering past exam questions?

You don't need to write out a full answer every time, though the occasional timed practice at that would be useful, particularly if you are not used to handwriting an answer or if English is not your first language.

Probably the single most useful revision activity of all for most people is to attempt old exam questions. A quick exercise which you can do frequently (and which you should try to do over and over during the final stages of revision) is to rehearse the vital first few minutes of working on a question – in other words, the minutes when you examine the question carefully and sketch out rough notes for an answer. Give yourself, say, 10 minutes to produce an outline answer to a question you haven't looked at before, then look back at your notes and see what you have left out.

As you tackle each question, go through the routine of answering the following points.

Key word underlining is dealt with in Chapter 5 Section 5.

- What is the question getting at?
- Which section of the course does the question relate most directly to and to which topic(s) within that section?
- What themes, examples, evidence and ideas can I draw on from the course?
- In what way is my (or others') management experience applicable?
- What would be a good order in which to take the points (i.e. a sketched outline of the content)?

The reason this is worth doing many times is that it helps you develop the intellectual agility to do what examiners clearly want you to do, which is to answer questions precisely and to draw on relevant parts of the course in doing so. It helps you organise your knowledge in the right sort of way for the job in hand. You get used to going quickly through the processes of:

- sorting through what you know of the course material
- selecting the most relevant items for the question, and
- arranging them in a suitable order for a coherent answer.

You don't need practice at writing out full answers quite so urgently because, once you have an outline, the writing itself is pretty much the same as writing an assignment, except that you have less time. In other words, you have already practised that area of skill in your assignment writing during the course. What you have not had practice at is 'thinking on your feet' and deciding very quickly on a line to take. Our normal modes of thinking about assignment questions are too reflective and slow for an exam. You need to practise a much more nimble style to prepare yourself for the exam.

If your exam has a case study, you would be well advised to give yourself some special practice in tackling this kind of question. Unless you are provided with the case beforehand (which occasionally happens) you will have to read and analyse it on the day. Although case study questions are usually allocated more time and marks than other questions, to equate with the demands they make, you will need to work systematically and purposefully in order to achieve the best results in the time available. A plan for getting the issues and problems in the case into a manageable form before you begin writing is essential. To attempt to keep on returning to the case text as you write your answer is to invite disaster. Thus, you must practise tackling this type of question beforehand. Chapter 2, page 44 should help you.

Where your exam involves some numerically based questions, don't reject these out of hand in your practice just because you perhaps feel less comfortable with numbers than words. You may find on inspection that they are more straightforward than you think and that where there are multi-part questions, you could relatively easily begin to accumulate marks. Indeed, the longer a question is, the likelier it is to have a number of sub-sections which may mean there are some relatively straightforward marks to be picked up early on.

If you run out of questions from sample papers, you can always make up some more of your own (as I suggest below) or, better still, exchange made up questions with another student.

One of the greatest benefits of this exercise of regularly sketching out quick outlines for answers is that you begin to discover that the ground you covered early in the course soon comes back into sharp focus; you find that you have learned much more than you had realised.

Try to think up exam questions for yourself

It is an excellent exercise to try to think up questions that you could be asked in the exam. Apart from stretching your mind, this will make you step over to the examiners' side of the fence. This, in turn, helps you to develop insights into the way they are likely to think. It helps you to take a broad view of the course, looking for the important issues and the underlying themes. On the other hand, you might guess badly, so don't pin all your hopes on your own hunches.

Should you set yourself a full-scale 'mock exam'?

Don't be discouraged if the answers you produce look unimpressive compared with your course assignments. Answers produced under exam conditions are bound to be less perfect than your assignments.

If you haven't taken exams for a long time, it is obviously useful to get some practice at working on exam questions 'against the clock', particularly if you habitually use a PC or use English as a foreign language. On the other hand, you might find it hard to make the time, or find the stamina, for a full-length practice. It depends on your own abilities and inclinations as to how useful it is to spend time this way. It might be just as useful and more practical to set yourself the task of writing a single timed answer every now and then. After all, you will have the benefit of a lot more nervous energy to help you perform great feats on the exam day; this is hard to summon up in a practice session, so you may find that you underestimate your powers in an informal try-out.

Have you time to take part in other course activities during the revision period?

Make time! It is easy to develop a distorted perspective on exams during revision. You begin to think your problems are much worse than they really are, or you bias your revision too sharply in one particular direction. The best way for most people to keep a sense of proportion is to talk to other people, whether face to face or otherwise, about what they are doing. This is probably the time when contact is *most* useful. I don't want to imply that, if you prefer, or are obliged, to study on your own, your chances are necessarily poor. It's just that if you *can* get to a tutorial or a study group, or contact other students or your tutor by telephone or computer, you will probably find it will make your revision a lot easier and more pleasant. It is a mistake to think that time spent in such contact is simply time lost from revising at home. Group revision can be extremely efficient. It throws up all sorts of insights into problems and misperceptions which might otherwise remain hidden, and is very helpful if you get stuck. It helps you sort out your ideas and offers many valuable clues and tips. For instance, one group very quickly brainstormed the key course concepts, topic by topic, for their course. Much to the reassurance of all those present, the size of the revision task then looked much more reassuring when they saw that the range of key concepts and ideas was in reality quite narrow, as Figure 8.3 illustrates for one topic in their course.

Indeed, it can be very valuable, particularly if you are new to exams, to meet fairly regularly with other students, even if you are only able to meet with one other, to compare your revision strategies and your progress, to set each other questions, to comment on and criticise each other's outline answers, and to provide mutual support in general.

PEOPLE

Job design
systematic training model
appraisal & feedback
expectancy theory
Needs theories — Maslow, Alderfer
McGregor theory x/y
satisfiers/dissatisfiers Herzberg   Job design/
                                                    enrichment
Counselling/handling discipline & grievance
managing rewards communication
                          Consultation Participation
4 Cultures Power Role Task Person
     Leadership - trait, style, contingency
Adair Blake and Mouton
     Boss v. subord. centered leadership
Tannenbaum and Schmidt model
     Employee representation (Unions, etc.)

Figure 8.3 A student brainstorm on the 'People' area of their course

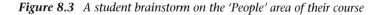

Key points

Strategies for revising for an exam

- Study *old exam papers* and specimen papers thoroughly.
- *Focus* your revision.
- Make a *timetable* for revising.
- Seek out the central *questions* in each part of the course.
- *Condense* the content of your revision into brief notes/diagrams.
- Think up *questions* you might be asked.
- Practise jotting down *outlines* for answers to questions.
- Practise *writing* out one or two answers in full against the clock.
- Check your progress at intervals.
- *Keep in touch* with other students and with your tutor to broaden your ideas and maintain contact with reality.

5 Final preparations

Is it a good idea to relax and get plenty of sleep and outdoor exercise in the day or two immediately before the exam? Perhaps you ought to get away for a short holiday? Probably for part-time students it isn't even within the bounds of possibility, given all the other demands of daily life. More importantly, it is not at all obvious that it would be good for your exam performance anyway – although in my case I couldn't perform without at least something approaching my normal sleep and exercise needs. That last day or so is when you should be gradually building yourself up to a peak of preparation. You can concentrate wonderfully when it's too late to worry about the frills. You can forget your plans for re-reading that book, or the thorough going-over you were going to give to that theory you never really understood. With all those possibilities left behind, you are in a position to concentrate all your energies on making the best job you can of marshalling what you do know.

Changes to your mental powers

The last couple of days, then, are about loading your plans and strategies into your head, going over your summary note sheets and generally getting yourself ready for action. Because the pressures build up in these final days, your mental powers will change. You will probably be less good at deep thinking tasks, such as sorting out the underlying meaning of a difficult chapter of a set book. But you will be better at working at routine things like checking over your notes, practising answering questions, or reminding yourself of your strategy for the exam. So it would be very unwise to leave basic revision to the last few days. Plan to switch your mode of work. Use these days as your polishing-up period for the exam. As with the actor at the dress rehearsal, it's too late to learn new lines or decide on a different interpretation. You just have to accept the way it is, and keep running over your material in your head, to make sure everything is in place.

Exam stress

It is possible that, as the exam draws closer, you will begin to find the tension gets on top of you. This is nothing to be ashamed of just because you are a manager. There are several varieties and levels of anxiety which can develop at exam time. You may experience a general uneasiness about the task ahead that builds up gradually over a long period until (very usefully) it provides the spur to getting down to a really intensive burst of work. This is a normal precursor to any kind of performance. What you need to do is to make sure you use this tension productively. Set yourself practical tasks in preparation for the exam so as to keep yourself busy. Remind yourself from time to time that this is your exam; you are doing it because you have chosen to, and because the tension it creates is a very productive force which will help you with some difficult learning. In other words, the ideal situation is that you learn to live with the pressures and to use them to achieve things for yourself.

Your feelings of stress may, however, develop to the extent that they spoil the last part of the course. You may find that all your thoughts become centred on the exam. In this case, you will find it useful to keep talking to other students and to your tutor. You need to share your thoughts about the exam and about your plans for tackling it. Talking to others will release tension and will help you to keep things in a realistic perspective. Your work colleagues, mentor, line manager or training manager may be useful sounding boards.

For a few students, though, particularly those who have had a previous bad experience, this is not enough and they may become very stressed. If you find this happening to you, then seek help. Some people find breathing exercises helpful, or meditation, or some other way of focusing intensively on reducing the physical manifestations of tension. If you feel bad, don't suffer in isolation and bottle up your stress. Look for help – there's no shame in seeking it just because you're a manager. It's not for nothing that stress workshops are so popular among managers!

Checking the arrangements

In fact, because you need to get so 'geared up' in the last day or two, you may become rather inattentive to the ordinary details of life. People sometimes make quite odd mistakes, like turning up for the exam on the wrong day or at the wrong place. Yes, it has happened, even to experienced managers! So it is a good idea to get all the details of the exam sorted out well in advance. You don't want to be worrying about anything trivial on the day. Mark the time very clearly on your calendar. You might even consider making a practice journey to the exam centre and finding the room, so that you don't have any last minute panics about the route, where to park, which train or bus to catch, where you left the address of the exam centre, or where the entrance to the building is. At least do a mental dry run to think of any likely hazards, such as the scheduled roadworks on the motorway that you may have forgotten about. Don't forget the elementary precaution of packing whatever you need for the exam on the previous evening – including a packet of sweets and a soft drink, if you feel the need. If your exam requires the use of a calculator, are you sure the battery won't run out at the crucial moment? Have you a reserve supply of pens and pencils? Have you all the necessary documentation?

Unlike in other circumstances, an apology for lateness won't retrieve the situation.

On the day

On the day itself, try to approach the exam calmly. Go about the normal business of getting up and starting the day in an unhurried way. Take a short stroll, perhaps, or do a few exercises, to get yourself tuned up and functioning properly. Get to the exam in good time and keep walking around if you have to wait to get into the exam centre. Don't let the other candidates disturb you. Remain aloof if you need to.

When you are in the exam room, find your desk and calmly settle yourself in. Set out whatever you have with you on the desk and check that you have everything you need. This act of 'housekeeping' is calming in

Some people feel glancing over their notes will only disturb their carefully stored ideas. Others find that a last-minute flick through their final condensed notes is reassuring.

itself. The exam room always seems a strange place, full of people you may not know, all deep in their own thoughts – but don't let the strangeness distract you. Just keep your mind ticking over. If you have prepared yourself sensibly, there is no point in worrying. In fact, once the exam has started you may find it surprisingly exhilarating and challenging. It's astonishing how much you can do in only three hours when you have keyed yourself up to a peak of mental alertness.

6 Working out your tactical plan for the exam

We need finally to consider in detail what you are going to attempt to achieve in the examination itself. You need to leave as little to chance as possible. You need to work out exactly what has to be done and exactly how you think you will tackle it. If you do, you will improve your performance enormously. So planning at every stage is vital.

ACTIVITY   What do you think are the keys to successful exam performance? Write a brief list of points. Check them after you've read this section. If there are any surprises, ask your tutor about them.

The nature of the task ahead of you

When you enter the exam, you have to be ready to work at peak efficiency. You have three hours to make the best show you can of all the work you have done during the course and during the final revision stages. You cannot afford to waste time. *You have to have a clear plan of attack for the task in front of you.* It is important that you are clear at all times about what you intend to do next.

In order to give a very practical flavour to the discussion, and for the sake of simplicity, I shall assume, as I said earlier, that you will be sitting a three-hour unseen exam in which you are asked to answer four questions, from a selection, the questions being similar in style and all carrying equal marks. I will assume also that you can take them in any order you like, that you can write any notes and jottings in the exam answer book, so long as you cross them out afterwards, and that you are allowed to have only a dictionary in the way of books.

Some exams allow you to take in course books or even notes. However, in most management exams, as you need to work fast, you need the ideas in your *head*, where you can think with them, not scattered around you in books.

As with all helpful advice, of course, it all depends on what suits you as an individual.

If your exam is different from this you need to find out how it differs and make the necessary adjustments to what I suggest below. I will, however, offer advice on two major variants, which are exams which involve a case study, and those with numerical questions.

Reading and thinking about the exam paper

The signal that the exam has started is when the invigilator tells you that you can turn the exam paper over. The general appearance of the paper should not be a surprise to you, if you have done your work on the specimen paper or past papers, but do check the instructions carefully first of all. If you are rather keyed up, you may find it difficult to take in the wording of the questions at first. So, although it might seem sensible to read carefully through the whole paper first, you may not be able to do that effectively. It may be better to do something more active to get you moving. Thus, some people find it helpful and reassuring to start jotting down a few key names, concepts, or theories on to their exam answer paper before they do anything else. It gets them going and thus reassures them that they have them to hand when needed; they put a line through them to show they are rough work and then turn to the question paper.

Certainly, it is no bad idea to scan quickly through the questions, putting ticks against possible ones and crosses against ones you definitely won't attempt. This will give you a first impression of what is on offer. But don't ponder over every question in detail. Search out the questions you are best prepared for. It is a gamble to allow yourself to be deflected from a well prepared topic on to an unprepared one, just because of the wording of the question. Don't do it! Your chosen topic may look more difficult to you simply because you know so much about it. Other questions may look easier because you don't know enough to realise their full import. Choose those questions where you can best demonstrate your knowledge and application of course ideas. You are much more likely to produce a solid answer on one of your prepared topics, even if you feel unhappy with the question.

How soon to start writing an answer

It may be a good idea to find a question you *know* you are going to attempt and begin straight away. If you are inclined to freeze up under pressure, or if your mind tends to go blank, then starting to write can be a good way to get yourself past those opening moments and into action. There is no reason to worry about starting your first question before reading the rest of the paper, if you are sure it is on one of your well prepared topics. Many people prefer to scan through the whole paper first, but if it suits you better to jump straight in, do it. However, you *will* need to think about the wording of the question and work out a basic plan before starting to write the answer proper. As with all advice, however, 'it all depends...'. It all depends on how *you* feel about the exam and also on the nature and style of the paper. You may wish to adopt a different strategy. Some people prefer to jot down a few basic ideas on a number of questions, possibly even more than is required, and *then* choose their first question. This has the advantage of allowing for further thoughts before they tackle the remaining questions and also for the selection of a balance of questions to best use the materials at their disposal.

You face a different problem if there is a compulsory question which is worth a greater number of marks than the others. I shall return to this below. But, whatever you do, remember to stick to your timetable, which must include time for planning.

The order in which to take the questions

You are usually allowed to tackle the questions in any order you like, so you may as well follow your own best interests. Some people recommend starting on your very best question, so as to build up your confidence. Others advise you to take your best question second, when you are nicely warmed up and when you are not so likely to be tempted to run wildly over your time allowance for it. In any case, it is a good idea to take your best questions earlier rather than later, to make sure that you have enough time to score well with them, to give you confidence, and to allow you to relax into your stride.

In the case of exams which have a compulsory case study worth, say, 50% of the marks with, say, two more questions to choose worth 25% each, most students prefer to tackle the case study question first. However, if, after your quick read through the paper, there is one of the 25% questions for which you are totally prepared, then by all means do that one first and safely gain those marks. But limit yourself strictly to your time budget and do the major question next. You would be most unwise to leave the latter question till last.

Examining a question

It's worth checking back to the question at intervals when you write your answer. In spite of careful planning, it's still possible to get side-tracked in the heat of the moment.

As with course work or written assignments, it is an excellent idea to underline or highlight the key words in the questions you intend to do. It makes you adopt a positive approach from the outset, and it focuses your attention on developing an answer to the precise question set, rather than producing a string of vaguely relevant information. The words you highlight are the ones you will have to think about carefully in deciding what material you can use and how to organise it. They will also help you to decide if you will need to define any key terms in your answer. If you rush into the question and make mistakes about the issues it addresses, you will seriously damage your marks.

Drawing together material to put into your answer

For some people, this may be in the form of a diagram such as a mind map.

As soon as you have highlighted the key words in the question, the next thing is just to jot down very quickly those sections of the course and topics you think are intended to be used in answering it. Don't worry at first about *how* to use them. Just write words down to reassure yourself that you have enough material to work on. You need whatever concepts, theories, examples and names you can conjure up. This is where you think back to the summary sheets you produced from your condensed notes. When you have a brief preliminary list or diagram (it may contain only five to 10 words), you can begin to sort out what to use and what to leave out.

The point to hold in mind is that exam questions are *always* asking for material from the course, so you need to write down a few headings and names from the course before you start taxing your mind with working out your plan of attack on the question. Once you are grappling with the challenge of constructing an effective answer to the question, your mind will be fully occupied. You will then be in danger of suddenly discovering that an important aspect of the argument has completely slipped from your mind. A single word is usually enough to trigger your memory and enable you to retrieve the point. Work fast and uncritically to get your list of potential material and don't hesitate to make a mess of your exam answer book. You can cross out all your jottings later.

Strike a balance between what you know and what the question asks for

The routine for tackling questions in the section entitled 'Should you try answering past exam questions?' on page 246 holds good.

As you answer a question, you have to steer a course between what you know and what the question asks for. Remember, the answer lies in the course material but you need to select what is relevant from your store of knowledge. You have to avoid the temptation to spill out all you know, disregarding what the question is specifically asking for.

What I propose is that you move back and forth between the question (or part question, where a question is divided into sections) and the knowledge stored in your mind. In this way, you can make sure that each has due influence upon the other. In other words, you choose the question and do a quick check on what it is about. Then you leave the question and go to your knowledge of the course to jot down some possible content. You then return to the question to get it more sharply focused in your mind. Then you go back to the preliminary list of course material to knock it into the shape you need. And finally, with a quick look back at the question, you start answering it in a way which brings the two together (see Figure 8.4).

Taking time to plan your answer

Appendix 8.1 shows just how brief such a plan can be.

These preparations for your answers sound all very well – but will you have time to spare for such refinements? It takes a lot of nerve to spend precious time in the exam preparing your answers. But bearing in mind the comments of examiners on undisciplined answers, it is time very well spent. Of course, you will have to carry out your preparatory activities at high speed. So how long should you spend? In the end this is something you will have to judge for yourself, but, to draw on a marketing analogy, the 20/80 rule is a reasonable target: if 20% of your effort will achieve 80% of your results, then in exam terms, you'd best devote it to planning! If you can do it efficiently in less time, then fine, but if you don't sketch out a plan, you will run the risk of 'going blank' in the middle of an answer.

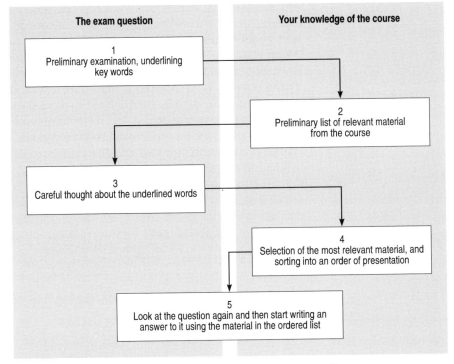

Figure 8.4 Five steps in preparing an answer to an exam question

Expressing your arguments in writing tends to absorb the whole of your attention. Then, when you get to the end of a paragraph and reach for the next point, it's gone. The argument stalls and you may find it difficult to retrace your plans. At this point you will waste far more time than writing a plan would have done or, even worse, you may repeat yourself and thus waste precious time for no extra marks. But don't go to the opposite extreme of spending so long on a detailed plan that you don't have time to answer the question. The examiner can't really give you marks for your plan, but only for your answer.

Sticking to the point

In your enthusiasm to show your knowledge of the course, don't forget the importance of keeping to the question. Check back at intervals when writing your answer, even though you've planned carefully. Of course, you must make sure to draw in plenty of material from the course, but you must always do it with a clear purpose so as to avoid appearing to be padding out your answers to conceal your ignorance. Everything you write, and that includes diagrams, should have a clear relevance to the question. Anything else is just wasting your time and the examiner's.

When to plan your later questions

When they have their first question safely out of the way, some people find it is a good idea to prepare rough plans for all of their other three answers, before writing out their second answer. The reason for this is that you need time on your side when you are planning. It is very hard to think straight in the final stages of the exam, as you become aware of the approaching deadline. You may have passed beyond the stage of thinking in a coherent way about such broad issues as the relationship of a question to the course content. On the other hand, you will probably be able to write at your fastest during the last hour of the exam, provided you know what you intend to say. So do the thinking, which requires calmer analysis, in the second quarter of the exam, when you have passed through the initial tension and have settled into a steady working mode. Then you will be in a position to take advantage of your final burst of energy in the later stages to get a great deal of useful material down.

Drawing up a time plan

With time at a premium, it is important to be realistic and think clearly about how you are going to use it. To assist with this you can draw up a plan of how, ideally, you would hope to use the time in the exam. Figure 8.5 shows one possible version.

Time

10·00 Turn over the paper and glance through it, marking the
       questions you think you might attempt   5 mins.

10·05 Start planning your first answer. Underline key words
       in the question. Jot down relevant course material.
       Return to the Question and work out a plan.   10 mins.

10·15 Start writing out your first answer   35 mins.

10·50 Finish the first answer and plan out the other 3   [ie. 3 x 8·3 mins] 25 mins.

11·15 Write out the second answer   35 mins.

11·50 Write out the third answer   35 mins.

12·25 Write out the fourth answer   35 mins.

13·00 Finish

Figure 8.5 *Sample time plan for a three-hour exam*

Some would advocate leaving time for checking through at the end, though it can be very hard to read with close concentration at this stage. And given your state of mind, there's always the possibility of altering something in haste that was, in fact, correct. This also applies to numerical questions. I suggest you do your checking as you go. It may be too late at the end of the exam.

This is, of course, a very idealised plan. You wouldn't be able to stick to it exactly. In fact, you would certainly have to modify it as you went along in the exam. Other people might suggest different allocations of time, as I have shown earlier. But it is not important whether this is the 'best' possible plan. What is important is that you draw up your own plan so that you have a clear idea of how you intend to use the time.

If you find that you are falling behind schedule as you answer a question, draw the answer to a close as quickly as you can. Don't leave the question half finished in the hope that you will have time to come back to it later. It is most likely that you won't because you are running late. But, more importantly, by then you will have lost your train of thought. Make the best of a bad job and write out whatever conclusions you can manage to draw while the question is still clear in your mind.

What to do if your time runs out

If, in spite of all your plans, you do end up with too little time for your last question, it will help to write out some notes showing how your answer would have developed if you had had time. If you present an answer entirely in note form, you are unlikely to scrape a pass on the question. But, if all else fails, notes are better than a few paragraphs which end abruptly without being developed. However, if you have part of an answer already written out, then some clearly written notes indicating where you intended to go might convince the marker that you are worthy of a reasonable mark. But it would scarcely be fair on the other candidates to allow you the benefit of the extra time you spent on the earlier questions *and* a generous benefit of the doubt on an uncompleted question. The marker will probably give you *some* credit for good notes, but basically you need to write out an answer in full to be safely in the running for a reasonable mark. So make sure you *don't* run out of time!

Presentation

If you include a diagram in your answer, don't waste time in presenting a beautifully polished, multi-colour work of art. An adequate sketch appropriately modified and labelled to suit the question is all that is needed to support the written word.

Most people write less tidily and legibly than their best in an exam. But do try to do the best you can to make your work legible. Unless instructed otherwise, start each question on a new page. Number the questions clearly. Draw a line across the page between your jottings and the answer itself and put one diagonal line through the former. If your handwriting or your command of written English is poor, it is too late to worry. You can't do much to change your basic style of expression or your handwriting at short notice. You can only work to improve them gradually over your years of study. On the other hand, try to remember your reader a little as you write and avoid being so overwhelmed by the need for speed that your writing descends to an illegible scrawl.

Special points to note with regard to exams that involve numerically based questions:

- Do show all your workings: if you get the answer wrong, the examiner cannot do other than give you no marks if you show none of your workings. You may have made a simple arithmetical error or a careless calculator input but have used a correct method of working. If you show how you arrived at your answer, you will gain the marks allocated for method of working.

- Do lay out your answer clearly. Help the examiner to follow your logic.

See the section on the dangers of calculators and computers in Chapter 7.

- Clear layout is also a way of helping yourself when it comes to checking your calculations, since people do make simple errors under pressure. Similarly, do ask yourself, as a rough check, whether your answer *looks* reasonable. Hitting the wrong button on your calculator can throw up an answer that an elementary reasonableness check would instantly throw doubt on. As a rough rule of thumb, most questions don't involve your manipulating very awkward fractions or decimals to arrive at your answer. Clear layout will help you to check your own logic easily.

Practical tips for the exam itself

- Scan through the paper finding the questions you are well prepared for.

- Start writing soon if it helps to 'unfreeze' you.

- Take your best question first or second.

- Compulsory questions that carry high marks should be tackled first or second.

- As you tackle the question:
  - Examine the wording carefully; use a highlighting pen for key words.
  - Very quickly list some relevant points from the course.
  - Move back and forth between the question and your list as you sketch an outline plan for your answer.
  - Take the time to plan your answer before you start writing.
  - Ensure what you write is relevant to the specific question asked.
  - Ensure your answers are in the required format, e.g. a report.

- Consider planning later questions in advance.

- Draw up a time plan for the exam.

- Don't run wildly over your deadlines.

- Do your best to write legibly and set numerical workings out clearly, but don't waste time on over-embellishing diagrams.

- If you do run out of time, notes are better than a few paragraphs which aren't developed.

- For numerical questions, check for elementary errors and ask yourself if the answer looks reasonable.

7 Handling stress in the exam

All the foregoing advice on planning, preparing and practising should enable you to perform effectively and efficiently in the exam. Suppose, however, in spite of all you do, you become overawed by the occasion when you are in the exam room itself. First of all, you can prepare yourself by visualising yourself beforehand in the exam room as you practise exam questions and techniques. Imagine yourself going into the exam room, laying out your kit, opening the paper and calmly beginning. You can practise this 'for real' in your own home.

This advice draws on the OU's *Open Teaching Toolkit: Revision and Examinations* compiled by Sue Cole and Pauline Harris.

Should you still experience a moment of panic or blankness in the exam room, remember the *Emergency Stop* routine:

- Say sharply, but silently, to yourself, 'STOP!'
- Breathe in and hold your breath for a moment before slowly exhaling. As you do so, relax your shoulders and hands.
- Pause for a moment, then breathe in again slowly – hold – breathe out, this time relaxing your forehead and jaw.
- Stay quiet for a few moments, then go back to what you were doing, only more slowly and smoothly.
- Say to yourself, 'My mind has gone blank, but blankness will pass. If I'm patient with myself and write down whatever comes into my head, then the information I know *will* resurface.'

Here is another basic relaxation technique adapted from the same source.

- Sit comfortably in your chair.
- Let your hands fall into your lap in a relaxed fashion with the palms facing upwards.
- Close your eyes and begin to calm your mind and breathing.
- Let your breath out; breathe in gently through your nose, feeling your abdomen rise, wait and breathe out slowly through your mouth, relaxing into the chair.
- Repeat, but on this breath feel the tension draining out of your feet.
- Work up your legs; pelvis; abdomen; chest; hands; shoulders; neck; over the top of your head and face, each time feeling the tension draining out during the exhalation. Concentrate on the feelings of heaviness.
- If your mind wanders, try repeating a simple word to yourself such as 'peace' or 'relax'; alternatively, follow the patterns on the insides of your eyelids.
- Gradually become conscious of the world around you again; continue working at a slightly slower pace.

8 Final thoughts

Now I suggest you think back over what you have read. If you are a total newcomer to exams, the advice in this long and detailed chapter may, at first reading, have been overwhelming. You may have wondered how you could possibly cope with all this *and* prepare for the exam as well. Remember, however, that most of it is really only common sense. I suggest you take a realistic view and undertake this final Activity.

ACTIVITY Take a blank sheet of paper. Check back to the first Activity in the chapter and then complete the following sentences.

The most important things for me that have emerged from reading this chapter are:

As a result I will:

Now pin this contract with yourself in a prominent place where you do your revision. It will serve as a reminder as you work towards a successful exam performance.

Finally, remember that this chapter is not one to read through once only. You will probably wish to return to it on a number of occasions, not only for your current exam, but also for future ones.

Appendix 8.1 An approach to an exam question

This question was the one I chose to tackle on the exam paper. (Don't worry if the question and the details of my notes are unfamiliar to you. The important thing to consider is my approach.)

> You have applied for promotion in your organisation and, as part of the selection process, you have been asked to write a paper on 'Leadership'. Write the paper in which you include:
>
> (a) a summary of the main theories of leadership style   (10 marks)
>
> (b) an example of **one** theory of leadership style, showing how it can be applied in practice.   (15 marks)

I first analysed the question and used a highlighting pen to emphasise the essential tasks I was expected to carry out.

I had 40 minutes to answer the question, so I allowed myself just under 10 minutes for planning. I then had 12 minutes to write Part A and 18 minutes to write Part B to reflect the distribution of marks for the two parts of the question. I got my thinking going by reminding myself first of all of the relevant parts of my course and the key concepts relevant to the question. On that basis, I knew I had the bones of an answer. I checked back to the question and reminded myself that Part A was worth 10/25 marks and thus not quite as important as Part B, which was worth 15/25 marks. I thus felt I should not get carried away with the fine detail in Part A provided I got down the main thrust of the theories. This would be a quick, mechanical process. I then developed a rough diagram (Figure 8.6) and branched out ideas as they occurred to me, because that suits my style of approach to planning answers. It would have been equally possible to make a rough list instead.

Figure 8.6 *Planning an answer*

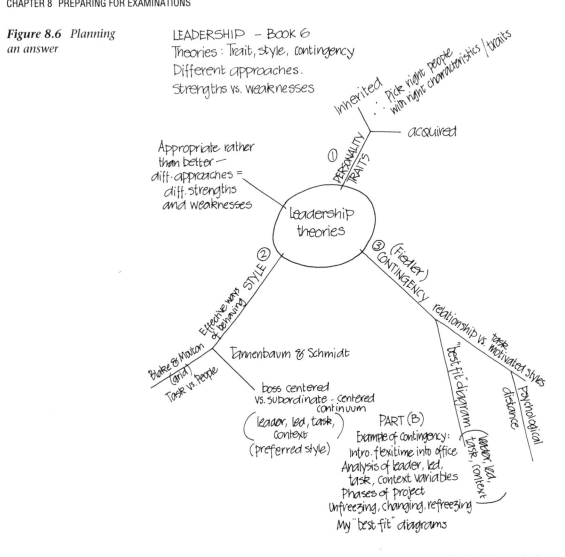

The numbers on the diagram show the order in which I intended to tackle the theories in Part A so that I could end up with Contingency Theory which would lead nicely into Part B, as I intended to use that theory in answering the latter question. My rough sketchy notes on Part B represent how I intended to tackle the question, using the *example* of introducing flexitime into the office. My brief notes tell me that I intended to *analyse* the phases of the change which this involved in terms of the concepts of the leader, the led, the task and the context, and *use* 'best fit' diagrams. I would thus be *applying* the theory in *practice* as the question asks and not merely regurgitating abstract material from Part A.

I did not write so much under this heading as I could easily remember the context. What I *had* to remember was to show how I applied the theory in practice and the triggers were there to remind me. There would have been no point in sketching out the best-fit diagrams in my notes. That would have merely wasted time. Better to do them freshly in my written answer, provided I knew what I intended to do.

So, using my notes and checking back from time to time to the question, I got on with writing my answer, keeping a strict eye on the clock.

Chapter 9 What next?

At the beginning we suggested that this book was not one to read from beginning to end, chapter by chapter. We do not therefore assume that when you come to this chapter you will have read everything in the book. You may well be about to dip into it as part of a reading strategy to get a feel for what the book is about before you select what is in it for you. On the other hand, you may have got from the book what you want and you may now be casting around for what to do next. So this chapter does not provide a conclusion, since there can be no conclusion to the development of study skills. You will never reach the stage where you can say, 'I've done it all and have no need for further effort.'

It's very easy to lose fitness for study. It's like physical training – you soon get out of condition after a long break. So don't forget to go back to parts of the book from time to time to refresh your study skills and to improve them. Thinking about this book has made us think again about our approaches on a number of occasions. It's very easy to get into a pattern of taking things for granted and to become complacent.

If, when you receive your tutor's comments on a written assignment, you think you could have done better, then that might be the time to glance through the chapter on assignment writing once more to check whether there is anything else you could have done to sharpen your approach. Whenever you take an exam, remind yourself about revision and exam techniques. When you have a mountain of reading to do, remind yourself about reading purposes and techniques.

We hope that you have not just accepted all we have said in this book. We hope that you will have added material of your own and made a note of any reservations you have, such as 'not for me' or 'not my style' against some of our suggestions. That's fine, providing you have been made to *think* about your style and approach.

During your management course you may well work on learning styles. You will probably encounter people such as Kolb, Honey and Mumford, and Kirton. You will possibly learn more about learning. We have decided not to go into learning theories here, as we wanted to give a practical, hands-on emphasis to the book. However, we hope you have been encouraged to reflect on your own approach to studying and that you are now in a better position to remove any barriers that hinder you from studying effectively.

The Activity overleaf asks you to consider yourself as a learner and to think about how you might develop further. We all study in different ways, at different times, and for different tasks. We each study using a range of strategies and approaches. You might find that at the start of a management course you study in a different way from the way in which you study at the end. It would, therefore, be an idea to photocopy the Activity below so that you can complete it at various stages in your management education. You may not be able to answer all of these questions now but you can start to think about them and return to the Activity later.

ACTIVITY

1(a) What conditions and tools are (i) essential and (ii) not essential but useful for your study (e.g. a room where you won't be disturbed, a computer)?

essential	useful

1(b) Consider your responses to 1(a). Do you have these tools and can you study in these conditions? If not, what could you do about it?

2(a) Think about times for studying. When do you work best – for example, before or after work, in the mornings or late at night? Do different study activities incline you to work at different times? For example, I read best in the evening and write best in the morning. How long do you spend at any one period of study? Again, does this depend on the task?

2(b) Do you find it easier to tackle difficult study activities at particular times? If so, note these below.

2(c) How long can you study for without losing concentration or suffering a deterioration in your performance? If it's different for different tasks, note these differences below.

3(a) What motivates you to study?

3(b) Can you think of any ways in which you are able to maintain your motivation if it seems to be dwindling?

4(a) How do your family, friends or colleagues contribute towards your studying? List their contributions below.

4(b) Can this support be developed further?

5(a) How do your family, friends or colleagues make studying difficult (if they do)?

5(b) If you have written an answer to 5(a), can you think of ways in which you could improve things?

Tutor comments on your
written work and
appraisal reviews at work
may help you here.

6(a) How good are you at relating your study of management to your
      work?

6(b) How, if at all, could you improve your relating of management study
      to your work?

7(a) Are you relating your study of management to other aspects of your
      work and life?

7(b) How could you improve or extend this?

8   Do you question what you study or do you sometimes just accept it?
      If you sometimes just accept it, how could you get more involved
      with what you are studying?

9   Do you ever finish reading something and realise you haven't really
      taken anything in?

      Are there any particular times when this happens?

      If so, what could you do about it?

10(a) How do you assess the worth and validity of new knowledge? What tools do you use to make this assessment?

10(b) Is there any way in which you can develop your ability to be constructively critical of theories and new ideas?

11(a) What are your weaknesses as a student?

11(b) What can you do about anything you have listed above?

12   What are your strengths as a student?

13   Can your strengths help you to overcome any weaknesses (if you listed any weaknesses in Question 11)?

'Learning as such is a continuously rotating wheel of four quadrants: questions – ideas – tests – reflections. This process lies at the heart of individual growth and of corporate success.'
Charles Handy,
European Foundation for Management Development (efmd) Forum 93/1, page 13.

You may have completely ignored some of the chapters in this book – that's fine and it's what we would expect. However, keep the contents of the book in mind as you progress through your course. It may be that a quick look at, for example, Chapter 7 on numbers would be useful if you find you are not interpreting numerical data very well or if you realise you are ignoring such data. Similarly, if you are using English as a first language you may well have ignored Chapter 6. However, if you are working or studying with colleagues using English as a second or foreign language, you might gain something from looking at the chapter written with them in mind. Moreover, you might like more practice in time management or in reading activities. If so, look at Chapter 6.

If you've worked through the relevant chapters and Activities in this book, you should now be more aware of study strategies that you can use to help you. However, don't put this book away and think you've 'done it'! Keep it handy, add your own notes to it and use it as a reference source during your course.

One area we have not touched on, because it seemed to us beyond the scope of this book, is that of the Accreditation of Prior Learning (APL) and the development of evidence such as a management portfolio. If this is something which interests you, then the Open University for instance offers a route to NVQ Levels 4 and 5.

What next? You may well wish to study for a further qualification, such as an MBA or eventually for a doctorate. You may wish to carry out business research, whether for a qualification or for internal organisation purposes. For any of these purposes you will need more specialist books than this one. What you can be sure of, however, is that they will build on the skills you have developed from using this book. None of your work will have been in vain.

We welcome any thoughts or observations you have on this book. Please send your comments to us at the Open Business School, The Open University, Walton Hall, Milton Keynes MK7 6AA, United Kingdom.

Finally, we offer our good wishes for your success in your studies. We hope this book will make a real contribution and that you will feel confident about getting in control of your learning and staying in control of it. Never forget that good study management is an integral part of good management education.

Reading appendix 1

As you will see the paragraphs in these Appendices are numbered. It is often a good idea to do this with texts you are using.

Successful versus effective real managers

by Fred Luthans, Professor of Management, University of Nebraska

1 What do *successful* managers – those who have been promoted relatively quickly – have in common with *effective* managers – those who have satisfied, committed subordinates and high performing units? Surprisingly, the answer seems to be that they have little in common. Successful managers in what we define as 'real organisations' – large and small mainstream organisations, mostly in the mushrooming service industry in middle America – are not engaged in the same day-to-day activities as effective managers in these organisations. This is probably the most important, and certainly the most intriguing, finding of a comprehensive four-year observational study of managerial work that is reported in a recent book by myself and two colleagues, titled *Real Managers*[1].

2 The startling finding that there is a difference between successful and effective managers may merely confirm for many cynics and 'passed over' managers something they have suspected for years. They believe that although managers who are successful (that is, rapidly promoted) may be astute politicians, they are not necessarily effective. Indeed, the so-called successful managers may be the ones who do not in fact take care of people and get high performance from their units.

3 Could this finding explain some of the performance problems facing American organisations today? Could it be that the successful managers, the politically savvy ones who are being rapidly promoted into responsible positions, may not be the effective managers, the ones with satisfied, committed subordinates turning out quantity and quality performance in their units?

4 This article explores the heretofore assumed equivalence of 'successful managers' and 'effective managers'. Instead of looking for sophisticated technical or governmental approaches to the performance problems facing today's organisations, the solution may be as simple as promoting effective managers and learning how they carry out their jobs. Maybe it is time to turn to the real managers themselves for some answers.

5 And who are these managers? They are found at all levels and in all types of organisations with titles such as department head, general manager, store manager, marketing manager, office manager, agency chief, or district manager. In other words, maybe the answers to the performance problems facing organisations today can be found in their own backyards, in the managers themselves in their day-to-day activities.

The current view of managerial work

Through the years management has been defined, as the famous French administrator and writer Henri Fayol said, by the functions of planning, organising, commanding, coordinating, and controlling. Only recently has this classical view of managers been challenged.[2] Starting with the landmark work of Henry Mintzberg, observational studies of managerial work have found that the normative functions do not hold up. Mintzberg charged that Fayol and others' classical view of what managers do was merely 'folklore'.[3]

On the basis of his observations of five CEOs and their mail, Mintzberg concluded that the manager's job consisted of many brief and disjointed episodes with people inside and outside the organisation. He discounted notions such as reflective planning. Instead of the five Fayolian functions of management, Mintzberg portrayed managers in terms of a typology of roles. He formulated three interpersonal roles (figurehead, leader, and liaison); three informational roles (monitor or nerve centre, disseminator, and spokesman); and four decision-making roles (entrepreneur, disturbance handler, resource allocator, and negotiator). Although Mintzberg based this view of managers on only the five managers he observed and his search of the literature, he did ask, and at least gave the beginning of an answer to, the question of what managers really do.

The best known other modern view of managerial work is provided by John Kotter. His description of managers is based on his study of 15 successful general managers. Like Mintzberg, Kotter challenged the traditional view by concluding that managers do not so simply perform the Fayolian functions, but rather spend most of their time interacting with others. In particular, he found his general managers spent considerable time in meetings getting and giving information. Kotter refers to these get-togethers as 'network building'. Networking accomplishes what Kotter calls a manager's 'agenda' – the loosely connected goals and plans addressing the manager's responsibilities. By obtaining relevant and needed information from his or her networks, the effective general manager is able to implement his or her agenda. Like Mintzberg, Kotter's conclusions are based on managerial work from a small sample of elite managers. Nevertheless, his work represents a progressive step in answering the question of what managers do.

Determining what real managers do

The next step in discovering the true nature of managerial work called for a larger sample that would allow more meaningful generalisations. With a grant from the Office of Naval Research, we embarked on such an effort.[4] We used trained observers to freely observe and record in detail the behaviours and activities of 44 'real' managers.[5] Unlike Mintzberg's and Kotter's managers, these managers came from all levels and many types of organisations (mostly in the service sector – such as retail stores, hospitals, corporate headquarters, a railroad, government agencies, insurance companies, a newspaper office, financial institutions, and a few manufacturing companies).

Exhibit 1

The Activities of Real Managers

**Descriptive Categories
Derived from Free Observation**

**Real Managers'
Activities**

Exchanging Information

Paperwork

Communication

Planning

Decision Making

Controlling

Traditional Management

Interacting with Outsiders

Socializing/Politicking

Networking

Motivating/Reinforcing

Disciplining/Punishing

Managing Conflict

Staffing

Training/Developing

Human Resource Management

10

11

We reduced the voluminous data gathered from the free observation logs into managerial activity categories using the Delphi technique. Delphi was developed and used during the heyday of Rand Corporation's 'Think Tank'. A panel offers independent input and then the panel members are given composite feedback. After several iterations of this process, the data were reduced into the 12 descriptive behavioural categories shown in Exhibit 1. These empirically derived behavioural descriptors were then conceptually collapsed into the four managerial activities of real managers:

1 *Communication.* This activity consists of exchanging routine information and processing paperwork. Its observed behaviours include answering procedural questions, receiving and disseminating requested information, conveying the results of meetings, giving or receiving routine information over the phone, processing mail, reading reports, writing reports/memos/letters, routine financial reporting and bookkeeping, and general desk work.

12

2 *Traditional management.* This activity consists of planning, decision making, and controlling. Its observed behaviours include setting goals and objectives, defining tasks to accomplish goals, scheduling employees, assigning tasks, providing routine instructions, defining problems, handling day-to-day operational crises, deciding what to do, developing new procedures, inspecting work, walking around inspecting the work, monitoring performance data, and doing preventive maintenance.

13

3 *Human Resource Management.* This activity contains the most behavioural categories: motivating/reinforcing, disciplining/punishing, managing conflict, staffing, and training/developing. The disciplining/punishing category was subsequently dropped from the analysis because it was not generally permitted to be observed. The observed behaviours for this activity include allocating formal rewards, asking for input, conveying appreciation, giving credit where due, listening to suggestions, giving positive feedback, group support, resolving conflict between subordinates, appealing to higher authorities or third parties to resolve a dispute, developing job descriptions, reviewing applications, interviewing applicants, filling in where needed, orienting employees, arranging for training, clarifying roles, coaching, mentoring, and walking subordinates through a task.

14

4 *Networking.* This activity consists of socialising/politicking and interacting with outsiders. The observed behaviours associated with this activity include non-work-related 'chit chat'; informal joking around; discussing rumours, hearsay and the grapevine; complaining, griping and putting others down; politicking and gamesmanship; dealing with customers, suppliers and vendors; attending external meetings; and doing/attending community service events.

15

These four activities are what real managers do. They include some of the classic notions of Fayol (the traditional management activities) as well as the more recent views of Mintzberg (the communication activities) and Kotter (the networking activities). As a whole, however, especially with the inclusion of human resource management activities, this view of real managers' activities is more comprehensive than previous sets of managerial work.

16

After the nature of managerial activity was determined through the free observation of the 44 managers, the next phase of the study was to document the relative frequency of these activities. Data on another set of 248 real managers (not the 44 used in the initial portion of this study) were gathered. Trained participation observers filled out a checklist based on the managerial activities at a random time once every hour over a two-week period. We found that the real managers spend not quite a third of their time and effort in communication activities, about a third in traditional management activities, a fifth in human resource management activities, and about a fifth in networking activities. This relative frequency analysis based on observational data of a large sample provides a more definitive answer to the question of what real managers do than the normative classical functions and the limited sample of elite managers used by Mintzberg and Kotter.

How the difference between successful and effective real managers was determined

Discovering the true nature of managerial work by exploding some of the myths of the past and extending the work of Mintzberg and Kotter undoubtedly contributes to our knowledge of management. However, of more critical importance in trying to understand and find solutions to our current performance problems is singling out successful and effective managers to see what they really do in their day-to-day activities. The successful-versus-effective phase of our real managers study consisted of analysing the existing data based on the frequencies of the observed activities of the real managers. We did not start off with any preconceived notions or hypotheses concerning the relationships between successful and effective managers. In fact, making such a distinction seemed like 'splitting hairs' because the two words are so often used interchangeably. Nevertheless, we decided to define success operationally in terms of the speed of promotion within an organisation. We determined a success index on a sample of the real manager's level in his or her organisation by his or her tenure (length of service) there.[6] Thus, a manager at the fourth level of management, who has been with his or her organisation for five years, would be rated more successful than a manager at the third level who has been there for 25 years. Obviously, there are some potential problems with such a measure of success, but for our large sample of managers this was an objective measure that could be obtained.

The definition and measurement of effectiveness is even more elusive. The vast literature on managerial effectiveness offered little agreement on criteria or measures. To overcome as many of the obstacles and disagreements as possible, we used a combined effectiveness index for a sample of the real managers in our study that represented the two major – and generally agreed upon – criteria of both management theory/research and practice: (1) getting the job done through high quantity and quality standards of performance, and (2) getting the job done through *people*, which requires their satisfaction and commitment.[7]

We obviously would have liked to use 'hard measures' of effectiveness such as profits and quantity/quality of output or service, but again, because we were working with large samples of real managers from widely diverse jobs and organisations, this was not possible.

What do successful real managers do?

To answer the question of what successful real managers do, we conducted several types of analyses – statistical (using multiple regression techniques), simple descriptive comparisons (for example, top third of managers as measured by the success index vs. bottom third), and relative strength of correlational relationships.[8] In all of these analyses, the importance that networking played in real manager success was very apparent. Of the four real manager activities, only networking had a statistically significant relationship with success. In the comparative analysis we found that the most successful (top third) real managers were doing considerably more networking and slightly more routine communication than their least

17

18

19

20

successful (bottom third) counterparts. From the relative strength of relationship analysis we found that networking makes the biggest relative contribution to manager success and, importantly, human resource management activities makes the least relative contribution.

21 What does this mean? It means that in this study of real managers, using speed of promotion as the measure of success, it was found that successful real managers spent relatively more time and effort socialising, politicking, and interacting with outsiders than did their less successful counterparts. Perhaps equally important, the successful real managers did not give much time or attention to the traditional management activities of planning, decision making, and controlling or to the human resource management activities of motivating/reinforcing, staffing, training/developing, and managing conflict. A representative example of this profile would be the following manager's prescription for success:

> 'I find that the way to get ahead around here is to be friendly with the right people, both inside and outside the firm. They get tired of always talking shop, so I find a common interest – with some it's sports, with others it's our kids – and interact with them on that level. The other formal stuff around the office is important but I really work at this informal side and have found it pays off when promotion time rolls around.'

22 In other words, for this manager and for a significant number of those real managers we studied, networking seems to be the key to success.

What do effective real managers do?

23 Once we answered the question of what successful managers do, we turned to the even more important question of what effective managers do. It should be emphasised once again that, in gathering our observational data for the study, we made no assumptions that the successful real managers were (or were not) the effective managers. Our participant observers were blind to the research questions and we had no hypothesis concerning the relationship between successful and effective managers.

24 We used the relative strength of correlational relationship between the real managers' effectiveness index and their directly observed day-to-day activities and found that communication and human resource management activities made by far the largest relative contribution to real managers' effectiveness and that traditional management and – especially – networking made by far the least relative contribution.[9]

25 These results mean that if effectiveness is defined as the perceived quantity and quality of the performance of a manager's unit and his or her subordinates' satisfaction and commitment, then the biggest relative contribution to real manager effectiveness comes from the human oriented activities – communication and human resource management. A representative example of this effectiveness profile is found in the following manager's comments:

> 'Both how much and how well things get done around here, as well as keeping my people loyal and happy, has to do with keeping them informed and involved. If I make a change in procedure or the guys

upstairs give us a new process or piece of equipment to work with, I get my people's input and give them a full story before I lay it on them. Then I make sure they have the proper training and give them feedback on how they are doing. When they screw up, I let them know it, but when they do a good job, I let them know about that too.'

26

This manager, like our study of real managers in general, found that the biggest contribution to effectiveness came from communicating and human resource management activities.

Equally important, however, was the finding that the least relative contribution to real managers' effectiveness came from the networking activity. This, of course, is in stark contrast to our results of the successful real manager analysis. Networking activity had by far the strongest relative relationship to success, but the weakest with effectiveness. On the other hand, human resource management activity had a strong relationship to effectiveness (second only to communication activity), but had the weakest relative relationship to success. In other words, the successful real managers do not do the same activities as the effective real managers (in fact, they do almost the opposite). These contrasting profiles may have significant implications for understanding the current performance problems facing American organisations. However, before we look at these implications and suggest some solutions, let's take a look at those real managers who are both successful *and* effective.

27

What do managers who are both successful and effective do?

The most obvious concluding question is what those who were found to be both successful and effective really do. This 'combination' real manager, of course, is the ideal – and has been *assumed* to exist in American management over the years.

28

Since there was such a difference between successful and effective managers in our study, we naturally found relatively few (less than 10% of our sample) that were both among the top third of successful managers and the top third of effective managers. Not surprisingly, upon examining this special group, we found that their activities were very similar to real managers as a whole. They were not like either the successful or effective real managers. Rather, it seems that real managers who are both successful and effective use a fairly balanced approach in terms of their activities. In other words, real managers who can strike the delicate balance between all four managerial activities may be able to get ahead as well as get the job done.

29

Important is the fact that we found so few real managers who were both successful and effective. This supports our findings on the difference between successful and effective real managers, but limits any generalisations that can be made about successful and effective managers. It seems that more important in explaining our organisations' present performance problems, and what to do about them, are the implications of the wide disparity between successful and effective real managers.

30

Implications of the successful versus effective real managers findings

31   If, as our study indicates, there is indeed a difference between successful and effective real managers, what does it mean and what should we do about it? First of all, we need to pay more attention to formal reward systems to ensure that effective managers are promoted. Second, we must learn how effective managers do their day-to-day jobs.

32   The traditional assumption holds that promotions are based on performance. This is what the formal personnel policies say, this is what new management trainees are told and this is what every management textbook states *should* happen. On the other hand, more 'hardened' (or perhaps more realistic) members and observers of *real* organisations (not textbook organisations or those featured in the latest best sellers or videotapes) have long suspected that social and political skills are the real key to getting ahead, to being *successful*. Our study lends support to the latter view.

33   The solution is obvious, but may be virtually impossible to implement, at least in the short run. Tying formal rewards – especially promotions – to performance is a must if organisations are going to move ahead and become more productive. At a minimum, and most pragmatically in the short run, organisations must move to a performance-based appraisal system. Managers who are *effective* should be *promoted*. In the long run organisations must develop cultural values that support and reward effective performance, not just successful socialising and politicking. This goes hand-in-hand with the current attention given to corporate culture and how to change it. An appropriate goal for cultural change in today's organisations might simply be to make effective managers successful.

34   Besides the implications for performance-based appraisals and organisational culture that came out of the findings of our study is a lesson that we can learn from the effective real managers themselves. This lesson is the importance they give and effort they devote to the human-oriented activities of communicating and human resource management. How human resources are managed – keeping them informed, communicating with them, paying attention to them, reinforcing them, resolving their conflicts, training/developing them – all contribute directly to managerial effectiveness.

35   The disparity our study found between successful and effective real managers has important implications for the performance problems facing today's organisations. While we must move ahead on all fronts in our search for solutions to these problems, we believe the activities basic to the effective real managers in our study – communication and human resource management – deserve special attention.

Endnotes

1 The full reference for the book is Fred Luthans, Richard M. Hodgetts, and Stuart Rosenkrantz, *Real Managers*, Cambridge, MA: Ballinger, 1988. Some of the preliminary material from the real managers study was also included in the presidential speech given by Fred Luthans at the 1986 Academy of Management meeting. Appreciation is extended to the co-authors of the book, Stu Rosenkrantz and Dick Hodgetts, to Diane Lee Lockwood on the first phase of the study, and to Avis Johnson, Hank Hennessey and Lew Taylor on later phases. These individuals, especially Stu Rosenkrantz, contributed ideas and work on the backup for this article.

2 The two most widely recognised challenges to the traditional view of management have come from Henry Mintzberg, *The Nature of Managerial Work*, New York: Harper & Row, 1973; and John Kotter, *The General Managers*, New York: Free Press, 1982. In addition, two recent comprehensive reviews of the nature of managerial work can be found in the following references: Colin P. Hales, 'What Do Managers Do? A Critical Review of the Evidence', *Journal of Management Studies*, 1986, 23, pp. 88–115; and Stephen J. Carroll and Dennis J. Gillen, 'Are the Classical Management Functions Useful in Describing Managerial Work?', *Academy of Management Review*, 1987, 12, pp. 38–51.

3 See Henry Mintzberg's article, 'The Manager's Job: Folklore and Fact', *Harvard Business Review*, July–August 1975, 53, pp. 49–61.

4 For those interested in the specific details of the background study, see Luthans, Hodgetts and Rosenkrantz (Endnote 1 above).

5 The source that details the derivation, training of observers, procedures, and reliability and validity analysis of the observation system used in the real managers study is Fred Luthans and Diane L. Lockwood's 'Toward an Observation System for Measuring Leader Behavior in Natural Settings', in J. Hunt, D. Hosking, C. Schriesheim, and R. Stewart (Eds.) *Leaders and Managers: International Perspectives of Managerial Behavior and Leadership*, New York: Pergamon Press, 1984, pp. 117–141.

6 For more background on the success portion of the study and the formula used to calculate the success index see Fred Luthans, Stuart Rosenkrantz, and Harry Hennessey, 'What Do Successful Managers Really Do? An Observational Study of Managerial Activities', *Journal of Applied Behavioral Science*, 1985, 21, pp. 255–270.

7 The questionnaire used to measure the real managers' unit quantity and quality of performance was drawn from Paul E. Mott's *The Characteristics of Effective Organizations*, New York: Harper & Row, 1972. Subordinate satisfaction was measured by the Job Diagnostic Index found in P. C. Smith, L. M. Kendall, and C. L. Hulin's *The Measurement of Satisfaction in Work and Retirement*, Chicago: Rand-McNally, 1969. Subordinate commitment is measured by the questionnaire in Richard T. Mowday, L. W. Porter, and Richard M. Steers' *Employee–Organizational Linkages: The Psychology of Commitment, Absenteeism, and Turnover*, New York: Academic Press, 1982. These three standardised questionnaires are widely used research instruments with considerable psychometric back-up and high reliability in the sample used in our study.

8 For the details of the multiple regression analysis and simple descriptive comparisons of successful versus unsuccessful managers, see Endnote 6 above. To determine the relative contribution the activities identified in Exhibit 1 made to success, we calculated the mean of the squared correlations (to approximate variance explained) between the observed activities of the real managers and the success index calculated for each target manager. These correlation squared means were then rank ordered to obtain the relative strengths of the managerial activities' contribution to success.

9 The calculation for the relative contribution the activities made to effectiveness was done as described for success in Endnote 8. The statistical and top third–bottom third comparison that was done in the success analysis was not done in the effectiveness analysis. For comparison of successful managers and effective managers, the relative strength of relationship was used; see *Real Managers* (Endnote 1 above) for details.

Fred Luthans is the George Holmes University Distinguished Professor of Management at the University of Nebraska. His major books include *Organizational Behavior* (McGraw-Hill), now going into its 5th edition; *Organization Behavior Modification and Beyond* (Scott Foresman), which won the annual ASPA award for outstanding contribution to human resource management; and *Social Issues in Business* (Macmillan), currently in its 5th edition. His most recent book, coauthored with Dick Hodgetts and Stu Rosenkrantz, is *Real Managers* (Ballinger), upon which this article is drawn. A consulting coeditor for the McGraw-Hill Management Series, Professor Luthans is also on the editorial boards for a number of journals and is currently an associate editor of *Decision Sciences Journal*. He is a past president of the Academy of Management and a fellow of both the Academy of Management and the Decision Sciences Institute. He has been an active consultant over the years to business and government both in the United States and abroad. His major consulting work at present is with Wal-Mart Corporation.

Reading appendix 2

Germanity – reflections on a people

by Susan Stern, Lecturer in Applied Linguistics, Frankfurt University

1   Next stop Germany. You don't know the country well (maybe not at all or only through books) and the Germans you have met so far haven't been on their own home turf. You wonder what they're like, the Germans – really like, that is, beyond the handshake and the smile (or is it no handshake and a nod, or a click of the heels and a bow?) Certainly, as someone planning to visit the country as more than a tourist in transit, you will have to do some homework. That means learn the language, you may think, and that, most definitely, is a worthy goal. However, acquiring a language (and especially German, as Mark Twain and others have discovered) is a long-term project, and you can't wait forever to move into the German market.

2   Assume, therefore, that the language barrier can be overcome, either because the Germans you will be talking to can speak your language (or English as a lingua franca) or because you can rely on translators and interpreters. Unfortunately, getting round the language problem doesn't get you all that far. Until you have got to know the people and figured out what makes them tick, your communication remains superficial and rudimentary. You are in a position to exchange words, but not to interact effectively. Operating on unknown territory with unknown rules puts you at a distinct disadvantage.

3   ... Perhaps you will address a German business associate by his first name, put your arm around his shoulders or slap him on the back in a fit of camaraderie; perhaps you will call him at home in the evening, or worse, drop by unexpectedly; perhaps you will walk into his office without an appointment, change dates on him, cancel a meeting at short notice. Perhaps, to simplify what seem like unnecessarily complicated procedures, you will cut through red tape and avoid proper procedures (of which you may not even be aware); perhaps you will praise or complain too much or too little or in the wrong way. You won't intend to insult or irritate; more often than not, you will simply be operating on the unconscious assumption that what works at home must work in Germany too. Although you can expect many Germans, especially the better-travelled ones, to make allowances for foreign behaviour (yours), you may still end up with an atmosphere that is slightly off. And possibly, a lost opportunity.

Germanity

4   Who are the Germans and what makes them tick? Experts write volumes on the subject, and just about everybody else seems to have some wisdom to contribute, more often than not unflattering. Misunderstood maybe, the

Germans are definitely much maligned, especially by those who don't know them.

Which of us has not heard at some time or another that the Germans are … aggressive, pedantic, assertive, stiff, unapproachable, humourless, full of angst? Even normally positive attributes such as 'efficient' and 'punctual' can quiver with negative connotations when applied to the Germans. A good number of the clichés in circulation can be written off to fear or envy (or both), and in view of the bellicose history of the Germans in the first part of this century, and the almost indecent prosperity of (West) Germany in the second part, this is perhaps not too surprising. But clichés they still are, and stereotypical Germans are of no practical use whatsoever.

What we need is a succinct portrait of a nation, one that captures its spirit, gives us an objective body of information which is concrete enough to be meaningful and yet broad enough to apply to one and all of its 80 million population, and which (above all) provides sufficient insight into the nature of the people to understand and predict their behaviour patterns. In short – we are searching for the core of Germanity.

Different – but the same

Does Germanity exist? Is it possible to lump all Germans together and make global statements about them? The best answer is probably the German *jein* – a mixture of *ja* (yes) and *nein* (no). To start with the latter: although Germany is neither a melting pot of different cultures and ethnic groups (like the former United States), nor a composite of groups arbitrarily united by political boundaries (like the former Soviet Union), it still does not have a homogeneous population.

This is hardly surprising given the fact that what we call Germany has always been a collection of states (in the past principalities, in more recent times, federal states). That every region and community thinks itself unique may raise a smile; but there is some basis to the widespread belief (on the part of most Germans themselves) that northern and southern Germans differ in everything from temperament to taste and that eastern and western Germans have scarcely more in common than their language (and wags have it that not even this is the case).

That said, and with all the reservations I have mentioned above, I still assert: Germanity exists. Quite simply, the Germans (homogeneous or not) differ from the Egyptians, the Chinese or the Italians. Something shared makes them (and the others) what they are and distinguishes them from the rest. And it is entirely possible to make intelligent comments about so-called typical German characteristics without falling back on cliché and prejudice; that is, to isolate, describe, explain a number of attitudes and behaviour patterns which most Germans have in common.

The key to this identification and interpretation process lies in cultural analysis. Some 10 years ago, the American anthropologists Edward T. Hall and Mildred Hall had a great success with their handbook *Hidden Differences* on how to communicate with the Germans, then published by the German magazine *Stern*. With their concepts of time, space and information-flow they have delved deep into the core of what I call Germanity. Let me therefore follow their lines.

Linear time

German punctuality is the stuff that jokes are made of. Is it a fixed idea or is there something to it? Insofar as punctuality reflects a very basic (learnt) attitude towards time, it can be seen as part of cultural programming and thereby take on new meaning. The Germans as a whole are highly time-oriented. They like to make schedules, which they then hold fast to; they tend to divide up and compartmentalise their time and go about one thing after another in sequence; they work by the clock and don't like to be interrupted; they keep track of time, they respect it by being in time and on time (thereby saving time as opposed to wasting it).

A culture which organises itself in such a way around linear or chronological time, which proceeds steadfastly along a timeline, can be called monochronic. Most northern European countries as well as the United States are basically monochronic (M-time) cultures and differ from one another primarily in degree.

By contrast, Mediterranean and Middle East countries are polychronic (P-time cultures); to these cultures, time is a quality which swirls rather than flows and because time is non-linear, actions tend to be performed spontaneously or simultaneously – at any rate, not according to a pre-planned linear schedule.

The importance of time does not lie in keeping it religiously (being on time); appointments may be made, but they are not taken too seriously. Time appears to be more plentiful in P-time cultures than in M-time cultures, and the notion of wasting time does not really exist.

Obviously, interaction between unenlightened M-time culture and P-time culture people can cause major frustrations and headaches on both sides. Both groups consider their way of going about things to be 'the right way' and anybody who does things differently is 'acting badly', 'breaking the rules', 'wrong'.

Even among people who belong to the same time culture, problems can arise. Both the British and the Germans are monochronic, but their notion of punctuality, for example, is not identical. An invitation to dinner at 8 will mean between 8.15 and 8.30 to the former and the dot of 8 to the latter. To say that the Germans are more punctual than the British would, however, be wrong. They are differently punctual.

Encapsulated space

Thus, to consider a culture in terms of its attitude towards time can have practical value; it gives the outsider a point of orientation. In the same way, attitude towards space (both literal and figurative) provides important clues to national behaviour.

Not surprisingly, attitude to space correlates closely with attitude towards time. The Germans, especially northerners, place great value on space. They need both physical and psychological room, no matter how limited that room may be. This translates in practical terms into an overall need for privacy. Germans as a rule dislike being crowded or jostled (physically or psychologically), they are uncomfortable under scrutiny. As a result, they tend to keep to themselves and make sure their doors (again, literally and figuratively) remain closed. They compartmentalise their lives in space as well as time; their activities are encapsulated, their work and home lives are usually kept strictly separate, their colleagues are rarely family friends.

19   All of this ties in with their need to work to the clock, keep schedules, move along the timeline with as few interruptions as possible. The overall result is the orderly and efficient work ethic the Germans are famous for.

Refined information

Since the Germans keep to themselves and lead a compartmentalised life, they tend to be cut off from the kind of information networks which would be available to them if they mixed more freely, worked with open doors, rubbed shoulders in the marketplace (so to speak). Information does not flow freely or easily in German society; information channels are narrow and well regulated. Germany is a low-context culture: lacking information surrounding an event, in any particular situation the Germans require highly detailed, refined information.

21   This need can easily give the impression that they are pedantic and irritatingly thorough, especially to someone from a high-context culture who already has the information (through the grapevine, forum, old boys' network) and doesn't need such meticulous filling-in. Turned around, the high-context person will not get through to his German associate unless he goes into what he himself might consider to be unnecessary detail.

22   I mentioned earlier on that the kind of information we need to get to the core of Germanity should enable us to understand and predict behaviour patterns. While it is obviously impossible in a short essay to give more than a few pointers to the deciphering of the Germans, I hope that these pointers will generate more of the same through a process of logical deduction and guesswork.

23   Through knowing, for example, that the Germans stick to their linear timeline, we should be able to figure out that they are likely to be thorough – and slow (no shortcuts). Through awareness of their need for space and privacy, we should not be surprised at their formality, their slowness to make friends. Attitudes and behaviour patterns are intricately linked; compartmentalisation is linked to decentralisation, the need for private territory to the need to possess (rather than borrow or share). Thus, a little knowledge can be stretched a long way.

Recommended texts

Most of the following publications can be found in good bookshops.

Career development

A Portfolio Approach to Personal and Career Development, The Open University. Available from the Learning Materials Sales Office, The Open University, P. O. Box 188, Walton Hall, Milton Keynes MK67 6DH. tel: 0908 653376.

This pack will guide you through the processes of self-assessment, action planning, skills development and personal reflection. It is also a guide to the development of your own personal portfolio or a record of knowledge, skills and experience that can be used and re-used in planning for personal and career development.

Dictionaries

Collins Cobuild English Language Dictionary, Sinclair, J. (ed.), Collins. A dictionary that provides excellent explanations and examples of words and how they are used.

Electronic Bilingual Business Dictionary, Peter Collins Publishing. English–German–English and English–Spanish–English. Just one of many. Ask an IT specialist for further references.

English Business Dictionary, Peter Collins Publishing (Bilingual: available in French, German, Spanish, Swedish, Greek).

Language Reference for Business English, Brieger, N. and Comfort, J., Prentice Hall International.

Oxford Dictionary of Business English for Learners: for learners of English, Tuck, A. (ed.), Oxford University Press.

General study skills

The MBA Handbook: an essential guide to effective study (1994) Cameron, S., Pitman Publishing, 2nd edition. If you are interested in going further, this is an excellent guide to assist your MBA studies.

Grammar and usage

Collins Cobuild English Usage, Sinclair, J. (ed.), Collins. An up-to-date explanation of how words are used.

Collins Cobuild English Grammar, Sinclair, J. (ed.), Collins. An excellent reference book if you are worried about grammar.

Numeracy

Mathematics for Secondary Schools 1 (1987) Blackett, N., Harper, E., Küchemann, D., Mahoney, M., Marshall, S., Martin, E., McLeay, H., Reed, P., Russell, S., Taylor, P. and Womack, D., Longman, Harlow.

This takes you back to basics and looks at many numeracy topics. It is wide ranging and written for those who want to 'begin again' with numbers.

Statistics for Business (1993) Gregory, D., Ward, H. and Bradshaw, A., McGraw-Hill, London, 4th edition.

This will give you an introduction to statistics, starting with data collection and moving through graphs and averages to more conceptually difficult ideas such as probability, regression and dispersion. This book is well illustrated with many examples and has an easy-going style.

Statistics (1994) Owen, F. and Jones, F., Pitman Publishing, London, 4th edition.

This book offers an excellent introduction to statistics. It starts with the assumption that you have no prior knowledge of statistics. The book covers basic statistics up to regression, correlation and significance testing. There is a study pack that you can buy to supplement the text.

The Economist Numbers Guide: the Essentials of Business Numeracy (1993) Penguin, London.

This is a well written book which examines numeracy from an economics viewpoint. It therefore covers forecasting, inflation, interest rates and decision making in addition to basic numeracy.

Research

Doing your research project: a guide for first-time researchers in education and social science (1987) Bell, J., Open University Press, Buckingham.

This book gives a clear and concise introduction to social science research. It will take you through the steps of planning projects, literature searches, keeping records, negotiating access, choice of research design, analysis and presentation of information, and writing your report. It offers a very good introduction to the many different types of research techniques.

Index

Page references for marginal notes are indicated by 'n'.

About the Open Business School

Since 1983, the Open Business School (OBS), as part of The Open University, has become one of the largest business schools in Europe. Continuing growth throughout the early 1990s is in part due to the innovations brought to management education through the application of The Open University's expertise in distance learning. To this must be added the recognition by individual managers and their organisations that the quality, flexibility and relevance of the programmes meets their business needs cost effectively.

The courses require considerable intellectual and practical commitment but success depends equally on the quality of the teaching and the support provided for study. One of the major strengths is the OBS's support network of more than 1000 local part-time tutors throughout Europe.

For further details of OBS Certificate, Diploma and Master of Business Administration (MBA) programmes, please contact the Customer Service Centre, The Open University, PO Box 222, Walton Hall, Milton Keynes MK7 6YY, United Kingdom. Tel (+44) (0)1908 653449.

Notes

Notes

Notes